FORTRESS
INTRODUCTION TO CONTEMPORARY THEOLOGIES

FORTRESS

Introduction to Contemporary Theologies

Ed. L. Miller
and
Stanley J. Grenz

Fortress Press ◆ Minneapolis

To Oscar Cullman and Wolfhart Pannenberg
Theologians who have decisively shaped our own theological thought

Fortress Introduction to Contemporary Theologies

Cover design by David Meyer

Library of Congress Cataloging-in-Publication Data

Miller, Ed. L. (Ed. LeRoy).
    Fortress introduction to contemporary theologies / Ed. L. Miller and Stanley J. Grenz.
       p.   cm.
    Includes bibliographical references.
    ISBN 0-8006-2981-7 (alk. paper)
    1. Theology, Doctrinal. I. Grenz, Stanley. II. Title.
BT77.3.M56 1998
230'.09'04—dc21   98-34169
                                                           CIP

Manufactured in the U.S.A.   AF 1-2981

5   6   7   8   9   10

CONTENTS

PREFACE

In the arts and literature, the technical meaning of "contemporary" is something that fits between the current and recent, on the one hand, and the modern, on the other. But contemporary also has a more general or popular meaning according to which it designates what has occurred in the last hundred years or so. Adopting this latter meaning gives us a definite place to start. Anyone who knows anything about contemporary theology knows that a decisive break with the old and an inauguration of a whole new scene began to take place about 1920. And this break—with its ongoing proliferations, reactions, detours, and dead ends—is what we mean by "contemporary theology."

But with repect to those many proliferations, detours, and so on—only someone very foolish would think to have captured all that in the space of a short book. The task of boiling down and straining out the most crucial people and ideas is bound to be a frustration for the authors. It gives us a new appreciation of the words of 2 Macc. 2:26: "For us who have undertaken the toil of abbreviating, it is no light matter but calls for sweat and loss of sleep" (NRSV). It will also be frustrating for some readers whose favorite theologian does not receive the expected attention or whose pet idea is not represented at all. But the alotted space is all that we have. We made the best choices we could.

Most of the major theological movements of the last hundred years or so have each been primarily associated with one thinker. This is reflected in our chapter subtitles, which draw our attention to the thinker or thinkers who might be regarded as the primary figures of the movement or idea or as the one who, for whatever reason, has come to be most obviously associated with it. On the other hand, most of the perspectives certainly involve other contributors, either as further exponents or antagonists. Therefore most of the chapters allow the discussion to extend beyond the contribution of the theologian named in the chapter title.

For the title of the book we have settled on *Fortress Introduction to Contemporary Theologies,* rather than the somewhat more usual "contemporary theology." If the plural suggests that the contemporary theological scene has moved in many and quite varied directions, that would be fine with us.

We wish to thank the editors at Fortress Press (most notably Hank French, Michael West, and Debbie Finch Brandt) for their interest in and support of this publication. We also must express our appreciation to Mr. James Watters and Mr. Michael McClosky for their assistance with this book.

All Bible quotations are from the New Revised Standard Version, 1989.

CHAPTER ONE

Back to the Basics
Karl Barth

Pratteln is a Swiss village on the Rhine, a couple of miles from Basel on the rail line to Zurich. One day, a lad was visiting his godfather, who was the pastor of the small parish in Pratteln. The playful boy was climbing around in the interior of the church. In his own words, many years later, he described what happened: "Feeling his way up the stairs of a dark church tower he unexpectedly caught hold of a bell-rope instead of the handrail, and to his horror heard the great bell ringing out above him, and audible not only to him but to others."[1] This boy grew into the man who is usually called the greatest theologian of the twentieth century. Even non-Barthians would come to acknowledge that he made an impact on all subsequent theologizing unparalleled in his time.

Karl Barth was born in Basel on May 10, 1886, to an extended family steeped in theology and preaching. He spent his youth in Berne, where his father taught theology. His education took him from the university in Berne to the German universities of Tübingen, Marburg, and Berlin. Following a decisive experience as pastor in the village of Safenwil, Switzerland, he assumed theology professorships in the German universities of Göttingen, Münster, and Bonn. Expelled from the latter because of his refusal to pledge allegiance to Hitler, he returned to Basel where he taught theology at the university from 1935 until his retirement in 1962. He himself never completed a doctorate, though he was eventually showered with honorary ones. He was a robust and good-humored man with a streak of sternness.[2] He was also one of the truly great pipe smokers of the twentieth century. He died in 1968 at the age of eighty-two.

◆

The Liberal Background

The young theologian Barth had been nurtured in liberalism, the reigning theological perspective of the late 1800s and early 1900s. This was an upbeat theology with roots in the work of Friedrich Schleiermacher (1768–1864) and empowered by Barth's older contemporaries, Albrecht Ritschl, Wilhelm Hermann (his teacher in Marburg), and Adolf von Harnack (his teacher in Berlin). The latter popularized this theology in a book that has been called the finest and most influential expression of Protestant liberal theology and the highwater mark of this movement. The book was the published version of sixteen lectures delivered at the University of Berlin during the winter semester of 1899–1900. In its English translation the book was entitled, *What Is Christianity?* The answer, according to Harnack: the Fatherhood of God, the Brotherhood of humanity, and the infinite value of the human soul.[3]

Harnack was an astute and critical scholar, an expert on the earliest periods of Christianity and the historical Jesus. He believed that while it was inevitable that Jesus' message found expression in the prevailing motifs of his time—motifs that would not prove effective for later times—it is possible to identify an essential meaning and application that is valid for all time. According to Harnack, when we strip away, say, the accidental apocalypticism (or imagery about the end of the world) that shrouds Jesus' teaching about the coming kingdom of God, which is actually something "within you" (Luke 17:21), and if we heed his statements about the human being as more valuable than the divinely attended sparrows (Luke 12:6) and the soul as worth more than everything in the world (Matt. 16:26) and his pervasive teaching about love of God and neighbor (Matt. 22:37–40), then we can begin to see the real substance of Jesus' proclamation.

It was a proclamation that had little to do with theological or philosophical speculations and everything to do with the individual's proper relation to God—the vertical relation— and to neighbor—the horizontal relation. In its outworking it was, thus, not only an individualistic but also a "socialistic" proclamation. The gospel, according to Harnack, "is profoundly socialistic, just as it is profoundly individualistic, because it establishes the infinite and independent value of every human soul. . . . Its object is to transform the socialism which rests on the basis of conflicting interests into the socialism which rests on the consciousness of a spiritual unity."[4]

It is no surprise, then, that this movement came to be called the "Social Gospel" movement. As for Jesus himself, Harnack argued that he is properly to be regarded as the supreme expression of what the gospel is all about:

> The consciousness which he possessed of being the *Son of God* is, therefore, nothing but the practical consequence of knowing God as the Father and as his Father. Rightly understood, the name of Son means nothing but the knowledge of God. . . . *He was [the gospel's] personal realization and its strength, and this he is felt to be still.*[5]

The far-reaching influence of theological liberalism in its day can hardly be overstated. It was clearly the reigning theology at the turn of the century and well into it. It is reported, for example, that the demand for Harnack's *What Is Christianity?* was such that attempted shipments resulted in a traffic jam of freight cars in the main rail station of Leipzig.[6] But this book was soon to be eclipsed by another, and liberal theology was soon to be eclipsed by another.

◆

The Bombshell Book

Books have poured from the pens, typewriters, and word processors of contemporary theologians like water from the Nile at flood season. But Karl Barth surely established some kind of a record. In addition to a large stack of volumes, he authored the magnitudinous *Church Dogmatics*—thirteen volumes, nine thousand pages, eight million words, and still unfinished at his death! It was said of him that he must have had ink in his veins instead of blood. And surely no book in twentieth-century theology made more of an impact than Barth's first major work, his *Epistle to the Romans,* first published in 1919. This book was subsequently described as going off like a bombshell on the playground of the theologians, and it was to the experience of publishing this book that Barth later likened his youthful experience of accidentally tolling the church bell in Pratteln and alerting the whole village. The theological world had been awakened, and it would never again be the same.

The book was written while the young Barth was getting his ministerial calling off the ground as pastor in the small, non-descript village of Safenwil, in the Swiss canton of Aargau. For Barth this was a time of inward foment, occasioned by several factors. One was the evident failure of theological liberalism in the face of the outbreak of the First World War. Even though Barth had been greatly influenced by his theological teachers in Germany, most notably Harnack in Berlin and Hermann in

Marburg, he was greatly distressed by a "a terrible manifesto" issued by ninety-three German intellectuals on the very day of the war's outbreak, identifying themselves with the war policy of Kaiser Wilhelm II. To his dismay, he discovered among the signatories the names of almost all of his German teachers. He said "it was like the twilight of the gods" when he saw there the names of Harnack and Hermann, illustrating how easily theology could be transformed "into intellectual 42cm cannons."[7] He realized that this ethical failure of his German theological masters displayed that "their exegetical and dogmatic presuppositions could not be in order.... A whole world of exegesis, ethics, dogmatics and preaching, which I had hitherto held to be essentially trustworthy, was shaken to the foundations, and with it, all the other writings of the German theologians."[8]

Another factor in the Safenwil foment was Barth's close friend and theological coworker, Eduard Thurneysen, who at the time was pastor in the neighboring village of Leutwil. The two pastors corresponded regularly and met together frequently,[9] thoughtfully seeking to forge an adequate theological perspective. It was Thurneysen who, in June 1916, during one of Barth's visits to Leutwil, whispered to Barth what were almost fateful words, involving a pun: "What we need for preaching, instruction and pastoral care is a 'wholly other' theological foundation."[10]

Still another factor was Barth's involvement in labor disputes in Safenwil. He had sided with the workers, whom he saw as exploited by the management in the small textile industry there. For a time he was called "the red pastor," and considerable trouble was stirred up, but his excursion into "religious socialism" reflected what would be a lifelong concern with politics.

Out of this early period—the Safenwil years—came *Epistle to the Romans*. Before it was over, this work would pass through six editions.[11] It is a biblical commentary, but not in the usual sense. Like most commentaries, it passes through the document (in this case the book of Romans) verse by verse, but its exegesis is pervaded by deep theological musings. In this volume, themes are introduced and stressed that would determine the contours of the theology that Barth would spend his whole life developing. In his discovery of "the strange new world within the Bible" he encountered, most notably, the stark doctrine of the wholly-otherness of God—he was fond of citing the line from Ecclesiasticus, "God is in heaven, and thou art on earth!" This God, upon which everything is absolutely dependent, is utterly unapproachable except by means of divine self-revelation. This is a God who sits in judgment on all sinful humanity, but also a God who graciously proffers forgiveness and salvation through the atoning gift of God's Son, Jesus Christ. It was such talk as this that really inaugurated twentieth century theology.

◆

The Kierkegaard Connection

The impact and controversy generated by *Epistle to the Romans,* along with other contributions Barth was making, resulted in the offer of professorships in German universities, first at Göttingen, then Münster, and finally at Bonn. It was during these years, 1921–35, that the systematic character of Barth's theology really took shape. Even so, it involved a false start.

It was during this time that Barth discovered a kindred spirit in the nineteenth-century Danish thinker Søren Kierkegaard (1813–55), often called the father of existentialism. It is impossible to summarize here the character of this philosophical perspective, which is so far-flung as to embrace both theists and atheists. It is enough for our present purpose to quote the influential twentieth-century atheist existentialist, Jean-Paul Sartre, who said that what all brands of existentialism have in common is that they claim that "subjectivity must be the starting point."[12] What this means, at a minimum, is that authentic reflection on human meaning is inseparably bound up with one's self-consciousness as an existing individual, caught in a web of ambiguity, transitoriness, and death.

But back to Kierkegaard, the Christian existentialist. Probably no one—not even Barth himself—laid so much stress on "the infinite qualitative difference between God and man."[13] Furthermore, in his pseudonymous writings[14] Kierkegaard contrasted with a vengeance the difference between the "objective" approach to God and Christianity and the "subjective" approach. In the objective approach God and Christianity are treated as facts or objective truths to be dispassionately apprehended in a historical, philosophical, or scientific manner. In the subjective approach they are treated as *existential* truths and realities that the individual must become passionately related to in a leap of faith. All this is epitomized in Kierkegaard's famous slogan: "Truth is subjectivity."[15] In contrast to the intellectual approximations involved in objective truth, Christian faith is a matter of inward appropriation—which constitutes an intellectual risk. The object of Christian faith is, indeed, an offense to the reason (1 Cor. 1:18ff.): the absurdity that the eternal God became a temporal human being in the concrete person of Jesus Christ.[16] Kierkegaard repeatedly warned of the dangers of confusing the sphere of intellectual abstractions with the sphere of faith as passionate assimilation:

> If Christianity were a doctrine, then the relation to it would not be one of faith, since there is only an intellectual relation to a doctrine.... Faith ... is not a lesson for slow learners in the sphere of intellectuality, an asylum for dullards. But faith is a sphere of its own, and the immediate identifying mark of every misunderstanding of Christianity is that it changes it into a doctrine and draws it into the range of intellectuality.[17]

It should be no surprise that such talk played right into Barth's hands. In fact, in *Epistle to the Romans,* Barth had announced, "If I have a system, it is limited to a recognition of what Kierkegaard called the 'infinite qualitative distinction': between time and eternity, and to my regarding this as possessing negative as well as positive significance: 'God is in heaven and thou art on earth.'"

It was during this time that Barth began what he thought would be his magnum opus. He called it *Christliche Dogmatik* (*Christian Dogmatics*). The first volume was published in 1927, and it was also the last. There were several reasons for this, including a study of St. Anselm's famous ontological proof for the existence of God as an example of "faith seeking understanding,"[18] which deepened Barth's notion of the impossibility of authentic knowledge of God apart from revelation, that is, the impossibility of any independent or "natural" theology. During this time he also acquired a still better understanding of the Reformed, or Calvinist, tradition that he was representing.[19] Furthermore, he began to see the dangers in any theology inspired by existentialism. Thus, in commenting on the new version of *Church Dogmatics* he explained: " . . . to the best of my ability I have cut out in this second issue of the book everything that in the first issue might give the slightest appearance of giving to theology a basis, support, or even a mere justification in the way of existentialist."[20]

What this meant, especially with reference to Kierkegaard, is evident in Barth's comments many years later in 1963 upon receiving the Danish-sponsored Sonning Prize.[21] He provided a sketch of his relation to Kierkegaard, extolling the contribution of the great Danish Christian but issuing a warning, too: "I regard him as a teacher through whose school every theologian must pass at some time. Woe to anyone who has failed to do that. But he should not remain in it, and he will do better not to return to it."[22] One of his most obvious complaints concerned what he called Kierkegaard's "holy individualism." This involved, on the one hand, a sort of anthropocentrism,

or human-centeredness, in that it made the human subject the
point of departure for theological reflection, which is exactly
what Barth from the start was trying to overcome. On the other
hand, he believed that Kierkegaard's preempting preoccupation with the individual's God-relation was both unhealthy and
inimical to the biblical teaching about the community of faith
and about the church as the divinely appointed witness to the
world: "Where in his teaching are the people of God, the congregation. the Church; where are her diaconal and missionary
charge, her political and social charge? . . . How strange that
we, who were just coming from an intense preoccupation with
the relation of Christianity to the social question, did not immediately become suspicious at the point of Kierkegaard's pro-
nounced holy individualism."[23]

◆

The Bible and the Newspaper

This criticism of Kierkegaard brings us back to the development of Barth's theology. One of the best-known lines from
Barth is: "We must hold the Bible in one hand and the news-
paper in the other." Nowhere is this principle better exemplified in Barth's own experience than in the case of his opposition
to the Nazi regime ("Nation, Race, and Fuehrer") while he was
in Bonn.

The mainstream churches in Germany had gradually yielded
to the overtures of Hitler and had coalesced into the Nazi-
oriented "German Christians." What this meant, among other
things, was a cooperation with the Nazi persecution of Jews.
The German Christians announced, among other things, that
"in the mission to the Jews we perceive a grave danger to our
nationality. It is the entrance gate for alien blood into our body
politic. . . . in particular, marriage between Germans and Jews

is to be forbidden. We want an evangelical Church that is rooted in our nationhood. . . . in our national mission that God has committed to us."[24]

Many Christians were, of course, aghast at the German Christians' weak-kneed posture, and there came into being an opposition Christian community, the Confessing Church, a sort of underground church, complete with its own clandestine leadership and seminaries. Barth was one of the spearheads of this organization. He was also the chief author of the Barmen Declaration—a document drafted on May 29–30, 1934, in Barmen, Germany, at a conference of Lutheran, Reformed, and other church bodies united for the purpose of resisting the Third Reich's usurpation of the proper role of the church. The Declaration was a self-conscious challenge to the Hitler regime, insisting on the autonomy of the church from political coercion. It was explicit in its denunciation of the reigning social order— actually a *dis*order—as in the following excerpts:

> We repudiate the false teaching that the church can and must recognize yet other happenings and powers, images and truths as divine revelation alongside this one Word of God, as a source of her preaching. . . .
>
> We repudiate the false teaching that there are areas of our life in which we belong not to Jesus Christ but another Lord, areas in which we do not need justification and sanctification through him. . . .
>
> We repudiate the false teaching that the state can and should expand beyond its special responsibility to become the single and total order of human life, and also thereby fulfill the commission of the church.[25]

According to Barth, the Nazi tyranny—an idolatry—is an example of what happens when the word of God gives place to the word of humanity, and Christian theology, rooted in the Bible, becomes confused with natural theology, rooted in human reason.

As for Barth personally, he refused to begin his lectures with the Hitler-salute, "Heil Hitler!" and he agreed to sign the oath of allegiance to Hitler only with the qualification that all such allegiance is subordinate to the dictates of the gospel. After some wrangling, he was summarily fired from this teaching post at Bonn and his lectures were canceled.

◆

God, Christ, and Election

No sooner had Barth been expelled from Bonn than he received an offer of a professorship in the city of his birth. It was at the University of Basel, from his appointment in 1935 to his retirement in 1962, that Barth produced the substance of what turned out to be his true magnum opus, his voluminous *Church Dogmatics*. The new project had already been conceived and started in Bonn. The title, *Church Dogmatics,* represented a new beginning and a theological enterprise even freer from extraneous factors and still more self-consciously "bound to the sphere of the church, where and where alone [dogmatics] is possible and sensible."[26]

The twelve volumes of Barth's *Dogmatics,* unfinished at his death, are divided up among four major topics—the Word of God, the doctrine of God, creation, and reconciliation—and innumerable subtopics. (Barth died before the final topic, eschatology, could be addressed.) Strewn throughout are immediately recognizable Barthian ideas, themes, doctrines, and emphases. These include: the transcendence of God; the trinitarian nature of God; the humanity of God in Jesus Christ; the sinfulness and helplessness of humanity; a theological anthropology in which authentic human nature is found in the man Jesus Christ; the rejection of all forms of natural theology; the indictment of "religion," including the great world religions, as demonic; the finality of Christian revelation; the necessarily dialectical character of Christian theology; and so on. But one idea towers above the rest as peculiarly Barthian—and particularly controversial: the Barthian doctrine of *election*. It also exemplifies what is often called Barth's "Christocentrism" or the "Christologically concentrated" character of his whole theology: Every teaching of Christian theology begins and ends with the biblical teaching about Jesus Christ, and every teaching about Jesus Christ begins and ends with election.

Divine election, or predestination, was of course a big thing in the Reformed theology of Calvinism. In fact, this is what often comes first to mind when one thinks of Calvinism—even "double predestination," the doctrine that God has positively predestined or elected some to eternal salvation and the rest to eternal damnation. Many are repulsed by this idea, but its importance in the history of theology, and especially Reformed theology, can hardly be overestimated. As faithful as Barth sought to be to the Calvinist reformers, it is at this point that he swerved in a different and innovative direction.

Repulsion aside, Barth could not allow that our eternal salvation lies with some mysterious and unfathomable *decretum absolutum,* some absolute decree about the eternal destiny of individuals. Soteriology—the doctrine of salvation—must do better at this point than fall back on this "blank" and a consequent shrug of the shoulders. We must fill in the blank. But how? What else can be done with the thoroughly biblical claim that God has elected sinners to salvation? Barth shifts our attention from the idea that God has elected or chosen us, to the idea that God has chosen *Christ,* and that "in Christ"—the crucial biblical phrase, as in Eph. 1:4—he has chosen *us.*

> Of Jesus Christ we know nothing more surely and definitely than this—that in free obedience to His Father He elected to be man, and as man, to do the will of God. If God elects us too, then it is in and with this election of Jesus Christ, in and with this free act of obedience, on the part of His Son. . . . It is in him that the eter-

nal election becomes immediately and directly the promise of our own election as it is enacted in time, our calling, or summoning to faith, our assent to intervention on our behalf, the revelation of ourselves as the sons of God.[27]

Let us make two points about Barth's distinction: First, Barth's is a radically substitutionary theory of the atonement. To be "in Christ" is first of all possible because Christ in his substitutionary death has borne the penalty for human sin and at the same time "transfers" his own perfection to sinful humans. Thus we are in Christ and by virtue of his perfection are acceptable to God. Second, it's not as if once upon a time God, foreseeing human sinfulness, decided to send his Son for the purpose of redeeming humans, though this imagery has its place. Rather, and more profoundly, the divine and eternal decision to redeem humanity through Christ is from the start inseparably involved in the divine nature itself. As the second person of the Holy Trinity, the Son possesses the divine nature and thus is both the subject and the object of election, the Elector and the Elected. It is, therefore, from start to finish, a matter of God's freedom and grace (to use typically Barthian language)—the self-sacrificing divine love for creation.[28]

We have already encountered the characteristically Barthian emphasis on the wholly-otherness and transcendence of God. Good portions of the *Dogmatics* are likewise filled with talk about God's sovereignty and other divine perfections. One of these, to which reference is made time and time again, is the divine freedom. This in turn is related to the divine love, as in Barth's definition of God as "the One Who Loves in Freedom."[29] This love issues in the divine condescension (Phil. 2:6-8), the revelatory and self-sacrificial act of God whereby he becomes one of us—"the way of the Son into the far country" where he takes upon himself what is ours and gives us what is his. Finally, this great drama is vindicated in the resurrection of Christ, God's "verdict" on the Cross of Christ (Rom. 1:4).

Unlike some, like Bultmann, who take the Easter event to have been a subjective event in the experience of the early disciples, Barth affirms the resurrection as a real and objective event which occurred in space and time.

All of this is concentrated in Barth's conception of the divine election of Christ, and of us "in Christ."

◆

"Neo-Orthodoxy" and Other Labels

Several labels have evolved in the interest of capturing the essence, or at least some aspects, of the theological perspective advanced by Barth and his associates. Though usually such labels are inadequate, if not misleading, in this case the labels are instructive and provide us with a quick summary of the broad contours of this theology.

Surely the most important and most widely used of these is "neo-orthodoxy." Nonetheless, this term has sometimes been misunderstood. "Orthodoxy," in this expression, doesn't refer generally to the sound teachings of Christianity pounded out during its formative and early periods. It refers more specifically and more technically to Reformed Orthodoxy, that is, the representation of Christian teaching worked out by the Reformed (as opposed to Lutheran) branch of the Reformation in the sixteenth and seventeenth centuries. Neo-orthodoxy is, thus, a theology rooted in John Calvin,[30] his colleagues, and his successors—the state church of Switzerland is reformed. But it is *neo*-orthodoxy, a teaching informed by a critical approach to the biblical literature, availing itself of the relevant insights of modern learning (history, science, psychology, etc.), and seeking to address the contemporary situation.

It is also called "dialectical theology." The word "dialectical" should suggest immediately a sort of give-and-take, as in the related word "dialogue." In the terms of Barth's theology, there is no continuity between God and humans, and divine revelation has required, therefore, a *dialectical* meeting of time and eternity in the God-Man Jesus Christ. Closely related is Barth's recognition that no human talk about God can ever be quite appropriate—it must inevitably fall short of its intent. Any theology, therefore, must involve a kind of crisscrossing of language with the purpose of coming closer and closer to its necessarily elusive object: First we say this and then we say that, recognizing that the truth lies in between. It is often suggested that a large-scale example of this dialectic in Barth is the way in which his earlier and negative view of our knowledge of God is corrected by a later emphasis on its positive character, and the way in which his early emphasis on the transcendence of God is balanced by a later stress on God's humanity in Jesus Christ.

Finally, Barthian theology has also been called a "theology of the Word." Here, too, a word of caution: "The Word" does not refer to the Bible, at least not primarily. For Barth, the only source and ultimate reference of any and all theologizing is the Word of God. But this can mean one of three different things, or all of them together. First, the Word means Jesus Christ—called "the Word" in John 1:1 and 1:14—whose life, death, and resurrection stands at the center and provides the meaning of the whole history of God's saving activity. Second, the Word refers to the Bible, but not in a fundamentalist sense, as we will see in a moment. Third, the Word signifies the church's ongoing and vibrant proclamation of the gospel. There is, of course, a sense in which the written word of the Scriptures and the proclaimed word of the church are subordinate to and dependent upon the actual revelation that lies in Christ and the salvation-history that culminates in him. They are witnesses to the revelation.[31]

A special note on Barth's view of the Bible: On the one hand, Barth accepted the historical-critical approach to the biblical literature and rejected any notion of its inerrancy. On the other hand, he stressed that even though the Bible is a human product and bears the marks of human frailty, it is, after all, the divinely inspired witness to, the interpreter of, and the proclaimer of the saving Event that is centered in Christ. Both sides of this coin are succinctly stressed in the following:

> Without an act of intellectual dishonesty no one can deny the relativity or the problematical character of the Bible. And the great danger is that the elimination of the human relativity of the Bible may lead to the elimination of the very thing the Bible is intended to bear witness to: the revelation of God. For is it not the very nature of revelation that the form in which it confronts us is relative and problematical?[32]

(It should be noted that this last sentence makes a claim for the relativity of all revelation, and also exemplifies, again, the "dialectical" at work.) Barth claimed also that our revelatory encounter with the Bible is a salvific event in that it works in us a miracle, the creation of faith. In this way the Bible becomes for us the Word of God—an idea that led many to think, falsely, that Barth had a sort of subjectivist view of revelation. As with the church's proclamation, "from time to time," the Bible becomes the Word of God when the Holy Spirit uses it to produce faith.[33]

◆

Barth vs. Brunner

While Barth was churning out his monumental *Church Dogmatics* in Basel, in Zurich, less than an hour away by train, another theologian was also producing an impressive theology. Emil Brunner was born and died in Zurich, the city of the great Reformation figure Huldrych Zwingli, where he taught at the university from 1924 until his retirement in 1955. During this time he taught for one year (1938–39) at Princeton Theological Seminary and for two years (1953–55) at the Christian University of Tokyo. He was very much at home with international students, and was especially influential among American thinkers.

Barth's contribution proved, eventually, to be so powerful and controversial as largely to eclipse Brunner's. But were it not for Barth, Brunner's would have been hailed as the dominating contribution of his time. Though it struggled for recognition in the shadow of Barth, it was a truly great theological production. It came to expression in a great number of publications, the heftiest and most influential of which were: *The Mediator* (a Christology), *Man in Revolt* (a Christian anthropology), *The Divine Imperative* (Christian ethics), *Reason and Revelation* (Christian epistemology, or theory of knowledge), and the three-volume *Dogmatics* (a systematic treatment of major Christian doctrines). Brunner's theology might be characterized as, more obviously than anything else, a "theology of encounter." He sought to provide a Christian application of the "I-Thou" relationship made famous by the Jewish thinker Martin Buber. The idea had roots also in Kierkegaard's notion that God is not an object to be related to in an intellectual manner, but rather a subject to be related to in a passionate faith-relation. In a way, Brunner's whole theology is pervaded by an emphasis on the divine approach to the human being by means of a self-disclosing revelation and the divine-human encounter that this makes possible. But Brunner's way of developing and explaining this was the cause of a great rift between himself and Barth.

From the standpoint of recent theology generally, one would rightly think of both Barth and Brunner as occupying the same theological ground. After all, they were both Swiss, they both saw themselves as representing and continuing the Reformed theological tradition, they both regarded themselves as exponents of neo-orthodoxy and dialectical theology, and they both saw themselves as emphasizing the transcendence of God over against the immanence-oriented liberal theology. Nonetheless, an issue arose between them that came to constitute the great theological debate of the mid-twentieth century. In a way, it all revolved around the German word *Anknüpfungspunkt,* "point of contact." The question was: Is there, apart from divine revelation, any point of contact between God and the human being? It seems like an innocent enough question. But it spawned a great controversy, and left Barth and Brunner characterized (by Barth himself) as "the Elephant and the Whale," both creatures of God but destined never to meet.

In the mid-'30s, Brunner published an essay entitled "Nature and Grace." Defending what he took to be the Calvinist understanding, he argued that whatever devastation may have been wreaked by the Fall, it could not have resulted in the complete obliteration of the *imago Dei,* the image of God in which humans were created (Gen. 1:26), for this would have deprived the human being of the very capacity of entering into an I-Thou relation with God. This relation is the twofold capacity of being addressed by God and responding to him:

> The Word of God could not reach a man who had lost his consciousness of God entirely. A man without conscience cannot be struck by the call "Repent ye and believe the Gospel." What the natural man knows of God, of the law and of his dependence upon God, may by very confused and distorted. But even so it is the necessary, indispensable point of contact [*Anknüpfungspunkt*] for divine grace.[34]

Brunner unpacked the idea of the human response to the divine address in terms of its "formal" and "material" aspects. The formal aspect is the capacity that all humans have—by virtue of being persons and possessing the faculty of speech—of being addressed by God. The material aspect, however, consists in how fallen humans actually do respond to the divine address. It is this material aspect of human nature that has been devastated by sin, not the formal.

There is then, says Brunner, a natural point of contact between the divine and the human, something in the divine nature that is analogous to human nature. Is this the *analogia entis*, the "analogy of being" taught by the scholastic thinker St. Thomas Aquinas and held so dearly by the Roman Catholic tradition? Yes and no. Brunner certainly granted that there is a natural analogy of divine and human nature in that both involve Person and Word, which makes possible the divine-human encounter as well as meaningful talk about God as "Father," "Son," "Spirit," "Word," and so on. But there is no natural knowledge of God, at least not apart from revelation. In stark contrast to the Roman Catholic tradition, Brunner denied any possibility of a knowledge of God or talk about God attained independently of grace and revelation.[35] (Unfortunately, he repeatedly represented his position by means of the expression "natural theology," as in his challenge: "It is the task of our theological generation to find the way back to a true *theologia naturalis*.")[36] Brunner also taught that there is a certain legitimate role for Christian apologetics, the rational defense of Christianity. It is appropriate for the Christian, seeing things aright by the light of divine revelation, to employ his or her rational faculties to point out the general reasonableness of Christianity and the truth of many of its claims.

How did Barth react to this? His response is summarized in the one-word title of the essay in which he answered Brunner: "Nein!" ("No!"). He would have none of it. Furthermore, he regarded Brunner as all the more dangerous because he was so close to the truth that he was misrepresenting.

It is important to note that Barth wrote this essay soon after his involvement with the Barmen Declaration, with its indictment of any and all attempts to supplant God's authority with any "natural" theology that could issue in something like Nazism. Indeed, he charged Brunner with opening the floodgates to natural theology, denying any status to "true" natural theology; he charged Brunner with distorting Calvin's teaching about the *imago Dei;* he claimed that the only point of contact between God and humans is the miraculous one that God, though the Holy Spirit, creates in the human. Alluding to an old-fashioned hearing device, he hoped for "an angel from heaven who would call to Brunner through a silver trumpet of enormous dimensions" that the "new creation" of 2 Cor. 5:17 is not the result of a repair job.[37] As for the *analogia entis,* "it is an invention of Anti-Christ, and I believe that on this account it is impossible to be a Catholic."[38] In place of all this Barth substituted the *analogia fidei,* "analogy of faith," an expression taken from Rom. 12:6 and employed by Barth to suggest that the divine-human relation is constituted not by nature or reason but solely by faith.[39] And as for Christian apologetics, Barth contemptuously characterized it as theology that has lost its nerve.

Brunner was unchastened. He did later recant his unfortunate use of the expression "natural theology"—he thought he had been clear that he meant a true natural theology, accessible only in the light of revelation. In the end, though, he claimed the victory. Writing somewhat later, in his *Dogmatics,* he noted that Barth had himself in the meantime altered his position and now granted what Brunner had insisted on all along. Brunner comments:

> The *Imago Dei,* in the sense of Gen. 1, the "over-againstness of I and Thou" he calls "the analogy between God and man." . . . And Barth asserts that *this* element in man as "made in the image of God, has not been lost, as we see from the legend of the Fall." . . . This is exactly what I said in my pamphlet, "Natur und Gnade" ["Nature and Grace"] some time ago. I am happy to know that this controversy, which caused so much discussion, may now be regarded as settled.[40]

The disagreements between Barth and Brunner (which extended beyond the matter of the Anknüpfungspunkt) took on, regrettably, a personal and acrimonious dimension. Barth's attacks on his colleague in Zurich were inordinately severe. Brunner, for his part, was bitter at having to live and work in the shadow of the great Barth and became somewhat obsessed with exposing weaknesses in Barth's theology. In their later years, a well-intentioned American student arranged for a meeting of the two dialectical giants with a view to a personal, if not theological, reconciliation. It was a pleasant meeting, a picture was taken of the Elephant and the Whale together, but nothing of consequence came of it. On the other hand, following a long and disabling illness, the last words that Brunner heard on his deathbed was a message from Barth sent by means of a friend: "Tell him . . . that the time when I thought I had to say 'No' to him is now long past, since we all live only by virtue of the fact that a great and merciful God says his gracious Yes to all of us."[41] It was April, 1966. A year and eight months later, in 1968, Barth too would be gone.

◆

The Fallout

The story is told that in 1936 Barth attended a conference where the very first presentation was on religious experience, liberally seasoned with references to psychology. Shortly into the paper, Barth stood up, interrupted the speaker, and demanded whether his presentation was on theology or on the psychology of religious experience: "If the paper is on the psychology of religion, why should we here listen to it? This is a conference of Christian theologians; only the word of God, not talk about psychology and religious experience, is appropriate here." With that, the meeting was thrown into turmoil.[42] In a sense, Barth interrupted and threw into turmoil the whole course of contemporary theology.

However, "the old man in Basel" has not gone uncriticized. Indeed, the criticism has come from all sides. He was always regarded with suspicion by those of a more conservative stamp who said, among other things, that he embraced a historical-critical view of the Bible and that he seemed to advocate a subjectivist view of revelation. The former was true and the latter was false. But at the same time, he was rejected by those of a more liberal stamp who complained, among other things, that he seemed to endorse a naive, uncritical view of the Bible and that he affirmed a narrow, exclusive, and definitive authority for Christianity. The former was false and the latter was true.

Two more specific issues came under repeated attack. First, Barth's utter rejection of natural theology was utterly rejected by many. We saw above how Brunner responded to Barth's denial of any natural "point of contact," and many followed Brunner in this. But of course Brunner himself opposed any actual natural theology. So others have thought that in this respect *both* of them failed. It was as if they both, especially Barth, had allowed a conclusion about a natural, philosophical knowledge of God to be dictated *a priori* by their biblical theology; Barth, at least, had claimed that no natural knowledge of God can possibly be sound because the Bible says that there is no natural point of contact. But of course that just begs the question. If, say, a particular natural, philosophical argument for God's existence should prove to be sound, then it must be accepted, and our biblical understanding of the matter must be adjusted accordingly. That is, it is not enough simply to reject such arguments as being unbiblical; rather, their failure to deliver the goods must be *shown*.

A second well-known criticism of Barth concerns his doctrine of election, or at least one of its implications. This criticism was leveled by Brunner and many others, who charge that Barth's doctrine of election leads naturally and inexorably to universalism, the idea that everyone will eventually be redeemed. It is, in fact, difficult to avoid this conclusion, given Barth's declarations about Christ's substitutionary atonement for sinful humanity and God's election of that humanity in his election of Christ. While universalism has seemed to most to be flatly incompatible with biblical teaching, Barth himself could find no satisfactory reply to this criticism and more or less left the matter to the hidden will of God. This seemed to be a very unrobust resolution in an otherwise very robust theology.

In the end, though, Barth's various critics seem like termites gnawing away at an impregnable edifice. The prediction made in 1966 has turned out to be true:

> When the curtain is rung down on the twentieth century and the annals of the its church history are completed, there will surely be one name that will tower above all others in the field of theology—that of Karl Barth. In him a church Father has walked among us, as theologian of such creative genius, prodigious productivity, and pervasive influence that his name is already being associated with that elite group of thinkers that includes Athanasius, Augustine, Anselm, Aquinas, Luther and Calvin.[43]

CHAPTER TWO

Christian Realism
Reinhold and
H. Richard Niebuhr

Though neo-orthodoxy was introduced into the contemporary theological scene mainly by Karl Barth, it was, as we have seen, hardly a one-man show. Nor was it limited to Europe. It gained a large following in the United States, too, where it found an especially forceful voice in Niebuhr—actually, *two* Niebuhrs: the brothers Reinhold and H. Richard. Their father, a German immigrant, was a pastor in the German Evangelical and Reformed Church, and they were nurtured in this pietistic tradition in the Midwest. H. Richard Niebuhr (1892–1962) spent the substance of his theological and teaching career at Harvard Divinity School, and Reinhold Niebuhr (1892–1971) at Union Theological Seminary. Reinhold became, surely, the towering figure of the first half of twentieth-century American theology.

◆

American Neo-Orthodoxy

Actually, Reinhold resisted the label "neo-orthodox," and he didn't even care much for the term "theologian"; he liked to think of himself as a social critic and moralist. Though both he and H. Richard clearly represented important variations on the neo-orthodox theme, their approach has been called "Christian realism," with a strong dash of pragmatism. It is useful to pay attention to these terms. This theology was called Christian realism because, first, it entertained no illusions about the human situation as defined by sin; it was realistic about sin's inevitability and universality. Second, it found in the biblical and Christian perspective the most adequate account of sin—its nature and origin—and of the fallenness of humanity. It was a "pragmatic" endeavor because it was driven by an interest in practical solutions, or at least responses, to the sinful human situation. More than most Christian postures that have sought to be more or less orthodox, Christian realism wanted to be relevant to social, political, and economic problems that extended beyond the Christian community and address a Christian word to people generally.

Like neo-orthodoxy in Europe, American neo-orthodoxy took shape in direct response to what was perceived as the naive optimism of liberalism. As Barth was to Harnack, so were the Niebuhrs to Walter Rauschenbusch (1861–1918). Rauschenbusch, also the son of a German immigrant, was a Baptist and the most influential representative of liberal theology in the United States. His first pastorate was in the notorious slum called "Hell's Kitchen" in New York. Here he was deeply disturbed by the plight of the poor and become profoundly involved in the question: What does the gospel say about this? Eventually he became a professor of church history at Rochester Seminary and also the leading exponent, this side of the Atlantic, of the Social Gospel movement. His most influential book was *Christianity and the Social Crisis,* published in 1907.

In this book, and in the 1912 *Christianizing the Social Order,* Rauschenbusch argued that the Christian message must be allowed to cut more deeply—or more broadly—than issues of merely personal morality, such as adultery or drunkenness, would allow; it must address the social and economic evils that spawn poverty, inequality, and despair. Thus he attacked laissez-faire capitalism, the profit motive, and industrial greed, and he preached the value of labor unions and the socialization of big industry. All of this, he claimed, is an essential part of the inauguration of the reign of God on earth, a reality to be brought about through self-conscious and concerted human effort stirred by love. Jesus' proclamation of the kingdom of God, said Rauschenbusch, is the touchstone of all Christian doctrines: "The Kingdom of God is . . . a collective conception, involving the whole social life of man. It is not a matter of saving human atoms, but of saving the social organization. It is not a matter of getting individuals to heaven, but of transforming the life on earth into a harmony of heaven."[1]

Such "Rauschenbuscharian" interest in the social order may seem, in fact, to cohere with what we have already said about the Niebuhrs. But while this is true at one level, it must be recalled that we have presented the Niebuhrs as rejecting liberal theology, and at a deeper level the similarities quickly disappear. The social gospel simply underestimated the reality and depth of human sin and was too optimistic in its vision of a humanly-produced reign of God. It was also cavalier in its reduction of all the major tenets of biblical Christianity to the single idea of working for the Kingdom. The Niebuhrian indictment of liberalism as a vapid distortion of authentic Christianity is nowhere better expressed than in H. Richard's famous characterization: "A God without wrath brought men without sin into a kingdom without judgment through the ministrations of a Christ without a cross."[2]

◆

Sin, the Empirical Doctrine

As the tiny village of Safenwil was to Barth and as the slums of New York were to Rauschenbusch, so was the metropolis of Detroit to Reinhold Niebuhr. It was there that he became quickened to the social implications of the gospel. At Bethel Church in Detroit where, beginning in 1915, he was pastor for thirteen years, Niebuhr was confronted with the exploitation and plight of Henry Ford's auto workers. His vexation during that time is evident in the following, written in 1927: "What a civilization this is! Naive gentlemen with a genius for mechanics suddenly become the arbiters over the lives and fortunes of hundreds of thousands. Their moral pretensions are credulously accepted at full value. No one bothers to ask whether an industry which can maintain a cash reserve of a quarter of a billion ought not to make some provision for its unemployed."[3]

The trouble, of course, is sin, a central theme of Niebuhr's most important work, the two-volume *The Nature and Destiny of Man,* published in 1941.[4] In this work he rejects the rationalistic conception of human nature, with its elevation of reason as the defining feature of humanity, and rejects the romantic or naturalistic conception, with its reduction of humanity to the categories of physics, chemistry, psychology, and the like. The first deifies human nature and the second debases it. For Niebuhr, the realist and pragmatist, the human being is a synthesis of and stands at the juncture of nature and spirit, the finite and the infinite (to use language that echoes Kierkegaard). With a foot in both worlds, the human being and human experience resists any systematic and coherent account. Therein lies the relevance of Christian anthropology—the Christian view of human nature. It is more realistic about human nature, respecting both its upside and its downside: "The Christian view of human nature is involved in the paradox of claiming a higher stature for man and of taking a more serious view of his evil than other anthropology."[5] Niebuhr saw this dialectical appraisal of and response to the human situation both as overcoming the idealistic-rationalistic/romantic-naturalistic dichotomy, and also as rooted in the biblical vision of human nature and the realities of life.

But whence comes this evil? According to Niebuhr, the awareness of our rootedness both in transcendence and nature spawns anxiety or insecurity; this in turn finds expression in sin, which Niebuhr conceived as rebellion against God grounded in the will; and sin, in its turn, finds expression in one direction in sensual self-indulgence and in another direction in self-assertive and self-elevating pride of power, of knowledge, or of virtue.

Niebuhr was, in fact, one of contemporary theology's most vociferous defenders of the doctrine of original sin. He is well-known for having approved the claim in the *London Times Literary Supplement* that "the doctrine of original sin is the only empirically verifiable doctrine of the Christian faith."[6] It is true that he came to regret his earlier use of the phrase "original sin," with its association with the traditional idea of inherited guilt—as if a sinful nature was passed along in the genes from our first parents, Adam and Eve. But call it what you may, it is a tragic, universal, and inevitable reality, but a reality for which each of us is responsible—inevitable but not necessary. And we all have a bad case of it! So bad, says Niebuhr, that we cannot extricate ourselves from it and are driven, thus, to the grace and forgiveness of God. The Cross of Christ is, in fact, the sign both of God's judgment of human sin and divine forgiveness, as well as the disclosure of the meaning of history.

According to Niebuhr, it is true that at some important biblical and theological level we are all hopelessly and equally sinful before God. But it is also true that in our practical and social existence some sins and situations are clearly worse than others: "Men who are equally sinners in the sight of God need not be equally guilty of a specific act of wrong-doing in which they are involved. It is important to recognize that biblical religion has emphasized this inequality of guilt just as much as the equality of sin."[7] Niebuhr was critical of any Barthian-type theology that, because of an exclusive emphasis on human sinfulness, fails to reckon with the relatively good or evil contributions of humans. With respect to the evil, Niebuhr echoes the biblical prophets:

> Specially severe judgments fall upon the rich and the powerful, the mighty and the noble, the wise and the righteous.... The simple religious insight which underlies these prophetic judgments is that the men who are tempted by their eminence and by the possession of undue power become more guilty of pride and of injustice than those who lack power and position.[8]

Though we live in anticipation of the eschaton and the inauguration of God's reign on Earth ("May your Kingdom come"), it is certainly our Christian responsibility to do what we can in the here-and-now: to practice love and to cultivate justice.

———————————————————◆———————————————————

Love and Justice

Love and justice are the key words for understanding the Niebuhrian application of the principles of Christianity to our practical, social, and political existence. By "love" Niebuhr means agape, self-sacrificing love. It is non-prudential, that is, it is moved by absolute obedience and out of concern for others— as in the example and teaching of Christ—rather than a concern for reward or happy consequences accruing to oneself; it is moved by sacrifice, abnegation, and personal loss. As such it is, for the sinful individual, an "impossible possibility," that is, an ideal that we must strive for despite its full unattainability.

Justice, on the other hand, is love making its way in the world, the attempt to embody love in the concrete situations and structures of our social life. More specifically, this would mean a more equitable distribution of public power and all that this implies socially, politically, and economically. Niebuhr himself was continually involved in programs of social reform, such as "Democrats for Social Action," of which he was one of the founders. (He was, thus, on the liberal side of politics and the conservative side of theology, a position that he insisted was not inconsistent.) But here, too, we have an impossible possibility. Niebuhr argued that we must have no illusions about the relativities and ambiguities that inevitably cloud and compromise the attempt to embody love in our social relations, organizations, and institutions. In our attempt to practice love and to do what is right we are constantly forced back and forth between extreme courses of action. An example of such tensions and dialectical responses was when Niebuhr found it necessary to abandon his pacifist stand and to advocate the American entrance into the war against the Nazis. Nor must we have illusions about the way self-interest inevitably obstructs and impedes justice. But even this must be turned, pragmatically, to serve the good:

> To understand the law of love as a final imperative, but not to know about the persistence of the power of self-love in all of life . . . results in an idealistic ethic with no relevance to the hard realities of life. . . . To know both the law of love as the final standard and the law of self-love as a persistent force is to enable Christians to have a foundation for a pragmatic ethic in which power and self-interest are used, beguiled, harnessed and deflected for the ultimate end of establishing the highest and most inclusive possible community of justice and order.[9]

The struggle for the social embodiment of love is a continuing one, characterized by responses and counter-responses, and one that ever approximates its goal but never attains it. But Niebuhr held that we dare not let up. It is the Christian responsibility to God and neighbor—in spite of sin, doubt, and confusion—to transform our world as best we can.

◆

Telos vs. *Finis*

In spite of such talk and concern about this world, however, Niebuhr's vision includes the next one, too. That is, we do not have in Niebuhr a preoccupation with this present life to the exclusion of eschatology—a doctrine of the consummation of all things, future life, judgment, and the like. We have seen this aspect of Niebuhr's theology in his conviction about the eschaton and the establishment of the kingdom of God.

At the broad horizon of Niebuhr's perspective we encounter an unmistakably *teleological* emphasis—from the Greek *telos,* meaning completion, fulfillment, or perfection. That the universe, history, and human life are propelled by a purpose, a plan, and an "end" in the sense of a goal, is an incontrovertible and essential part of the biblical-Christian vision. It has everything to do with human freedom, responsibility, and authenticity because it means that the human being is not reducible to the blind and irrational forces of nature. On the other hand, because we are nonetheless to some degree the products of nature, it is also evident—painfully evident—that each of us has an "end" in the other sense, too, in death or *finis.* This twofold meaning of "end" gives us exactly the sort of ambiguous and dialectical existence that, by now, we would expect from Niebuhr: The human experience of finis constantly confronts the experience of telos with the threat of nonbeing and meaninglessness. "The problem is that the end as *finis* is a threat to the end as *telos*. Life is in peril of meaninglessness because *finis* is a seemingly abrupt and capricious termination of the development of life before it has reached its true end or *telos*."[10]

On the other hand, says Niebuhr, Christianity understands this aspect of the human situation, and it addresses the tension between time and eternity. In the biblical-Christian view the ambiguities, threats, doubts, and vulnerability of our present existence will be overcome in that future event, represented in the biblical idea of the reign of God, when "God will be all in all." Then, too, the meaning and the purpose of the whole of history will be displayed for all.

Niebuhr sees this bipolar teaching about our present situation and our future hope expressed vividly in the New Testament teaching about the two comings of Christ. In the first coming, God appeared decisively in history, defeated the enemy, and, through Jesus' teaching and miracles, imparted a foretaste of the coming kingdom. The second coming will signal the consummation of all things, the complete disclosure of the reality and rule of God in God's kingdom. In the meantime, though, we live in the interim period between the first and second comings. This is a time when we look both backward to the first coming with its promise and forward to the future with its prospect. It is inevitably also a time of ambiguity.[11] (In the next chapter we will see that it was Oscar Cullmann who most emphatically articulated this "already/not-yet" character of New Testament eschatology.)

It is clear, then, that Niebuhr took biblical eschatology seriously. It is also clear that he did not take it literally. The traditional talk about the return of the Son of man on clouds of heaven, the last judgment, and a general resurrection of the dead must be taken as imagery, to be interpreted for its real— and serious—point. In fact, says Niebuhr, any theology that does not reckon seriously with such symbols will not take history itself seriously either. He addresses, for example, the traditional imagery just mentioned. The symbol of the triumphant and glorious second coming of Christ, the suffering Messiah, (often called the *parousia,* a Greek word meaning "presence") expresses God's sovereignty over the world and the final supremacy of love over the forces of self-love. The last judgment expresses the reality of Christ as the judge of all history, the reality of the distinction between good and evil, and the truth that there is no escape from our responsibility for sin and guilt. The symbol of the resurrection of the body expresses that the mystery of the life's fulfillment can be accomplished only by God.[12]

Niebuhr provides a fitting summary statement of his teleological and eschatological perspective. It also brings us back to the points made earlier.

> The Christian hope of the consummation of life and history is less absurd than alternative doctrines which seek to comprehend and to effect the completion of life by some power or capacity inherent in man and his history. It is an integral part of the total biblical conception of the meaning of life. Both the meaning and its fulfillment are ascribed to a centre and source beyond ourselves. We can participate in the fulfillment of the meaning only of we do not seek too proudly to appropriate the meaning as our secure possession or to effect the fulfillment by our own power.[13]

◆

The Niebuhr Prayer

Predictably, Niebuhr's theology has sometimes been judged as a one-sided and negative preoccupation with impossible possibilities. Some argue that it needs to be supplemented with the more upbeat and promising Christian emphases on the resurrection of Christ, the Holy Spirit at work in the Christian community, and a reign of God that has already made its presence felt in the world. On a different note, Niebuhr's theological-social perspective is surely frustrating and disappointing to those who need to see things in black and white. It will be objected that there is too much room for interpreting, accommodating, and otherwise "fudging" in the interest of an application of Christian principles. But, of course, that is just the point. According to Niebuhr, the actual world in which we live is in fact characterized by particularities, relativities, and ambiguities— the consummation of all things has not yet occurred. That may be unfortunate, but that's the fact. So a truly meaningful application of Christian principles will necessarily be realistic about our situation and willing to give and take in the interest, as is were, of striking the best deal at the moment.

At any rate, many of those who have reflected on the course of twentieth-century theology would say that Reinhold Niebuhr was, with his particular insights and contributions, surely the right person, at the right place, at the right time. Certainly everyone remembers the prayer he composed in 1934:

> God, give us grace to accept with serenity the things that cannot be changed, courage to change the things that should be changed, and wisdom to distinguish the one from the other.[14]

CHAPTER THREE

Jesus Christ and Mythology
Rudolf Bultmann

If it is true that Karl Barth was, in an important sense, the greatest theologian of the twentieth century, there is no doubt that Rudolf Karl Bultmann (1884–1976) was the greatest New Testament scholar. Of course, this doesn't mean that everyone has agreed with his views. Hardly. But his views—sometimes controversial in the extreme—established a framework that determined the character of subsequent New Testament scholarship to the present day. Further, not only did his methodological and exegetical insights hold obvious implications for the larger world of theology, but he made distinctive contributions to theology itself; he was a major shaper of one of the dominant strands of twentieth-century theology, namely, "existential" theology. Born in Bremen in northwest Germany, the son of a Lutheran pastor, and educated in the universities of Tübingen, Berlin, and Marburg, he settled into an academic career at the University of Marburg and wielded a decisive influence over the entire theological world from 1921 until his retirement in 1951.

Like Barth, Bultmann studied at Tübingen, Berlin, and Marburg. Like Barth, he was greatly influenced by his liberal teachers, Wilhelm Hermann and Adolf von Harnack. Like Barth, he reacted to theological liberalism. With Barth he was initially united in the development of dialectical theology. But then he took a quite different turn.

◆

The New Testament

Though our concern is mainly with Bultmann's contribution to theology, some notice should be given to his closely associated legacy to New Testament studies. This latter necessarily involves many considerations, but we mention here just two: form criticism and the history of religions approach to the New Testament literature.

The historical-critical approach to the Bible—which insists on bringing to bear on the Bible the same sorts of interpretive tools that would be brought to bear on any literature—goes back to the eighteenth century with Hermann Reimarus. Since then the method has been increasingly refined, but probably the single biggest boost was provided by the introduction of *Formsgeschichte,* almost always rendered in English as "form criticism." Though applied first to the Old Testament, in the 1920s and '30s it became for many an indispensable tool of New Testament interpretation, mainly through the work of, first, Karl Ludwig Schmidt and Martin Dibelius and, then, Rudolf Bultmann. Form criticism—which has been applied mainly to the New Testament Gospels, and especially to the first three Gospels (the Synoptics)—begins with the recognition that the original oral content of these Gospels has been altered by superimposed layers of subsequent tradition. It then attempts to uncover that original content through analysis of the differing linguistic forms or types of expression present in the text, which point to differing and developing concerns in the early Christian communities. In this way, not only do we more correctly identify the authentic sayings of Jesus in the Gospels but we reconstruct somewhat the development of early Christian doctrine and the church.

Form criticism was, of course, attended by yet other critical tools employed in the interest of identifying authentic Jesus-material in the Gospels. Bultmann was one of the first to apply what came to be called the "criterion of dissimilarity": Only those sayings of Jesus can assuredly be accepted as authentic that stand in contrast both to Jewish teaching and practice, on the one hand, and to Christian teaching and practice, on the other. The idea is that only thus can we be certain that the saying or material wasn't read into the Jesus-story from either the Jewish or Christian side. Bultmann was also one of the first to emphasize the relevance of linguistic factors: Rhythms, phraseology, and particular expressions, especially Semitisms, can often reveal a Palestinian and thus early date for the material in question.

The historical-critical approach to the New Testament literature continued to be refined into the latter part of the twentieth century with the addition of many other criticisms—source criticism, redaction criticism, literary criticism, and the like—and other criteria of authenticity. But for all their importance, none of these hit the scene, so to speak, with the force of form criticism. It was a kind of new beginning for New Testament studies. In this respect, Bultmann's *The History of the Synoptic Tradition* (published in German in 1921), a largely form-critical scrutiny of the traditions about Jesus contained in the first three Gospels, became a sort of agenda-setting work.

Like form criticism, the history of religions approach was largely a German-sponsored methodology. In German it is known as the *religionsgeschichtliche Schule*—a real mouthful that means the "history of religions school." As the label suggests, this is the attempt to relate some of the most important material in the New Testament to its religious and cultural environs. This approach claims that the New Testament material was largely derived from non-Jewish or extrabiblical settings. Thus, for example, Egyptian mysticism, Hellenistic philosophical speculation, mystery religions, and Roman religious rites figure as relevant background to and explanations for central New Testament ideas. This even includes some of the Christological titles by which the New Testament writers attempted to represent the person and work of Jesus. The Pauline "Lord," for example, was seen to derive not from the Jewish-biblical tradition but from a Hellenistic religious milieu, and likewise with "Son of God" and "Savior."

In this approach Bultmann was not an originator. Heavy-duty work had already been done prior to Bultmann, perhaps most notably by Wilhelm Bousset (d. 1920) and Ernst Troeltsch (d. 1923). But again, it was the Marburg professor who brought this approach to the forefront. Without minimizing the Jewish-biblical contribution, Bultmann emphasized that with the spread of early Christian teaching a division was bound to rise between Palestinian and Hellenistic forms of that teaching. In the latter case, it was inevitable that many Hellenistic elements would intrude into the original Gospel, and this is indeed evident in the New Testament documents as they now stand before us. In this respect one should note Bultmann's book, *Primitive Christianity in its Contemporary Setting,* which includes discussions not only of the Jewish background but also of the Greek city-state, Platonic idealism, astrology, Stoicism, mystery religions, and the like. The book includes a chapter entitled, "Primitive Christianity as a Syncretistic Phenomenon." Even though Bultmann believed, as we will see, that Christianity embodied a unified and distinctive "existential" teaching, he recognized that the New Testament confronts us with a syncretism, a drawing upon many diverse cultural strands—in addition to the Jewish strand—to formulate and express that central teaching.

One of those strands calls for special note: Gnosticism. It itself was a hybrid, involving in its various forms elements drawn from late Jewish speculation, Greek philosophy, Persian religion, and the like. It was called Gnosticism (from the Greek word *gnosis*, "knowledge") because it taught that redemption of the human soul was attained by a secret knowledge. Generally, this was a knowledge of the spiritual world of light from which a heavenly redeemer had descended into this world of matter and darkness to engage in combat the Powers of Darkness and to liberate enlightened souls into fully spiritual existence. Bultmann believed that such a mythology lies behind the image of Jesus Christ we encounter especially in the fourth Gospel, the Gospel of John, with its pervasive descending-ascending Savior motif, its unmistakable light-darkness dualism, its talk about the vanquishing of the evil one, and its emphasis on the believer's release into eternal and spiritual life. Some of this, naturally, figures into Bultmann's monumental commentary, *The Gospel of John,* published in German in 1941. It is hard to overstate the influence of Bultmann's view of the Gnostic presence in the New Testament literature. It is also hard to overstate the controversy it started.

Bultmann's work on the New Testament contributed dramatically to a distinction that would have ever increasing consequences for theology: the distinction between the Jesus of history—the historical Jesus as he actually lived and taught—and the Christ of faith—the One who is encountered in the New Testament documents and who is believed in, proclaimed, and worshiped. It was a distinction thrown into clear relief in the title of Martin Kähler's important book, *Der Sogennante Historische Jesus und der Geschictliche, Biblische Christus,* or "The So-called Historical Jesus, and the Historic Biblical Christ" (second edition, 1896).[1] Indeed, the distinction would prove crucial to Bultmann's own theology.

◆

Demythologization

Now the more theological and apologetic aspect of Bultmann's contribution comes into view. It also becomes apparent how closely intertwined, for Bultmann, are the interpretive and theological tasks. Recalling Barth's treatment of the book of Romans, exegesis involves not just an exegesis of the text but also *Sachexegese,* "exegesis of the subject-matter." That is, a *theological* analysis of, evaluation of, and response to what the text says. As Bultmann made clear already in the introduction to his 1926 (German) *Jesus and the Word,* the point is to be led to a "highly personal encounter with history."[2]

In 1941 Bultmann exploded his own bombshell when he issued a mimeographed pamphlet, eventually published in English under the title *New Testament and Mythology: The Problem of Eliminating the Mythological Elements from the Proclamation of the New Testament.* The result was that the world of theology would never again be the same.

Bultmann begins, rather abruptly, with the judgment that much of the New Testament is, for moderns, irrational and utterly meaningless. To take his own example, the New Testament cosmology is obsolete. The New Testament writers believed in a three-storied universe: Heaven is up above, we are here, and hell is down below someplace. Now the fact is that this view of the world is wrong and we can never again believe it. But is it not possible to reject the world view of the New Testament while continuing to affirm its essential teachings? Not quite. As Bultmann explains, the New Testament three-storied universe is built right into our essential doctrines and creedal statements:

> No one who is old enough to think for himself supposes that God lives in a local heaven. There is no longer any heaven in the tradi-

tional sense of the word. The same applies to hell in the sense of mythical underworld beneath our feet. And if this is so, the story of Christ's descent into hell and of his Ascension into heaven is done with. We can no longer look for the return of the Son of Man on the clouds of heaven or hope that the faithful will meet him in the air.[3]

At many other points, as well, the New Testament can no longer speak to our contemporary situation. A literal interpretation of the whole "eschatological" framework of the New Testament (that is, its teaching about the end of the age and the last events) must be abandoned, for the Son of man did not in fact return in glory on the clouds of heaven and the reign of God did not materialize as scheduled. The New Testament teachings about the atonement rest upon primitive ideals of guilt and righteousness. The idea of a pre-existent son of God who enters the world to redeem humans is drawn from Gnosticism. In fact, at almost every turn the New Testament reflects the mythologies of Jewish apocalypticism and Greek-inspired Gnosticism, with their dualisms, demonic powers, and divine interventions. What can all of this mean to modern technologically minded people, committed as we are to a scientific world view? A literal interpretation of the New Testament, with its three-storied universe and its demons, would mean for us today a *sacrificium intellectum*. Bultmann concludes that if the modern individual "is prepared to take seriously the question of God, he or she ought not to be burdened with the mythological element in Christianity."[4]

The question then becomes this: Can the *kerygma,* or essential message of the New Testament, survive this elimination of mythology? At this point Bultmann's more positive contribution begins to take shape. He believes that the essential truth and relevance of the New Testament can be preserved through the program of *Entmythologisierung,* "demythologization," the process of liberating the New Testament message from its mythical setting and expression. Actually, the word "demythologization," as Bultmann himself observes, is inadequate because the aim is not to eliminate or subtract the mythological elements in the New Testament but to interpret them. The older liberalism had attempted such a subtraction of the mythological elements with the result that it threw out the kerygma itself and left us with only the trite and sentimental ideals of the social gospel—love thy neighbor and collect used clothing for the poor. More accurately, demythologization is "the method of interpretation which tries to recover the deeper meaning behind the mythological conceptions."[5] What we must do is penetrate to the kernel of eternal truth hidden within the mythological husk. We must free the existential meaning, valid for all times, from its local mythological expression in the New Testament. The *kerygma* is the gospel proclaimed and experienced in faith. We must not allow it to be emptied of its power by tying it to a prescientific understanding of the universe. The task of freeing the existential meaning of the gospel, says Bultmann, will tax the time and strength of a whole generation, but it will be worth the trouble, for the New Testament does indeed offer even the contemporary individual "an understanding of himself which will challenge him to a genuine existential decision."[6]

Not that demythologization began in modern times. Bultmann believed that the earliest attempts at demythologization are to be found in the New Testament itself—for example, in the Fourth Gospel. Written to a generation for whom the apocalyptic Son of Man did not, in fact, return as expected, the Fourth Gospel attempts to translate the futuristic eschatology of the Synoptic Gospels into "realized eschatology"; it spiritualizes the message of a coming reign of God into a message, a truth, a *kerygma* for the present. In the same way, judgment and salvation—which Bultmann existentializes into self-understanding and authenticity—must be confronted and appropriated here and now. Though, for instance, we can no longer take seriously the biblical teaching about the imminent end of the world, we should take seriously the imminent end of the world of each one of us, that is, our deaths.

It should be apparent from all of this that Bultmann was in agreement with Barth over the rejection of the older liberal theology. But it should also be apparent that his interpretation and application of the kerygma was taking a quite different character that was, to use a word that Barth despised, "existential."

◆

The Heidegger Connection

In 1957 Bultmann published a brief but highly provocative article called, in the English translation, "Is Exegesis without Presuppositions Possible?" The answer, he said, was no. The problem is to identify the correct presuppositions. That he thought that the correct "preunderstanding" was provided by existentialism—a philosophical perspective then in its heyday—is one of the best known facts about Bultmann. One recognizes at this point the influence of the German philosopher Martin Heidegger, Bultmann's contemporary, who was in Marburg during 1923–28. In an autobiographical essay, Bultmann reflected on Heidegger's influence:

> The work of existential philosophy, which I came to know through my discussion with Martin Heidegger, has become of decisive significance for me. I found in it the conceptuality in which it is possible to speak adequately of human existence and therefore also of the existence of the believer. However, in my efforts to make philosophy fruitful for theology, I have more and more come into opposition to Karl Barth.[7]

Existential philosophy as mediated by Heidegger thus became the hermeneutical sieve through which Bultmann sifted out the real stuff, as it were, of the New Testament *kerygma*.

After his time in Marburg, Heidegger taught at the University of Freiburg. He was supportive of the Nazi party in the '30s and '40s (unlike Bultmann), but was in any case a major shaper of one important strain of twentieth-century philosophy—phenomenology, which, along with existentialism, focused attention on the immediate, inner, self-conscious experience of the individual. It should be remembered that these were the days when people like the French philosopher Jean-Paul Sartre were writing books with titles such as *On Being and Nothingness*. Heidegger's own most influential work was called *Being and Time*, published in German in 1927.

Heidegger talked of the human being as "thrown" into the universe, in a state of *Angst* and "forlornness" and in search of responsible or authentic existence. In diametric opposition to Barth, Bultmann solicited direct help from philosophy and sought to demythologize the Bible specifically in light of Heidegger's phenomenological-existentialist approach.

> Our question is simply which philosophy today offers the most adequate perspective and conceptions for understanding human existence. Here it seems to me that we should learn from existentialist philosophy, because in this philosophical school human existence is directly the object of attention.... Existential philosophy, while it gives no answer to the question of my personal existence, makes personal existence my own personal responsibility, and by doing so it helps to make open to the word of the Bible. It is clear, of course, that existentialist philosophy has its origin in the personal-existential question about existence and its possibilities. Thus it follows that existentialist philosophy can offer adequate conceptions for the interpretation of the Bible, since the interpretation of the Bible is concerned with the understanding of existence.[8]

The recurring references here to "human existence," "personal existence," and "personal responsibility" signal that we are in the presence of a perspective very different from traditional ontologies, or theories of being, which understood human nature as a sort of universal and fixed category. Here, rather, the accent falls on the particular individual, enmeshed in temporality and in the ambiguities of concrete situations and confronted by a call to decisions—and the decisions are what make us what we are. Bultmann believed that this is what the New Testament *kerygma* and Christian faith is really about—not the timeless ethical truths that the old liberal theology propounded. But Heidegger's existentialism was a humanistic existentialism, seeking to identify answers to the human quandary by looking within the human individual, apart from any input from the divine. In contrast, Bultmann, the Christian thinker, believed that we must be "open to the word of the Bible" because the message of the Bible confronts us with a special and gracious act of God, from the outside, in order to make possible the recovery of authentic existence.

But how?

◆

An Existentialist Christology

According to Bultmann, the event of Jesus Christ is a unique mixture of history and myth, and if we are to appreciate the existential truth and meaning of that event we must look beyond its mythological setting. After all, says Bultmann, myths are to be interpreted not cosmologically but anthropologically, not as objective pictures of the world but as expressions of our understanding of human existence.

Bultmann accepted the crucifixion of Jesus as a historical fact, but did not see Jesus as, in a literal sense, the Son of God expiating the sins of the world. Moreover, "an historical fact which involves a resurrection of Jesus Christ from the dead is utterly inconceivable!" The death and resurrection of Jesus Christ, which Bultmann took to be one event, is an "eschatological" event, an event the existential significance of which cannot be located in any historical fact but is apprehensible through the eyes of faith. And what does faith see there, hidden from ordinary historical, scientific, and objectifying understanding? It sees open and authentic existence supremely actualized in Jesus Christ, and it hears an invitation to participate in it ourselves. Such talk must not be mistaken for a mere slogan. What it means is that in identifying ourselves with the cross—death to the world—and resurrection—the Lordship of Christ—we forfeit the security of the world and of things and align ourselves with the hidden, transcendent, and divine Reality. Thus, though we can no longer interpret Jesus' proclamation of the coming reign of God in terms of space and time, Jesus may yet be for us the bearer of the "last" world—not a temporal but an existential last world, the ultimate and decisive word about God.[9] In such talk we see again the "existentializing" of biblical language.

There is, therefore, an important difference between *Historie* and *Geschichte,* that is, between history conceived as merely *chronological* events and history conceived as dramatic and consequential events, or *historic* events—echoing the title of Kähler's book. It is the latter kind of history that holds existential meaning, and it is the latter that theology is interested in. Theology is not concerned with whether or not something could be shown to have actually happened once upon a time, but with what it could mean for humanity. That is why Bultmann, when he was asked whether he believed that Jesus actually rose from the dead, responded: "I am a theologian, not an archaeologist." The historical (*historisch*) status of the cross and resurrection has no bearing at all on their existential (*geschichtlich*) significance. Again, there is a big difference between the Jesus of history and the Christ of faith. So much is this the case, that one encounters this rather startling assertion in the oft-quoted opening line of Bultmann's *Theology of the New Testament:* "The message of

Jesus is a presupposition for the theology of the New Testament rather than a part of that theology itself."[10]

◆

Bultmann vs. Cullmann

It is sometimes noted that no one hit more home runs than Babe Ruth and that no one struck out more times than Babe Ruth. Likewise, Bultmann was the most important New Testament scholar of the twentieth century, but no New Testament scholar was more ruthlessly criticized. The criticism of Bultmann usually centered on one or more of three Bultmannian ideas.

For one thing, Bultmann concluded that virtually nothing can be known about the historical person of Jesus himself and that what can be known of his teaching has to be wrung out from the texts by means of exceedingly complex methods. Second, he held that even what can be determined turns out to be quite unlike what has traditionally been held. In this respect, Bultmann believed that Jesus did not identify himself with the future coming Son of man but, like John the Baptist, proclaimed the imminent coming of that eschatological figure; and he concluded that it was during the development of the Gospel traditions that—to use a famous Bultmannian slogan— "the proclaimer became the proclaimed." Thus, according to Bultmann, Jesus himself had no "messianic self-consciousness." Third, he argued that the early Christian interpretations of Jesus and his mission were heavily colored by the redeemer myths of Gnosticism. As we have seen, he believed that the Gospel of John, especially, with its descending-ascending heavenly savior motif, clearly betrays a Christian adaptation of Gnosticism.

For all the power of Bultmann's contribution to the understanding of the New Testament, it was criticized by many of his fellow scholars. These included, to name a few, Werner

Kümmel (Bultmann's successor at Marburg), Joachim Jeremias (Göttingen), and most British scholars, to say nothing of Americans. But of all the critical responses to Bultmann, none was more systematic, sustained, and influential than that of Oscar Cullmann. Cullmann was born in 1902 in Strasbourg, France, began his long and distinguished career as a teacher of Greek and German, and spent most of his career as a professor of New Testament at the University of Basel in Switzerland and, simultaneously, at the Sorbonne in Paris. Though, like Bultmann, he employed a historical-critical approach to the New Testament literature (the great American Roman Catholic scholar, Raymond Brown, called him "a master of modern critical exegesis"), he delivered to his wide audience quite different conclusions from Bultmann's.

He argued, for example, that considerable and reliable information can be recovered from the New Testament and related literature about the historical Jesus and his teaching. To the satisfaction of many he demonstrated that Jesus had, indeed, possessed a messianic awareness of himself as the divine instrument through whom atonement for sin would be won, and further, that he had identified himself with that heavenly Son of man who would eventually return in glory and judgment for the inauguration of the reign of God on earth. He was also one of the strong resisters of Bultmann's Gnosticizing of New Testament texts, arguing, along with many others, that there is no good evidence of Gnostic influence on the New Testament. In fact, the truth is quite the opposite of what the Bultmannians claimed: It was early Christian teaching that imparted the Christian-sounding features to Gnosticism. The single most important work that reflects these conclusions was Cullmann's highly acclaimed *The Christology of the New Testament*.

This book was an attempt to document the several perspectives on the person and work of Jesus Christ through an investigation of the various titles accorded him in the New Testament.

According to Cullmann, these titles represent different aspects or *functions* of Christ and can be arranged to signal the different ways that Christ has functioned with respect to his pre-existent work (Word, Son of God, God), his earthly work (Prophet, Suffering Servant, High Priest), his present work (Lord, Savior), and his future work (Messiah, Son of Man). This view of Christ at work, as it were, in different periods of time reflects, in turn, the idea for which Cullmann was most famous. It began with his book, *Christ and Time*, which was published immediately after the Second World War. In spite of the title, it was hardly a philosophical treatise. Rather, it was an attempt to document from the biblical literature a theological view of history that came to be called *Heilsgeschichte*, "salvation history" or "redemptive history." The term had been used prior to Cullmann, but he gave it the particular twist and content that it was known for in the second half of the twentieth century. The idea was further refined in Cullmann's subsequent larger and more systematic book, *Salvation in History*, originally published in German in 1965.

In a nutshell, *Heilsgeschichte* is the view that God has acted redemptively throughout history; that these salvific events stand one to another in a two-fold relation of continuity and progression; that the event of Jesus Christ is the center of this salvation history (logically, not chronologically); and that this history will be consummated in the yet future coming of the reign of God. The underpinnings of the whole idea could be stated succinctly in Cullmann's slogan, which he himself italicized for emphasis, that *"all Christian theology in its innermost essence is Biblical history."*[11]

One particular feature of this vision is the idea that this divinely ordained salvation history, which extends from creation to consummation, is propelled by a progressive reduction or narrowing—from all creation to Israel, to the faithful remnant, to the solitary Individual who is Christ the Center—and then it expands again to the Twelve, to the church, and finally encompasses once again all creation, which is now a new creation in which God reigns. In such a scheme, the role played by Israel, elected by God to be the bearer of salvation (Jesus Christ, the Jew), is apparent. Another feature of the salvation-historical view, and one that proved to be especially influential, was the teaching that with the earthly ministry of Jesus Christ the reign of God has already broken into our realm and has dealt a death-blow to Satan and sin, but that the full consummation lies still in the future. Cullmann likened the earthly work of the incarnate Lord to a decisive battle that has determined the outcome of a whole war, and our present situation to those who know the outcome but must continue to struggle against a defeated enemy who doesn't realize that he is defeated.[12] It came to be called, "already/not yet eschatology," and became the standard view of a wide block of New Testament scholars—probably most.

Cullmann never tired of explaining that only the salvation-historical perspective could at once preserve the integrity of the biblical vision and provide a real basis for talk about meaningful Christian existence in the present. His target was Bultmann-ian existentialism, which constantly threatened to slip into an individualistic subjectivism and turn history into a matter of self-understanding. This is evident from the opening pages of *Salvation in History,* from which the following pointed questions are taken:

> Certainly the whole New Testament contains the call for the decision of faith and implies a new understanding of existence. But does not this call rest on the faith that a divine history has occurred, is occurring, and will go on occurring, which, while envisaging this faith, is first of all independent of it and stands over against the believer? Does not faith therefore mean *aligning our existence* with this series of events *hic et nunc?*[13]

It should also be noted that in the original German edition, *Salvation in History* bore the subtitle, *Heilsgeschichtliche Existenz im Neuen Testament,* "Salvation-historical Existence in the New Testament." Cullmann was no less interested in "Christian existence" than was Bultmann. But he thought that his own reading of the biblical material provided an adequate foundation for that existence.

Nonetheless, the salvation-historical approach was all frankly discarded by Bultmann himself, who called it a clever theological construction—an overly imaginative imposition on the actual biblical data.[14] The fact remains, though, that Cullmann provided what was perceived to be an intellectually responsible alternative to Bultmannian skepticism about the historical Jesus, Bultmann's view of the New Testament material as radically dependent on contemporary religious, theological, and philosophical milieus, and Bultmann's view that the original stuff of Christianity was significantly different from what soon hardened into the familiar tradition. Generally speaking, the Bultmann-Cullmann debate split the theological world, and the division continues, in a way, to this day.

◆

Other Responses

We have just seen how Bultmann's contributions to New Testament scholarship fared at the hands of some of his contemporaries—spearheaded most notably by Oscar Cullmann. Here we mention some of the criticisms of his more theological contributions, though it should be noted that, in the end, the two sorts of responses are hardly separable from one another.

Of course Bultmann was attacked sharply by those who feared, understandably, that he was dissolving the substance of the Christian gospel, right before their eyes, into some sort of self-understanding subjectivism. That is, instead of defining the Christian proclamation in terms of what God has announced and accomplished "out there" in biblical history and, centrally, in the ministry, cross, and resurrection of Jesus Christ, Bultmann defined it in terms of what individuals experience in their own personal confrontation with existence. However, Bultmann has been likened to a man driving his automobile toward a precipice at full speed and swerving to safety at the very last moment. According to Bultmann, though it is necessary to provide the modern individual with a demythologized and existential interpretation of the New Testament, there is a limit to this procedure. He acknowledged that at some point it is also necessary to affirm the objective reality of God's gracious act that provides for humanity the possibility of self-understanding and salvation. He did insist on the *kerygma* as the proclamation of God originating from beyond the world, and he did believe, as any Christian must, that in some very important sense the locus of God's revelation is the Christ-event.

Critics on the other side do not complain that Bultmann's swerve to safety comes so late but that it comes at all. For example, the Swiss theologian Fritz Buri objected that Bultmann's program of demythologization, if honestly carried through, would include finally the kerygma itself—a "dekerygmatization," which of course would be the end of the gospel.

Another objection, similar to Barth's central complaint against Kierkegaard, was that Bultmannian faith was an inner directed, privatized faith that seemed out of step with social responsibility, the sense of community, and even the doctrine of the church as a communion of believers. Still another objection was that all the high-flown talk about responsible and authentic existence does not really issue in anything concrete and real. What do responsibility, authenticity, openness to the future, and so on really *mean*? It reminds us of the cartoon of Heidegger, urging his students during the war, "You must decide!" To which his students responded, "Yes, Professor Heidegger, but decide *what*?" For all the urgency of Bultmann's existential language and the passion of his appeal, how does it actually help or guide us in the concrete situations in which we find ourselves? In any event, insofar as Bultmann's approach was hitched to the existentialist star, it began to fade when that star began to fade in the 1960s.

Still another and very common criticism is that Bultmann is rationalizing the New Testament message, making it intelligible and palatable to moderns when in reality it claims to be an offense. Barth, of course, was concerned to preserve undiluted the biblical statement of God's judgment on sin as well as his free offer of salvation through the atoning death and real resurrection of Christ—however offensive such talk may seem in a scientific and technological age. Bultmann, on the other hand, seemed quite willing, even anxious, to subordinate the expression and interpretation of the Christian kerygma to contemporary expectations. How is Bultmann's procedure compatible with the New Testament announcement that its own message is a "stumbling block" and "foolishness" (1 Cor. 1:18ff.)? Bultmann answered that what is indeed incomprehensible is not the way God relates to our theoretical thought but the way God deals with our personal existence. For Bultmann demythologization removes only a superficial or false stumbling block to Christian faith in order to lay bare the real one: the God who in the Word presents Godself to us as gracious.

Whether the personal and existential aspects of the gospel can be so neatly separated from their historical moorings is a good question. It is probably *the* question, and we will return to it at the end of chapter 4.

For the moment, we should note that one of Bultmann's own students, Ernst Käsemann, who became a leading New Testament scholar in his own right, had second thoughts about Bultmann's view of the historical Jesus. In 1953 he presented a paper entitled, "The Problem of the Historical Jesus."[15] Käsemann raised all over again the twofold question: What can we know about the historical Jesus? and Is what we can know relevant for an understanding of authentic Christian faith? On both counts he delivered an un-Bultmannian opinion. With that he launched what came to be called, in the title of James M. Robinson's 1959 book, *A New Quest for the Historical Jesus*.[16] The old or first quest was inaugurated by Albert Schweitzer, whose 1906 book, called in English *The Quest of the Historical Jesus*,[17] recovered for twentieth-century theology the eschatological character of Jesus, the proclaimer of the coming reign of God. This view in fact hardened into what has come to be called "the eschatological consensus" that is the dominating view of New Testament scholars by and large. Of course, at the very end of the twentieth century it has also been challenged by some engaged in what is called "The Third Quest for the Historical Jesus." These are, most notably, some members of the notorious "Jesus Seminar," which, even more skeptical than Bultmann, has reduced the authenticity of the traditional Jesus-sayings to 18 percent of what we find in our Bibles. They advocate the images of Jesus as the Spirit-Filled Sage or Jesus the Itinerant Cynic. But they have hardly carried the day.

Overlooking for the moment the differences between Bultmann and Cullmann, at the end of the twentieth century their broad perspective, centering on the historical Jesus and his proclamation of the coming reign of God, still stood as the framework from which most New Testament scholars and theologians attempt to understand his significance.

CHAPTER FOUR

The God Above God
Paul Tillich

In his autobiographical reflections in *On the Boundary*, Paul Tillich reflected on the times he spent as a youth gazing out over
the immense sea and the relevance of this for the development
of this theology:

> The weeks and, later, months that I spent by the sea every year
> from the time I was eight were ... important for my life and
> work. The experience of the infinite bordering on the finite suited
> my inclination toward situation and supplied my imagination
> with a symbol that gave substance to my emotions and creativity
> to my thought. Without this experience it is likely that my theory
> of the human boundary situation ... might not have developed
> as it did.[1]

Paul Tillich (1886–1965) was born and educated in Germany,
but fled to the United States in the 1930s because of the Nazi
persecution of nonconforming theologians. In the United States
he taught theology at Union Theological Seminary, the University of Chicago, and Harvard. He became the dominating fu-

ture of American theology. Unlike Barth, who spurned modern philosophy and culture as distractions to theology, Tillich embraced input from many secular quarters and sought to correlate philosophy with theology. Shifting even more than Bultmann to a decidedly philosophical and metaphysical platform, at home in every period in the history of philosophy and theology, and employing the contributions of recent thought, such as depth psychology, Tillich sought to work out his existentialist and "boundary line" theology for all phases of life and experience. He was called "the apostle to the intellectuals."

--------------------◆--------------------

The Method of Correlation

That Tillich's system has been called a "theology of culture" suggests its comprehensive character. Indeed, the phrase was used as the title for a collection of his essays on topics including science, morality, art, and education. It also reflects Tillich's belief that the political, scientific, and artistic life of every culture reflects an existential situation and an ultimate concern, be it a worthy one or an idolatrous one. It follows for Tillich that the expression of the Christian message must be translated for a given cultural situation and the existential questions that that situation poses.

As he expresses it in the opening lines of his *Systematic Theology*, the responsibility of any adequate theology is twofold, namely, "the statement of the truth of the Christian message and the interpretation of this truth for every new generation. Theology moves back and forth between two poles, the eternal truth of its foundation and the temporal situation in which the eternal truth must be received."[2] Persuaded that theology must begin with an existential analysis of the human being, and that biblical symbolism must be positively embraced as the only adequate vehicle of theological expression, Tillich develops his contemporary translation of Christianity by means of what he called the "method of correlation." This method, central to Tillich's whole theology,

> tries to correlate the questions implied in the [cultural] situation with the answers implied in the [Christian] message.... The method of correlation explains the contents of the Christian faith through existential questions and theological answers in mutual interdependence.... The answers implied in the event of revelation are meaningful only in so far as they are in correlation with questions concerning the whole of our existence, with existential questions.[3]

The method of correlation has several functions. First, "correlation" may mean correspondence or aligning of items; logical interdependence; or real or factual interdependence. All three meanings have important theological applications. A good example of the last is to be seen in revelation where genuine revelatory disclosure is conditioned by both objective and subjective contributions, the divine revealing and the human receiving. Second, the mutual interdependence and interdetermination of existential questions and theological answers is, for Tillich, symptomatic of our simultaneous unity with and estrangement from the infinite and, consequently, our ability to ask the questions and our inability to answer them. It is also suggestive of the "theological circle" in which the theologian necessarily finds himself or herself, theology being the outworking of one's own (sometimes hidden) ultimate concern—a fact to be frankly admitted. Third, through the method of correlation Tillich hopes to avoid the error of those theologies that try to deliver answers to questions that we in our particular situations haven't asked, and also to avoid the error of those theologies that fail to see that the answers must come from beyond the questions themselves. Finally, Tillich sees his method of correlation as having been employed in one form or another throughout the history of Christian theology, and he cites the opening lines of Calvin's

Institutes as expressing its essence: "The knowledge of ourselves is not only an incitement to seek after God, but likewise a considerable assistance towards finding him. On the other hand, it is plain that no man can arrive at the true knowledge of himself, without having first contemplated the divine character, and then descended to the consideration of his own."[4]

The several parts of Tillich's *Systematic Theology* are each divided into two sections witnessing to Tillich's thoroughgoing attempt to correlate existential questions with theological answers: "Reason" and "Revelation," "Being" and "God," "Existence" and "Christ," "Life" and "Spirit," "History" and "Kingdom."

◆

The Ground of Being

It is hardly possible even in outline to deal with the many dimensions of Tillich's imposing theology. We will, therefore, focus our attention on one of his themes, the foundational one: God as the symbolic expression of the Ground of all being and meaning.

Tillich is sometimes identified as a "Christian atheist." But is it possible to be a Christian theologian, like Tillich, and yet deny that God exists? The answer, of course, depends on what one means by "God" and what one means by "exists." When Tillich says that God doesn't exist, he refers to the traditional idea of God. Actually, in one sense Tillich and his brand of theology is to our age what the pre-Socratic philosopher Xenophanes (500 B.C.E.) was to his. Xenophanes had attacked the old Homeric, mythological concept of the gods as falling woefully short, in respect both to the popular depiction of their immoral escapades and of their anthropomorphic character. Likewise, Tillich suggests to us the inadequacy of our own popular idea of God. Traditional natural theologies, he says, are significant in that they articulate the existential question of God in a manner appropriate for a particular situation. Thus, a formulation of, say, the cosmological argument for God is not interesting for the sake of the soundness of its conclusion—logically, it is surely misguided—but for the sake of the way it expresses a culture's concern about the God-question.[5] But that culture is rapidly passing on and it behooves us to allow its old theology to give way to a new theology, one that can be correlated with the new situation.

Of course, we do not believe naively that God is a nice old man with long white hair sitting on a great white throne. We might, however, still think of God as a metaphysical Principle, transcendent First Cause, or Necessary Being. In short, we conceive God to be a supernatural *Thing*. Even this, says Tillich, relegates God to the level of a finite being like ourselves and other things in the universe: It "separates God as a being, the highest being, from all other beings, alongside and above which he has his existence."[6] By thinking of God as an individual thing or substance, by placing God in a supernatural world alongside our own, or by making God a cause alongside other causes, we transform the infinity of God into finitude. Tillich further warns against the biblical personalism that leads us to think of God as a being and a person: "The God who is a being is transcended by the God who is Being itself, the ground and abyss of every being. And the God who is a person is transcended by the God who is the Personal-Itself, the ground and abyss of every person."[7] Nevertheless, the concept of a personal God is for Tillich an existentially necessary symbol because only a person can grasp us and speak to us in our loneliness.

God is neither "up there" nor "out there," like substances, causes, principles, or people are. In this sense it is not appropriate to say that God either exists or doesn't exist.

The question of the existence of God can be neither asked nor answered. If asked, it is a question about that which by its very nature is above existence, and therefore the answer—whether negative or affirmative—implicitly denies the nature of God. It is as atheistic to affirm the existence of God as it is to deny it.[8]

For Tillich, God is surely above and beyond the traditional God of supernaturalism; God is not a superthing existing out there in the universe someplace. This is the first concept of God that Tillich rejects.

But he also rejects the God of naturalism. The naturalistic interpretation identifies God in some way with the universe itself, or at least with its essence of special powers. The trouble with this position, according to Tillich, is that it "denies the infinite distance between the whole of finite things and their infinite ground." The naturalistic identification of God with the world makes the word "God" superfluous and simply reveals the naturalist's insensitivity to "a decisive element in the experience of the holy, namely, the distance between finite humans, on the one hand, and the holy in its numerous manifestations, on the other. For this naturalism cannot account."[9] So the supernaturalist idea of God is inadequate inasmuch as it turns God into another thing out there, and the naturalist idea is inadequate inasmuch as it fails to distinguish God from the universe and to do justice to our experience of the holy. Both reduce God to an idol.

How, then, shall we speak of God? Tillich answers that there is a third way (grasped in part by classical theologians such as Augustine, Aquinas, Luther, and Calvin) that will liberate us from the two dangerous extremes. God is neither *in* the world nor *above* it; images drawn from the spatial realm can hardly describe God's relation to the world because that relation is hardly spatial. Rather, God is at the very depth of being and experience, the infinite ground, the condition, the power of all things. God is *Being Itself*—this is the only non-symbolic statement that can be made about God. Still, says Tillich, it may be possible for the naturalist to describe God in much the same way. We must therefore add an important qualification. Reality is self-transcending in that finite things point beyond themselves to their infinite depth. In fact, God the Ground of Being, infinitely transcends that of which he is the ground, a state of reality which has its counterpart in our own self-transcendence in the ecstatic experience of the holy. Tillich's third way thus steers between naturalism and supernaturalism and, as he says, underlies the whole of this theological system.[10]

◆

Christ, the New Being

We move now from Tillich's doctrine of God to his doctrine of the Christ—he was always fond of employing the "the" to emphasize that "Christ" is not a personal name but a function, office, or role.

According to Tillich, humans are guilt-ridden, painfully conscious of their finitude, and threatened with meaninglessness. They are estranged from their essential being and plagued with existential anxiety, a dreadful awareness of their possible nonbeing. Tillich urges us, nevertheless, to affirm meaning with meaninglessness, to have certitude within doubt, to have "the courage to be." But the source of this courage can never again be the idolatrous God of traditional theism. Our courage lies, instead, in the "God above God," the power of being itself, the God of the third way discussed above.

Tillich, espousing a partly "adoptionist" Christology, says that this God chose or adopted Jesus, who then became the Christ, that is, "the anointed." God has subjected himself to the conditions of spatio-temporal existence; he has shared in human estrangement; and he has conquered and transformed it through Jesus as the Christ who, as the Christ, was "united with the ground of his being and meaning without separation and disruption."[11] The subjection of the Christ to estranged existence is symbolized in the cross, and his conquest is symbolized in the resurrection. Estrangement thus stands conquered in principle, and the Christ becomes—for those who in faith receive him as such—the bearer and mediator of the "New Being." He also becomes the center and ultimate criterion of all reconciling revelations—such as those found in non-Christian religions—otherwise known as "ecstatic manifestations of the Ground of Being."

To be grasped by the healing power of the New Being is salvation or the recovery of our essential being and the fulfillment of our meaning. (Tillich is delighted to point out that the Latin *salus* means, most fundamentally, "healing.") This involves, first, a participation in God's participation in and victory over the cleavage (or "split," to use another of Tillich's favorite expressions) between humanity's essential meaning and its existential state, and therefore victory over humanity's estrangement from God, the world, and itself. It also means an acceptance of God's acceptance of us through God's reconciling and healing work. And it means a transformation in personality and community. The "regeneration, justification, and sanctification" of traditional theology is thus restated by Tillich as "participation, acceptance, and transformation."[12]

◆

The Protestant Principle

In all of this there is to be seen a new role for the Protestant doctrine of justification by faith alone. Tillich liberates the "Protestant principle" from its merely historical interest and extends it far beyond its traditional Lutheran and Calvinist interpretation, radicalizing and universalizing it for the contemporary situation.

When the Bible says, as it does in so many places, that we are justified not by works but by faith, Tillich understands "works" to include intellectual as well as moral works, especially in our age of anxiety and doubt. The intellectual Pharisee, like the sinner, stands in need of justification. But God is ready to receive the doubter, for the Ground of Being is present in every authentic act of doubt and faith, accepting and affirming the being of the one who quests for Being Itself. It is interesting to note that Bultmann also saw his program of demythologization as a means of enriching the doctrine of justification by faith, and, in this respect, he expressed himself in a very Tillichian way:

> Demythologizing is the radical application of the doctrine of justification by faith to the sphere of knowledge and thought. Like the doctrine of justification, demythologizing destroys every longing for security. There is no difference between security based on good works and security built on objectifying knowledge.[13]

The Protestant principle—at least in Tillich's understanding of it—protests against all idols and deabsolutizes religions and even Protestantism itself, an idea suitably stressed in Tillich's book *The Protestant Era*. He was, in fact, repulsed by the "absurd and demonic" doctrine, fostered by Christian exclusivism, that only those who hear and receive the Christian gospel will be saved. On the contrary, he believed, in a somewhat Platonic way, that all people participate more or less in the power of the New Being; otherwise, they would possess no being at all.

It is probably impossible to summarize succinctly the undergirding movement of Tillich's theology any better than he himself does in the closing lines of one of his most important works, *The Courage To Be:* The God above God, the power of being, has appeared in the New Being of Christ, and "the courage to be is rooted in this God who appears when God has disappeared in the anxiety of doubt."[14]

◆

Faith and Symbols

One of the most discussed issues of twentieth-century theology and philosophy concerns the nature of religious language. Paul

Tillich, with his focus specifically on religious symbols, was a major contributor to that discussion. Even those who reject the broad substance of Tillich's theology often acknowledge the importance of his treatment of religious symbols. He himself said, "My whole theological work has been directed to the interpretation of religious symbols in such a way that the secular man—and we are all secular—can understand and be moved by them."[15] We have already made several references to religious symbols, but we need now to spell out Tillich's view a little more.

It all begins with faith, which Tillich defines as "ultimate concern." For each of us there is a kind of center of gravity around which our existence revolves, which drives it and provides it with meaning. For everyone there is Something which we value above all else, Something about which we are ultimately concerned. However others may choose to use the word "faith," this is what Tillich means by it. But though everyone has faith in this sense, most people's faith, or ultimate concern, is centered in something finite—wealth, pleasure, political ideology, or the like. This is idolatrous faith because it treats something of finite significance as if it held infinite or ultimate significance. But how do we speak of the object of authentic faith? No ordinary, literal, or scientific language can possibly represent either the Ground of Being on the one hand or our existential experience on the other. Thus enters one of Tillich's central contributions: "The language of faith is the language of symbols."[16]

We can summarize here only a few of the many interesting points Tillich makes concerning religious symbols. For example, symbols differ from signs in that they point beyond themselves and participate in that to which they point; they have a life of their own, in that they are born (not invented), they live and die; they are reflective of a community's self-understanding; and they unlock dimensions of reality and of our own individual souls that otherwise remain concealed to us.

This is also the case with myths, the larger stories constituted by particular symbols. For example, the Biblical myths of the creation and the fall—with their symbols of the six days of creation, Adam and Eve, the serpent, fig leaves, expulsion from the Garden, and so on—confront us with our existential situation as utterly dependent on something beyond ourselves and woefully out of whack with our ideal nature. We have already seen that the essence of the Christian proclamation is expressed by the symbols of the atoning cross of Christ and his resurrection. And everything said about God is necessarily symbolic, except that God is Being Itself—the only non-symbolic thing that can be said about the Ultimate.[17]

Tillich's appeal to the role of religious symbols is strewn throughout his works, most notably, perhaps, in his famous little book *Dynamics of Faith* and his essay with the instructive title "Existential Analyses and Religious Symbols." From the former comes his most famous expression of his high estimation of the power and significance of religious symbols: "Never say *only* a symbol, but rather *not less* than a symbol!"[18]

◆

The Problem of Faith and History

Many have found the opaqueness of Tillich's language off-putting, a barrier to their understanding of his thought. An example might be his definition of miracles as "ecstatically received understanding of constellations of factors which point to the divine Ground of Being."[19] Some have regarded such talk as theological gobbledygook. More substantively, some have wondered whether Tillich's central concept—that of the Ground of Being—is really even meaningful. Does it have any real, identifiable content? What can one actually do with it, either from a theoretical or a practical standpoint. How can such a contentless concept provide a serious basis for the conceptual unpacking of Christianity, especially over and against competing religious visions? How does one get excited about, say, worship of and prayer and service to *Being Itself*? Surely something would be lost in Billy Graham's evangelistic benediction if he were to say: "May the Ground of Being bless you, real good!" Likewise, Tillich's denial of a real incarnation of God in Christ, his denial of the real resurrection of Jesus from the dead, and his separation of the Jesus of history from the Christ of faith, appear to many to be downright betrayals of the substance of New Testament Christology, and his ontological speculations appear to be simply alien to the character of biblical theology.

But let us focus for the moment on what may be the most crucial difficulty for Tillich—and, while we're at it, for Bultmann, too—at least as viewed from the standpoint of the mainstream of Christian thought: their view of faith's relation to history. In a way, this problem has plagued all of twentieth-century theology.

At best, Tillich's and Bultmann's explanation of this matter leaves something to be desired, but they do make a distinction that is both clear and crucial. We have seen that Bultmann claims a certain objectivity for the Christ event, and that Tillich's theology requires a concrete embodiment of the New Being, which means that the event of Jesus as the Christ has a "factual element." As it turns out, though, they both appear to lay the foundation of faith on a quite different ground. Both distinguish the *historischer Jesus* from the *geschichtlicher Christus*—that is, the Jesus who lived once upon a time and the Christ who lives in and for existential situations—and both point faith in the direction of the latter. Tillich puts his references to the "factual element" into perspective: "Knowledge of revelation, although mediated primarily through historical events, does not imply factual assertions, and is therefore not exposed to critical analysis by historical research."[20] In other words, historical events (for example, the life of Jesus of Nazareth) may be the occasion of revelation, but what is revealed is something not disclosed empirically, and the object of faith is thus insulated from any historical or factual investigation. Bultmann has already distinguished the theologian from the archaeologist, and Tillich avers that the truth of Christianity is entirely independent of whether Jesus Christ ever lived, much less died and rose again.[21]

One wonders whether those theologians who have abandoned as a failure the quest of the historical Jesus believe that it is not possible practically and technically to verify the Christ event, or as Bultmann and Tillich appear to mean, that the Christ event cannot even *in theory* be confirmed as a historical fact. While Bultmann, Tillich, and others were arguing that the Christ event has *existential* meaning, even if it was not a literal event, something else was going on. Philosophers were debating whether theological propositions were even *cognitively* meaningful (that is, even had truth-falsity status) if they were not in some way rooted in empirical and thus theoretically falsifiable events.[22]

Aside from what the "faith is independent of history" position may mean for the epistemological question as to the truth-value of Christianity, certainly it would be theologically vacuous for St. Paul, who saw Christian faith as inseparable from its historical moorings: "If Christ has not been raised, then our proclamation has been in vain and your faith has been in vain" (1 Cor. 15:14). For Paul the resurrection is indisputably an empirical and, in principle, falsifiable event. It would also be vacuous for countless others, including Barth, who have staked their salvation and hope on the objective, historical, and (at least in theory) investigatable fact of the miracles, suffering, and resurrection of Jesus Christ:

> The truth of Jesus Christ is also in the simplest sense a truth of facts. Its starting-point, the Resurrection of Jesus Christ from the dead, is a fact which occurred in space and time, as the New Testament describes it. The apostles were not satisfied to hold on to

an inward fact; they spoke of what they saw and heard and what they touched with their hands.[23]

Obviously there is a big difference between the opinion that a man died and was then raised from the dead, and the further opinion that this man was the Christ and that God has acted for our salvation in his death and resurrection. The latter can never be known historically or empirically. But the former can—at least in principle—and many maintain that such historical events or facts are necessarily involved in the network of divine-historical elements that constitutes the Christian gospel. In this view, it is not so much a question of self-understanding but of how we are in fact understood by God; it is not a question of what we hope but of what we are entitled to hope. Christian faith holds genuine existential-subjective significance only because it rests on a historical-objective foundation, that is, only because God did something "out there," in history, in reality. If a folksy metaphor may be permitted, Christianity issues checks under the name of the Bank of Historical Events. If it turns out that the bank is broke—well, Kierkegaard taught us a long time ago that risk is the measure of faith's intensity.

CHAPTER FIVE

Religionless Christianity
Dietrich Bonhoeffer

A remarkable strain of twentieth-century theology was inaugurated, unwittingly, by Dietrich Bonhoeffer, a German pastor and professor who was imprisoned and executed by the Nazis because of his involvement in the Resistance. It is clear that Bonhoeffer had no inkling that his several books and, especially, his fragmentary ideas conceived in prison would be all that interesting. Of course, he didn't live to see that he would be hailed as one of the most innovative and influential theologians of his time.

Bonhoeffer was born in 1906 in Breslau, Germany (now Poland), into a well-to-do and cultured family with eleven children. His father was an eminent psychiatrist who was eventually appointed to a professorship at the University of Berlin. As a child Bonhoeffer played with the children of the great theologian, Adolf von Harnack. Somewhat to the disappointment of his parents but with their support, he enrolled as a student in theology at the University of Berlin. Although Barth was of course not there, Bonhoeffer nonetheless fell under his influence. After completing his doctorate, he was a pastor in Barcelona, Spain; a student at Union Theological Seminary in New York; and then a professor of theology at Berlin until, in 1936, he was ousted from his teaching post by the Nazis. After pastoring for two years in London, he was summoned back to Germany to head up an underground seminary for the Confessing Church, which opposed the "German Christians." During this period he produced *The Cost of Discipleship* and *Life Together*. In 1939, during a lecture tour in the United States, he was invited to join the faculty of Union, but even this opportunity did not deter him from returning to Germany to participate in the church's struggle there. This struggle did, in fact, lead to his death in 1945, as we will see.

◆

Cox and Secular Theology

It is instructive to note right at the start that both radical and conservative theologians have been quick to claim Bonhoeffer as a champion for their causes. It is no wonder that Bonhoeffer was conscripted by several strands of radical thought, especially by what came to be called "secular theology." Bonhoeffer's rather startling thesis was that the world has "come of age" and can do without religion: "God is being pushed more and more out of life," and "we are moving towards a completely religionless time."[1] Moreover, he thought that this was a good thing.

Secular theology received its best-known expression in Harvey Cox's theological best-seller *The Secular City*, published in 1965. Before joining the Harvard Divinity School, Cox, a young Baptist theologian, was a professor at Andover Newton Theological School where he wrote *The Secular City*. For a time it was truly all the rage.

Cox's opening statement gets right to the point: "The rise of urban civilization and the collapse of traditional religion are the two main hallmarks of our era and are closely related movements."[2] Urbanization, or the contemporary cosmopolitan life-style, with its freedom of anonymity and mobility, has emerged against the backdrop of scientific and technological advances that were in turn spawned by the "wreckage of religious world-views." A corollary of urbanization, which is a way of living together, is the way in which modern people grasp and understand their life together, or *secularization*. More specifically, Cox defines secularization as "the loosing of the world from religious and quasi-religious understandings of itself, the dispelling of all closed world-views, the breaking of all supernatural myths and sacred symbols"[3] (as opposed to *secularism,* which simply substitutes one dogmatic ideology for another). Secularization is interested in this world, not some other world; it is interested in the human being, not some god beyond, as the one responsible for the world and history; and it no longer finds its morality or meanings in religious rules or rituals.

Even though the church has railed against all that is secular, Cox claims that the Bible itself lays the foundation of modern secularization. For example, the Genesis account of creation portrays nature as "disenchanted," or freed from the supernatural, something to be investigated and mastered by humans. The "civil disobedience" of the Hebrews in the story of the Exodus speaks of the desacralization of politics, the rejection of all sacral-political absolutisms. And the Sinai covenant, with its "Thou shalt have no other gods before me," represents, with its plural "gods," a deconsecration and relativization of cultural creations and human values. In the Creation, in the Exodus, and at Sinai, Cox sees God releasing people to their maturity, and calling people to maturity is the task of the church. In fact, the church must become God's avant-garde in the midst of the city; if anyone, the church must fully embody the biblical principle of secularization.[4]

Something like this, says Cox, is what Bonhoeffer means by the world "coming of age" in "a completely religionless time."

But is it?

◆

"God of the Gaps"

Some of the more traditionally inclined theologians have been distressed by such readings of Bonhoeffer, claiming that the radical interpreters grasped, at best, only one side of his position and made him a spokesman for a cause that in fact would have repelled him. What Bonhoeffer was responding to, they argue, was the preoccupation with the *forms* of traditional religion rather than with its *substance*. While it is, of course, impossible to say exactly what Bonhoeffer was getting at, we think that this "take" on his fragmentary and undeveloped thought is probably closer to the truth.

When Bonhoeffer claims that the world has come of age and can do without religion, he means that the world can do without *religiosity*. There is, for Bonhoeffer, a difference between superficial religiosity and genuine Christianity. This interpretation of Bonhoeffer agrees with his earlier and emphatic renunciation of the easy religion or "cheap grace" offered by the church, "sold on the market like cheapjack's wares," forgiveness without repentance, faith without involvement.[5] This interpretation also agrees with Bonhoeffer's evolving preoccupation with the church's relationship to the world come of age, an interest that can be traced from his *The Cost of Discipleship* through the uncompleted *Ethics* to its final and most dramatic and provocative (though fragmentary) expression in *Letters and Papers from Prison*. Of course, the radical interpreters make much out of the difference between the "earlier" and the "later" Bonhoeffer. But this exaggerated distinction does not do justice to the continuity of Bonhoeffer's works, the changing circumstances of his ministry, and the numerous friends and students who surely understand better than anyone else what he was saying.[6]

Bonhoeffer did believe, to be sure, that God was being pushed out of the world. The God of traditional religion was a

"God of the gaps," a God invoked to fill up the gaps in our understanding of the cosmos and ourselves. But the unswerving advance of science has made such a God increasingly unnecessary. With the rise of Darwinism, for example, the God of traditional religion took a giant step backward. For the hypothesis of an immediate and special creation of humans was now discarded in favor of a better one. That particular question was now answered, more naturally, without God. Nor can we allow this God, driven from the public side of life, to take refuge in the personal, inner, and private side of life. For this realm— the mysterious inner sanctum of the soul—is also being exposed and understood, in this case by the light of psychoanalysis. With the rise of Freudian psychology, God took another giant step backward. The world is coming of age and can fill up the intellectual and scientific gaps for itself.

It is not just a matter of filling up for ourselves the intellectual gaps; the emotional or spiritual gaps are being filled in without God, too. As Bonhoeffer sees it, people are not incurably religious in the sense that there is a God-shaped blank in the human soul and the human being remains unfulfilled until that blank has been filled in. More specifically, there is no religious *a priori*, as was maintained by the eighteenth-century German thinker Friedrich Schleiermacher; the "numinous consciousness," a deep sense of the divine presence emphasized as the core of authentic religion by Bonhoeffer's older contemporary Rudolf Otto, is for most people an alien and unrecognizable experience; and St. Augustine was simply wrong when he said that the heart is restless until it finds its rest in God.

On the intellectual, moral, and religious planes modern people can, as a matter of fact, get along without God, live, well, and be happy: "God as a working hypothesis in morals, politics, or science, has been surmounted and abolished, and the same thing has happened in philosophy and religion. . . . For the sake of intellectual honesty, that working hypothesis should be dropped, or as far as possible eliminated."[7] As Bonhoeffer expressed it in his oft-cited slogan, we must learn to live in the world *etsi deus non daretur,* "even if God were not given."[8]

◆

Religionless Christianity

Bonhoeffer believed that the demise of a God of the gaps is good because this is not the God of Christianity anyway. The sooner we rid ourselves of the felt necessity of this "religious" God, the sooner the God of authentic Christianity becomes a possibility for us.

In this respect there is a more positive side to Bonhoeffer's theology, apparently not always appreciated by his radical interpreters. The world's coming of age "opens up a way of seeing the God of the Bible," a God who helps us not by a transcendent and otherworldly omnipotence, but by weakness and suffering with us in the world. We must allow God, as God allowed Godself, to be edged out of the world and onto the cross. This, says Bonhoeffer, "will probably be the starting-point for our 'secular interpretation.'"[9]

This means, as Bonhoeffer says in his *Ethics,* that the church must reconsider its understanding of and relationship to the secular world. Indeed, the Church's ill-conceived distinction between the sphere of the sacred and the sphere of the secular (an echo of Barth's early emphasis on the transcendence and wholly-otherness of God) is one of the causes of its ineffectiveness in the modern world. The truth is that God entered the world in the incarnation and "in Christ . . . was reconciling the world to himself" (2 Cor. 5:19). The separation of the sacred from the secular denies the unity of God and the world achieved in the revelation and work of Christ. There is no God apart from the world, no supernatural apart from the natural, no sacred apart from the profane. Christ is the ultimate reality and the world is part of that reality.[10] In fact, the true Church "has essentially nothing whatever to do with the so-called religious functions of man, but with the whole man in his existence in the world with all its implications." The problem now is how to speak in a secular way about God and to live a kind of "worldly holiness."[11]

If we are moving, then, toward a completely religionless time, the Christian will have to abandon the *deus ex machina*— the convenient problem-solving God—as well as otherworldly and ecclesiastical involvements. Quite simply, the Christian must cease to be religious.

> He must ... really live in the godless world, without attempting to gloss over or explain its ungodliness in some religious way or other. He must live a "secular" life, and thereby share in God's sufferings. To be a Christian does not mean to be religious in a particular way, to make something of oneself (a sinner, a penitent, or a saint) on the basis of some method or other, but to be a man— not a type of man, but the man that Christ creates in us. It is not the religious act that makes the Christian, but participation in the sufferings of God in the secular life. The "religious act" is always something partial; "faith" is something whole, involving the whole of one's life. Jesus calls men, not to a new religion, but to life. But what does this life look like, this participation in the powerlessness of God in the world? I will write about that next time, I hope.[12]

By thus breaking in upon the secular world the Christian will be what he or she is supposed to be—a man or woman "for others." This is to be fully human, fully Christian.

◆

A Man for Others

A man for others is what Bonhoeffer was.

Reacting to Barth's early preoccupation with the divine Wholly-Otherness, bearing the imprint of von Harnack's social consciousness, and, in all, totally Lutheran in his biblicism and Christology, Bonhoeffer felt constrained to cast himself upon the political and moral crisis of his time. From the beginning he opposed the infamous Aryan Clause, which banned Jews from positions in the Church, and he was instrumental in the formation of the Confessing Church, which resisted the German Christians of the Third Reich. He was originally a pacifist, but this option steadily eroded for him in light of the harsh realities developing right before his eyes. Along with his brother-in-law Hans von Dohanyi, he eventually became implicated in the ill-fated plot to assassinate Hitler. He was arrested in April of 1943 and was shifted around from one prison to another until one day, at Flossenburg, he concluded a worship service for his fellow prisoners and then, summoned by the guards, he said, "This is the end. For me the beginning of life." He was hanged on April 9, 1945. A few days later, Flossenburg was liberated by the Americans.

Wayne Best, an imprisoned British officer, was an eyewitness of the last events:

> Bonhoeffer . . . was all humility and sweetness; he always seemed to me to diffuse an atmosphere of happiness, of joy in every smallest event in life. . . . The following day, Sunday, 8th April, 1945, Pastor Bonhoeffer held a little service and spoke to us in a manner which reached the hearts of all, finding just the right words to express the spirit of our imprisonment and the thoughts and resolutions which it brought. He had hardly finished his last prayer when the door opened and two evil-looking men in civilian clothes came in and said, "Prisoner Bonhoeffer, get ready to come with us." [13]

A poignant incident says a lot about the man. During a trip to America in the late '30s Bonhoeffer was a visiting professor at Union Theological Seminary in New York. Certainly he had good reasons to remain in the United States and was, in fact, invited by Union to become a permanent member of the faculty.

His decision and the reasons for it are made clear in a letter to Reinhold Niebuhr: He would have no good conscience about participating in the reconstruction of Germany if he was not willing to participate in its present crisis and sufferings.

> It was a mistake for me to come to America. I have to live through this difficult period in our nation's history with Christians in Germany. I will have no right to participate in the reconstruction of Christian life in Germany after the war if I do not share the tribulations of this time with my people. . . . Christians in Germany are faced with the fearful alternatives either of willing their country's defeat so that Christian civilization may survive, or of willing its victory and destroying our civilization. I know which of the two alternatives I have to choose but I cannot make the choice from a position of safety.[14]

So he sailed back to Germany and to his death.

Obviously, it is unfortunate that the writings and thoughts of this innovative theological mind must remain forever incomplete. Nonetheless, a central and consistent thrust is discernible in Bonhoeffer. And although he represented an exciting departure from the usual understanding (or misunderstanding) of what it means to be a Christian in the modern world, it is not necessary to yield to the temptation of interpreting him after the fashion of certain radical secularists or so-called Christian atheists. He was, after all, a man who until the very end continued to speak of the world of God, redemption, and the forgiveness of sins, and he was a man who prayed.

———————————————◆———————————————

A Theological Legacy?

There was a time in the 1960s when Bonhoeffer figured centrally, along with the likes of Bultmann and Tillich, in a sort of radical re-imaging of Christianity. In 1963 Bishop John A. T.

Robinson published a theological best-seller called *Honest to God,* and now it is hard to overstate the influence of that little book. Robinson outlined what he regarded as the only viable theological perspective for the time, and that perspective was self-consciously drawn from the insights of those three thinkers. With respect to Bonhoeffer in particular, Robinson said:

> I must register the impact of the now famous passages about "Christianity without religion" in Dietrich Bonhoeffer's *Letters and Papers from Prison.* . . . One felt at once that the Church was not yet ready for what Bonhoeffer was giving us as his last will and testament before he was hanged by the S.S.: Indeed it might be understood properly only a hundred years hence. But it seemed one of those trickles that must one day split rocks.[15]

At the time, it did seem that Bonhoeffer was "here to stay." On the other hand, Karl Barth, the greatest theologian of the twentieth-century, regarded Bonhoeffer as a man of good theological insights, but in the end not really profound, and he predicted for Bonhoeffer a brief theological influence. With respect to the latter, it appeared that Barth was right, as Bonhoeffer's star faded rather quickly. As will be said in the case of the death of God theology, which we consider in the chapter 6, Bonhoeffer's contribution resonated with a general social-cultural experience. It is easy to understand how Bonhoeffer, especially the "radical" Bonhoeffer, was relevant in the time of the Vietnam War, the martyred Che Guevara, and the American civil rights turmoils. But that experience eventually faded, making Barth's evaluation seem justified; perhaps it was not. Recent years have witnessed a renewed interest in Bonhoeffer, and the significance of his contribution to twentieth-century theology probably remains to be seen. Perhaps, as Robinson said, it will take a hundred years.

The Death of God
William Hamilton and Thomas J. J. Altizer

Surely the most radical movement within twentieth-century theology was the so-called death-of-God theology. Any perspective advertising itself as "Christian atheism" is bound to be an odd one, and in fact, to many onlookers at the time it all seemed rather outrageous. On the other hand, in retrospect it should not be so surprising that the tumults of the '60s yielded a theological perspective to complement the social and personal upheavals that captivated so many in those years. That it gained immediate attention (it even made the cover of *Time* magazine) is understandable. Whatever else the death-of-God theology was, it was a sort of ultimate extension of secular theology, which sought, in one way or another, to push God out of the world.

As we will see, many thinkers are associated with the death-of-God movement. Two Americans, however, were the primary movers: William Hamilton and Thomas J. J. Altizer.

Hamilton, a Baptist, received his seminary degree at Union Theological Seminary, where he enjoyed the tutelage of both

Reinhold Niebuhr and Paul Tillich. He took his doctorate in theology at St. Andrew's University in Scotland, where he studied with the famous theologian Donald Baillie. During the heyday of the death-of-God movement, Hamilton was a church history professor at Colgate Rochester Divinity School. In 1961 he burst upon the scene with a book with the revealing title, *The New Essence of Christianity.* Altizer received his B.A., M.A., and Ph.D. degrees from the University of Chicago. In the '60s he was professor of Bible and Religion at Emory University. In 1966 he published a book with an even more provocative title, *The Gospel of Christian Atheism.* Hamilton and Altizer together published, in 1966, *Radical Theology and the Death of God.*

◆

Variations on a Theme

What is not very understandable—and wasn't then either—is the meaning of the bizarre claim that "God is dead." Several thinkers were associated with this movement, representing variations on this theme.

Gabriel Vahanian published a book actually called *The Death of God,* but the title was intended to suggest rather the end of Christian *culture,* arguing that it is no longer possible to objectify God or caricature God through a traditional and antiquated religiosity. Paul M. van Buren was identified as another death-of-God theologian, though he wasn't happy about it. Prompted on the one hand by philosophical verificationism and on the other by classical Christology, van Buren attempted a reinterpretation of the gospel for modern empirical people by stressing the factual character of the Christ event. His interest in accommodating the insights of analytic philosophy—very much in vogue at the time—is reflected in the full title of his book, *The Secular Meaning of the Gospel: Based on an Analysis of Its Language,* and in his rejection of God-talk, including death-of-God-talk, as meaningless. On the Jewish side, Richard L.

Rubenstein, author of *After Auschwitz,* was interpreted as aligned with these thinkers. Writing pessimistically for a post-Holocaust Judaism, Rubenstein interpreted the death of God phenomenologically. The death of God had to do not with something going on with respect to God, but with something going on with human experience; it was a sort of cultural anthropological event. He preferred the observation that "we live in the time of the death of God" to the statement "God is dead." That is to say for Rubenstein, the death-of-God theology, like all theology, was an expression of a way in which the world is experienced.

But Thomas J. J. Altizer and William Hamilton unmistakably and clearly proclaim the actual death of God, and it is to them that one must turn for the most emphatic and authentic expression of this position.

◆

The Nietzsche Connection

Now at first it is difficult to believe that these thinkers were really affirming the actual death of God. Upon hearing this phrase we are apt to recall the German existentialist thinker and writer, Friedrich Nietzsche (1844–1900). In his *The Gay Science* he represented a madman running through the streets in search of God who, unable to find God, cries out:

> God is dead. God remains dead. And we have killed him. . . . Is not the greatness of this deed too great for us? Must not we ourselves become gods simply to seem worthy of it? There has never been a greater deed; and whoever will be born after us—for the sake of this deed he will be part of a higher history than all history hitherto.[1]

Nietzsche meant that the idea of God, especially as an absolute lawgiver for humans, could no longer be accepted. He himself explains his meaning: "The greatest recent event—that 'God is dead,' that the belief in the Christian God has ceased to be believable—is even now beginning to cast its first shadows over Europe."[2] In this sense, God is dead, and humans themselves must ascend the throne of God and become the measure of all things.

We rather naturally suppose that the death-of-God theologians meant something like that—the traditional idea or concept of God is irrelevant and dead. But this was not the case, at least not with Altizer and Hamilton. Their deicidal tendencies are to be taken quite seriously; they were affirming God's actual death.

◆

Hamilton's Angle

In a straightforward statement by Hamilton, which appeared (some would say appropriately) in *Playboy,* he lists the possible meanings of the phrase "death of God." The phrase may suggest, for example, that there is no God and there never was one. This is, of course, simply the standard atheistic line. Or the phrase may mean that the idea of God and the word "God" have become vacuous and require radical reformulation. It may mean that classical conceptions of God, like God as problem solver or God as necessary being, must be abandoned. But after listing these and still other possible interpretations, Hamilton explains that none of these are intended by death-of-God theologians such as himself. By "death of God" they mean, rather, that

> there once was a God to which adoration, praise and trust were appropriate, possible and even necessary, but that there is now no such God. This is the position of the death-of-God or radical theology. It is an atheist position, but with a difference. If there was a God, and if there now isn't, it should be possible to indicate why this change took place, when it took place and who was responsible for it.[3]

In another statement Hamilton says, "We are not talking about the absence of the experience of God, but about the experience of the absence of God." To those who still think that he must be speaking symbolically, Hamilton says, "We have insisted all along that 'death of God' must not be taken as symbolic rhetoric for something else. There really is a sense of non-having, of non-believing, of having lost, not just the idols or the gods of religion, but God himself."[4]

Yet to say that God has "died" is somewhat misleading inasmuch as it conjures up an image of a God who once upon a time was living, breathing, eating, and answering prayers, and then suddenly keeled over dead. It would be closer to the truth (though not nearly so dramatic) to say that God has been transformed, that the supernatural has become immersed in space and time, the spirit has become flesh, the transcendent God has become wholly immanent, that not only has our way of talking about God changed—*God* has changed. This is the real significance of the phrase "death of God."

It is, at best, difficult to say how and when this happened. Both Hamilton and Altizer agree that God died, or at least began to die, at the time of the incarnation, when God took on the spatiotemporal reality of Jesus Christ, entered human history, and accepted the burden of not only sin and suffering but morality as well. Hamilton saw God as still dying in the nineteenth century, as reflected in both American and European literary and political movements. He saw Melville's *Moby-Dick*, for example, chronicling the death of God: "Perhaps the most unforgettable image of the dying God in our language is that of Ahab finally fixing his harpoon in Moby Dick's side, as the two of them sink together, both of them God, both of them evil."[5] There is, therefore, a three-part answer to the question of when God died: "The coming and death of Jesus makes God's death possible; the 19th century makes it real. And today, it is our turn to understand and to accept it."[6]

◆

Altizer's Angle

More important than when and how God died is what God's death means. Here it is Altizer who provides the most vivid input. "Vivid" may be too weak a word. Altizer is more of an apocalyptic poet than a theologian. Hamilton himself said of him: "Altizer is all *elan,* wildness, excessive generalization, brimming with colorful, flamboyant, and emotive language."[7] That kind of style, along with his drawing upon everything from the Bible, Hegel, Nietzsche, Sartre, Blake, and Freud, makes for a "theology" not easily digested.

Altizer made much of the *kenosis* ("emptying") passage in Phil. 2:7-8, where Paul says that Christ "emptied himself, taking the form of a slave, being born in human likeness. And being found in human form, he humbled himself and became obedient to the point of death—even death on a cross." The more orthodox might cringe at Altizer's use of this biblical passage as a proof text for his strange theology. But on this particular point Altizer out-orthodoxes the orthodox; he carries the kenotic act of God further than the Bible itself does, claiming that the Godhead was entirely transformed into Jesus, an idea propagated already in the third century by the heretic Sabellius. At any rate, sifting out biblical passages to his taste and greatly influenced by Eastern mysticism, the dialectical thought of Hegel, and the poetic vision of Blake, Altizer was persuaded that God's self-emptying of Spirit in order to become flesh— as descent into the concrete—has achieved, or is achieving, a supreme *coincidentia appositorum,* a complete union of the sacred and profane.

This in turn means a liberation from the "alien transcendent," the oppressive shadow of the Wholly Other, and freedom to live in the immediate moment:

The death of God abolishes transcendence, thereby making possible a new and absolute immanence, an immanence freed of every sign of transcendence. Once a new humanity is fully liberated from even the memory of transcendence, it will lose all sense of bondage to the past, and with the loss of that bondage it will be freed from all that No-saying which turns us away from the immediacy of an actual and present "Now."[8]

For Altizer, God gives way to Jesus, otherworldly thinking gives way to this-worldly thinking, and guilt gives way to a theological-Dionysiac celebration of life. The death of God is a joyous and liberating event; God's withdrawal means for us a new openness to the world and an opportunity to bear on our own shoulders the responsibility of suffering and love.

Still, it is not altogether happy that God has withdrawn from our world, and Hamilton speaks of a kind of uneasiness and nostalgia for the absent God and a hope that it may someday be possible to speak of God again. Understandably, in the days of the death-of-God movement there was a great fondness for Samuel Beckett's *Waiting for Godot,* an uneventful dialogue, feebly reminiscent of half-forgotten religious images and theological dogmas, in which two characters base their ill-defined hopes on the arrival of some obscure personage named Godot. He never comes, but they continue to wait. This was a summary of the pathetic ambiguity and dim expectation of at least one state of mind in the '60s.

◆

"God is Dead" is Dead

During what might be called the "rush for relevance" that seemed to motivate many theological perspectives of those years, Rubenstein announced, rather triumphantly, "Radical theology is no fad. It will not be replaced by some other theological novelty in the foreseeable future. Too many tendencies in classical theology, philosophy, and literature have intersected in this movement for it to disappear as rapidly as it has gained attention."[9] He was wrong. Soon after he wrote those words it was frequently observed that God-is-dead was dead. The quick demise of the death-of-God theology, at least as *theology*, is in part to be explained by the fact that it was really 40 percent poetry, 40 percent social commentary, and only 20 percent theology; after the flush of novelty, it could hardly stand up against real theology. Also, it was so self-consciously wedded to the social and psychological situation of the day that after the passing of that situation it had no holding power. Its slogans, which sounded so good at the time, began to ring hollow. Talk about "openness to the world" or about "bearing on our own shoulders the responsibility of suffering and love" began to be perceived as a kind of theological posturing, devoid of much theological substance.

Now it is irresistible to put Mark Twain's words in the mouth of God: "Reports of my death have been greatly exaggerated."

CHAPTER SEVEN

Theology in Process
John B. Cobb Jr.

A young army recruit knelt beside his bed to offer his usual nightly prayers. Suddenly the room seemed to be filled with "a presence of the most blessed sort." For a few brief moments the young man was enveloped with a sheer and inexplicable joy. The divine presence he encountered that night, he later realized, was nothing less than an outpouring of God's pure grace, which came "as a gift totally disconnected from expectation, merit, or anything else in my own life." Determined to expose his faith to "the worst the world could offer," the young man enrolled in the University of Chicago to focus on the modern objections to Christianity. The result, however, was disastrous. Within six months his faith was shattered, and his prayer life, which had previously been the mainstay of his existence, evaporated—never to be retrieved.[1]

Having gone through a profound, personal experience of the death of God that Thomas Altizer would later speak about in his own writings, the young man set out on new course. He launched a quest to reconstruct not only his faith but also the faith of the church in a manner that could meet the challenges of the modern context. This quest produced the "dean" of American process theologians, John Cobb, Jr.

◆

A Theologian "in Process"[2]

In 1925 John Cobb, Jr., was born the youngest of three children to missionaries John and Theodora Cobb. Young John spent most of his first fifteen years on the Japanese mission field, until the outbreak of the Second World War forced him to return to his parent's home state of Georgia to live with his grandmother. During his high school and college days, Cobb was a deeply pious person with a profound sense of communion with God. Yet other students found his moralistic side offensive. A cartoon bearing the title "Spares" found its way into his college annual, picturing John with not only a halo around his head but also extra halos dangling from his arm.

In 1944 Cobb joined the U.S. Army. His missionary background made him an obvious candidate for the Japanese language program, but an experience of divine call to Christian ministry led him to abandon the prospects of a career in the foreign service. The presence of intellectually oriented Catholics and Jews in the army unit sparked Cobb's ill-fated decision to enroll in the master's program at Chicago.

In the face of the demolition of his faith that the Chicago experience produced, Cobb turned to the University of Chicago Divinity School to provide a context in which to discover the answers to his quest. In the midst of his personal turmoil, some stability came into the future theologian's life through his marriage to a high school friend. He began to receive direction along the path to intellectual stability as well. At Chicago, Cobb confronted Charles Hartshorne,[3] who directed his graduate studies leading to the completion of Ph.D. work in 1952. More significant, through Hartshorne, Cobb discovered the process philosophy of Alfred North Whitehead.

Meanwhile, family difficulties forced Cobb to launch his career in 1950. He took positions in several rural congregations and taught at a junior college. After completing his doctoral work in 1952, he was offered a post at Candler School of Theology on the campus of Emory University. But the situation at Emory proved difficult, and in 1958 Cobb moved on to what would become his final academic home. From that point until his retirement in 1990 he served as Ingraham Professor of Theology at the Claremont School of Theology and Avery Professor in Claremont Graduate School in southern California.

Cobb's twin passions have been process theology and the church. Interest in the former resulted in the establishment of the Center for Process Studies at Claremont together with the publication of the journal *Process Studies*. His commitment to the latter is evident in Cobb's involvement as an ordained minister in the United Methodist Church and his desire to write not only for the academy but also for laypersons.

Appropriately, Cobb is a theologian in process. His interpreters cite various transitional points in his theological career. Perhaps the most abrupt of these occurred in 1969. Prior to this, Cobb had sought to show how Whitehead's thought provided the means to overcome the concerns bequeathed to theology by Karl Barth and the neo-orthodox theologians. Cobb later spoke of his work during this early phase of his career as "Whiteheadian scholasticism."[4]

His sudden awareness of the ecology crisis, however, led to a radical shift in his thinking. Cobb now began to merge what he—in keeping with the widely-held distinction between theology and ethics—had previously kept quite distinct, namely, his political interests and his theological work.[5] In his later reflections on this transformative experience, he reports that in the summer of 1969 "my complacency was shattered and I went through a conversion experience. As with many such conversions, the changes appeared more drastic at the time than they do in retrospect. Nevertheless, something did happen to me, and my work in the 70s was different because of it."[6] What was this transformative experience?

> That summer, quite abruptly, I was forced to the awareness that the structures of society and the patterns of development which I had taken largely for granted are leading humanity toward global self-destruction. . . . That summer I realized that the very ways in which 'progress' was being made—e.g., dominant development policies as well as economic programs in the industrialized world—were all part of the total network of processes that were destroying the basis of human life on the planet. The issue of human survival seemed so overwhelming in its importance that I felt I must reorient my priorities at once.[7]

Cobb's immense shift was signaled by a little book written for church study groups bearing the provocative title, *Is It Too Late? A Theology of Ecology*. The volume revealed that, like Immanuel Kant nearly two hundred years earlier, Cobb had now "awakened" from his own "dogmatic slumber."[8]

The post-1969 Cobb became interested in other issues as well. His quest to think more holistically and to break down the barriers dividing the academic disciplines led him to cover the territory from economics[9] to education. His attempts at integrative theological reflection encouraged him to engage with older and newer developments, including the Buddhism he encountered as a "missionary kid"[10] and the rising liberation and feminist movements.

Yet even in the midst of these engagements, he looked to process thinking to provide not only his own theological moorings but also the basis from which to respond to the new situation. For example, he concluded that Whitehead's emphasis on the organic unity of all reality provided a philosophical foundation for the idea that all living beings are bound together in one planetary "web of life," as proponents of the ecology movement were articulating. He now "became more of a Whiteheadian than before."[11] But rather than mere metaphysical speculation, his process theology had become a political theology, as the title of his *Process Theology as Political Theology* indicated.

The transition that began in 1969 led Cobb to abandon any plans he may have had to write a systematic theology. Such a project, he concluded, assumes that theology is the attempt to understand and interpret the essence of the Christian faith in an abstract manner, whereas the actual goal of the enterprise is to transform reality.[12] Cobb, however, never abandoned completely his interest in articulating what he sees as the truth of Christianity on behalf of the church. Thus, after his retirement he offered a book-length attempt to come to terms with his own theological heritage as a Wesleyan.[13]

Throughout his career, Cobb has remained convinced of one central point. The process view of reality provides the foundation for living responsibly and transformatively in the world. This constitutes his abiding contribution to contemporary theology.

----------------◆----------------

The Process View of Reality

Strictly speaking, process theology is a twentieth-century phenomenon. Yet its roots lie much earlier. The philosophers of ancient Greece chose "Being," or immutability, rather than "Becoming," or change, as the foundational metaphysical concept. The champion of Being was Parmenides (c. 515–450 B.C.E.), who defined reality as what remains eternally the same—the change we perceive in sense experience is mere appearance. Parmenides' chief rival was Heraclitus (c. 540–475 B.C.E.), who said that all reality is involved in incessant change and subject to new modifications.[14] "You cannot step twice into the same rivers," Heraclitus declared, "for fresh waters are ever flowing in upon you."[15]

Parmenides' position dominated the Western philosophical tradition through most of history. But as the nineteenth century gave way to the twentieth, thinkers in many fields began to look for other options. They were naturally drawn to Heraclitus. Cobb is no different.

The ultimate goal of process theologians like Cobb is to indicate the relevance of the Christian faith to a culture increasingly imbued with the sense of Becoming.[16] To this end they borrow from process philosophy with its focus on dynamic rather than static categories. This philosophy declares that to be actual is to be in process, and that every entity is an integration of opposites—inner plus outer, past plus future, self plus other. Without a doubt, the most important articulator of the new process philosophy is Alfred North Whitehead (1861–1947).[17]

A mathematician in his native Britain until 1924, when he accepted a professorship of philosophy at Harvard University, Whitehead produced what one observer lauds as "the most impressive metaphysical system of the 20th century."[18] Thinkers like Cobb who draw their philosophical foundation from Whitehead's work would heartily concur with this conclusion. Yet, "process" remains a difficult view of reality for many people to understand, let alone to accept.

Although a pioneer, Whitehead actually saw himself as simply engaging in the traditional task of speculative philosophy, namely, "the endeavor to frame a coherent, logical, necessary system of general ideas in terms of which every element of our experience can be interpreted."[19] What is revolutionary in Whitehead is his assertion that reality is not static essence, but process. Alluding to the maxim of Heraclitus, he declares, "The ancient doctrine that 'no one crosses the same river twice' is extended. No thinker thinks twice; and, to put the matter more generally, no subject experiences twice."[20]

But how is it possible that "no subject experiences twice"? Whitehead's answer lies in a radically new understanding of what a "subject" is. For him, a subject or an "actual entity" is not a permanently enduring thing, not a neutral, objective, purely material substance. Instead, each of the fundamental building blocks of reality is an "occasion of experience" or a "drop of experience"—an activity or a "becoming" that comes into existence and then quickly disappears. Each "becoming" brings together past and future, or in process language, each is "dipolar," consisting of a "physical" pole—its relevant past— and a "mental" pole—its achievable possibility.

First is the past dimension: Each occasion is embedded in a temporal stream of past occasions climaxing in its immediate predecessor, from which it draws certain aspects and rejects others as it comes into existence.[21] Whitehead uses the term "prehension" to speak of the movement from past to present and of the relatedness of each occasion to its antecedent.

To the past must be added the future dimension. Not only is each occasion a product of its immediate predecessor, but each occasion also draws from its achievable potential. In the process of becoming, each occasion is confronted by, and either accepts or rejects its "initial aim," the best possible pattern whereby it might become an enjoyable experience and make a contribution to subsequent occasions.[22]

Occasions that are tied together by a common element into a self-sustaining whole form what Whitehead calls a "society of occasions." Societies come in various types, but the most unique is that of the human person.[23] Each human is a society that can remember its past, anticipate its future, and weave the two together. Every human remains a finite society, for its experience incorporates a limited past and a limited future.

God plays a crucial role in Whitehead's philosophical system. God provides the initial aim to every occasion of experience. In addition, God is the final "repository" of each occasion once it perishes.[24] Each entity not only forms the predecessor for the next occasion, it also adds to God's experience.

God, then, is similar to all other actual entities.[25] Like them, God is dipolar, consisting of a primordial and a consequent dimension.[26] In God's "primordial" or nontemporal, "mental" pole God supplies the "lure" or persuasion to actual entities in the process of becoming. But Whitehead's deity also sports a "consequent," temporal, or "physical" pole. God "prehends" the temporal world. By acting as the repository of all perishing actual entities, God retains the novelties achieved as the future becomes the present and vanishes into the past.[27] Thereby, God forms the world into a unity. Thus, in contrast to humans who are finite societies of occasions, God is the unbounded society.[28] God remembers all experiences and envisions all possibilities; this God weaves past and future together in a never-ending process.

The God of process philosophy, therefore, is not aloof from or unaffected by the world. Instead God and the world are interdependent. Both need the other, and both are bound up with the other.[29] Further, this God works in the world primarily through persuasion—through the power of the "lure"—rather than coercion. Thus, Whitehead's two favorite pictures of God's dealings with the world are "tender care" and "infinite patience."[30]

This outlook suggests a mutual faith between God and the world. Process thinker Lewis Ford explains: "Faith in this sense is reciprocal. Just as the world must trust God to provide the aim for its efforts, so God must trust the world for the achievement of that aim."[31]

Whitehead's God is neither all-powerful nor all-knowing.[32] Instead, like humans, God knows the future only as possibility, never as actuality. And as the one who "feels" every experience, God becomes, to cite Whitehead's widely-acclaimed definition, "the great companion—the fellow-sufferer who understands."[33]

◆

Cobb's Process Theology

John Cobb, Jr., is not the only theologian to draw from Whitehead's metaphysics the foundation for a reformulation of Christian theology.[34] Yet he became the most prominent exponent of the type of theology that emanates from the process philosophical system. Cobb's overriding concern is to construct a vision of reality for the contemporary world.[35] Such a vision, Cobb believes, could provide the intellectual underpinnings for a renewed Christian faith that can transform our world.

Initially, Cobb launched his project with an attempt to draw from process philosophy insights in developing a new—and as it turned out, highly controversial—Christian natural theology.[36] Actually, his desire to construct a Christian theological edifice upon a naturalistic foundation is in keeping with Whitehead's own concern to engage with a scientifically oriented culture.[37] Like his philosophical mentor, Cobb wants his theological starting point to be completely open to scientific investigation. But why choose process philosophy? Cobb finds Whitehead's structure of thought to be both intellectually superior and congenial to faith.[38]

Cobb's biggest theological bogeyman is the classic, but in his estimation now antiquated, concepts of God as the Cosmic Moralist, the Unchanging and Passionless Absolute, the Controlling Power, or the Sanctioner of the Status Quo.[39] More relevant in contemporary society, he believes, is the process understanding that views the deity as a participant in the temporal process.[40] To show this, he appeals to the human experience of being "called forward." We have a sense of being lured beyond what the past dictates, of being directed to something beyond. This experience, Cobb argues, cannot be explained solely by a mechanistic model that views all events as rising from a cause found in the prior conditions. Further, this experience of being lured to the future is not limited to humans. Rather, Cobb asserts that all nature is being called forward toward ever new possibilities.

Not only does this conception cohere better with contemporary science than does the God of classical Christian theology, Cobb is convinced that it is also more in keeping with biblical personalism. In fact, he believes that there is a convergence between Jesus' teaching about the coming reign of God and the scientific picture of an evolving universe. The link between the two emerges when we conceive of the source of the "teleological pull" within creation as "will" and "love," or personality. In this manner, Cobb concludes, both Jesus and the new scientific cosmology point to the same conception of God, namely, God as "the One Who Calls."[41]

Bolstered by this convergence between the scientific and biblical visions, Cobb replaces the classical view of God as the controlling power over the world with the Whiteheadian idea of God as Creative-Responsive Love.[42] This God relates to the world through persuasion, not coercion. While remaining the source of unrest in the world, the process God undergoes risk and adventure throughout the entire cosmic experiment. And the outcome of this experiment remains unknown, even to God.

◆

The Process Christ and Our Human Future

As we would expect, Cobb's project of reformulating the Christian faith moved from the doctrine of God to the doctrine of Christ.[43] Here his goal is to carve out a new incarnational Christology, an understanding of Christ as the incarnate Word, or *logos,* of God. In this enterprise, Cobb finds process thought helpful, especially Whitehead's concept of how actual entities come into existence.[44] As we noted already, according to process philosophy a present occasion is the product of past experiences and the initial aim God offers to it. In this manner, both the past and the initial aim may be said to be "incarnate" in the present.[45] Further, the aim for each occasion of experience arises from God's primordial nature.

On this philosophical basis, Cobb constructs his Christology. The primordial nature of God from which all initial aims emerge, he says, is none other than the Logos. Because these aims lure the world toward its own creative transformation, Cobb names them "the Christ." "Christ," then, is simply "creative transformation," or more specifically, the "incarnation of the Logos in the world of living things and especially of human beings."[46] This insight indicates how the divine Word can be both universally present throughout creation and specially present in Christians. According to Cobb, the divine primordial nature is universally present insofar as it is incarnate as the initial aim in all occasions of experience. At the same time, the work of the Christ is most discernibly present in humans to the extent that they "decide for" the Word, that is, insofar as they are receptive to the incarnation of the Word in the initial aim that comes to them in each occasion of experience. In this manner, "the Christ" becomes the principle of creative transformation in our lives as well as in the world as a whole.[47]

As a Christian, however, Cobb cannot stop here. He must also offer an understanding as to how Jesus of Nazareth is the Christ. According to Cobb, Jesus is the Christ in that Jesus brought into history a distinctive structure of existence. The incarnation of the Christ in Jesus constituted his very selfhood. On this basis, Cobb can conclude, "So far as we know, Jesus was unique." He then explains:

> The distinctiveness of Jesus can be spoken of in terms of Christ. Christ is the incarnate Logos. As such Christ is present in all

things. The degree and the kind of Christ's presence varies. The fullest form of that presence is that in which he coconstitutes with the personal past the very selfhood of a person. That would be the paradigm of incarnation. In that case Christ would not simply be present in a person but would be that person. The distinctive structure of Jesus' existence was characterized by personal identity with the immanent Logos. Hence it is a matter of literal truth to affirm the identity of Jesus with Christ. In all things Christ is present. Jesus *was* Christ.[48]

Insofar as the incarnate Christ "coconstituted" Jesus' identity, Jesus showed us the basic truth about reality. As David Ray Griffin indicates, for Cobb, "Jesus reveals the supreme incarnation of the Christly aims from God, and his achievement affects the continuing development of human history by opening history to new possibilities for transformation."[49] If we accept the truth Jesus incarnates, we open ourselves to the same creative transformation operative in Jesus. In this manner Cobb's process turns out to be what we might term an "exemplification Christology."[50] More important for Cobb than the qualitative uniqueness of Jesus is Jesus' role as the one who exemplifies a universal divine principle, a principle that characterizes the primordial nature of God.

The theme of creative transformation leads to Cobb's vision for the future. In process thinking, the future is radically open. As the one who journeys with us, God doesn't foreordain the future, but calls us to be cocreators in bringing to pass God's aims for the world. Cobb realizes that the openness of the future is a double-edged sword. It provides the basis for hope that progress will occur. But it also means that we may choose self-annihilation. Hence, God cannot guarantee that the divine reign will arrive at the end of the historical process. Nevertheless, Cobb elevates his vision of God's kingdom as the basis for our hope and the motivation for our actions.

But what does this ideal of the divine reign look like? Here Cobb chooses to remain vague. He does hint at an eschatological realm characterized by mutual participation[51] and by the perfect indwelling of the Logos. Hence, he concludes his volume on Christology with this poetic description: "All our images of hope . . . point toward a transcendence of separating individuality in a fuller community with other people and with all things. In this community the tensions between self and Christ decline, and in a final consummation they would disappear. This is the movement of incarnation. Christ is the name of our hope."[52]

Despite Cobb's use of the term "consummation," process thinkers do not typically speak about an actual end to history. Indeed, if Becoming takes primacy over Being, we cannot anticipate a actual future point when the process comes to rest.[53] In what sense, then, can we talk about an eschatology?

To resolve the problem of the "perishing" of actual entities, Whitehead introduced the concept of "objective immortality." By this he meant the final integration of all occasions of experience in the consequent nature of God. Occasions don't simply perish without a trace. Rather, they become the foundation for subsequent occasions. More importantly, they are taken into the divine life, where they add to God's experience.

The same holds true for our future as humans, as well as for the future of the world. Like occasions of experience, we too will enjoy immortality,[54] yet not through a literal historical resurrection. Instead, as we add to the enjoyment of God, are "remembered by God," and hence are "taken up into God's life" we enjoy "resurrection."[55] In the same way, the world itself is included into God's consequent nature. "In this inclusion of the world in God," Cobb writes, "the world is completed and becomes everlasting." According to Cobb's vision, even evil is taken up and overcome in the kingdom. He offers this explanation:

> God's reception of these creaturely events in the Kingdom of Heaven is not merely passive any more than is the reception of

the past in other actual entities. They are synthesized into a new whole. But whereas in the world the synthesis depends on extreme selectivity, so that most of what is offered is rejected, such limitation is not present in the Kingdom. God's aim is so inclusive that he can receive and synthesize into good what in worldly occasions would be mutually destructive elements, or elements incompatible with their limited aims. Even experiences whose intentions are evil or whose consequences in the world are destructive can be taken up into the Kingdom as contributions to its everlasting and growing harmony.[56]

◆

A Problematic Vision?

Cobb's reformulations of Christian themes along the lines of process philosophy triggered an elongated and often heated theological engagement involving both sympathizers and opponents.[57] Some critics, such as Wolfhart Pannenberg, have pinpointed problems in Cobb's Christology, going so far as to claim that it is merely a form of an ancient heresy called "dynamic monarchianism," the teaching that Jesus is divine in that God's power rested on him.[58] Others chide Cobb for proposing an overly optimistic view of humankind and an insufficiently radical understanding of evil, which in process thought appears to be a necessary part of the world's movement toward God.[59] The focus of the theological discussion, however, has been the process conception of God.

It would be incorrect for us to label Cobb's understanding of God as "pantheism." Cobb doesn't simply equate either the world or the world process with God. The more appropriate designation might be "panentheism," which, in fact, Cobb's teacher, Charles Hartshorne, preferred. According to process thinking, not only does the world, especially humankind, act as cocreator with God of itself, it also contributes to God's own life as it is taken up into God's consequent nature. Hence, process theology is panentheistic in that it envisions all reality being taken into God, so that God can no longer be conceived apart from the world.

We readily grant that process panentheism marks a crucial step away from the sheer monism of pantheism, which in the end blurs the distinctions between creation and Creator. But does the panentheistic view of God move sufficiently away from pantheism so as to maintain the central Christian conception of God and the Christian teaching about God's relation to the world? Critics say, "No!"

In their attempt to uphold the importance of human cooperation in the process of creation, Whiteheadian theologians such as Cobb give us a God whose only tool is persuasion; this God can only seek to convince us to make the best possible decisions while we are en route to the future. Cobb and his associates readily admit that in the end "God is not completely in charge." But at what cost? Sympathetic critic Joseph Bracken confirms our suspicions: "There is no way to legitimate the traditional understanding of God as Creator within the Whiteheadian scheme of things."[60] At the very least, the process model amounts to a completely new understanding of the Christian doctrine of creation.[61]

Another related problem glares at us from the pages of Cobb's writings. This problem is actually the flip side of the critique of the process concept of evil that we mentioned in passing earlier. Taking their cue from Whitehead's "fellow sufferer" God, process theologians have stood at the forefront in creating a theology that elevates God as one who suffers with the world. In fact, the suffering God has become one tenet of the new "orthodoxy" within contemporary theological parlance.

While we can applaud Cobb for his role in this development, his method of introducing this important point is unsettling. By relegating mastery over evil solely to the divine experience,

Cobb's vision borders on the old "pie-in-the-sky-by-and-by" theology he left behind him in the Georgia mountains. Where does this leave the holy God of the biblical story, who rejects sin and evil to the point of defeating them within the program of salvation history? Putting the two criticisms together, we are left thinking that Ted Peters may be right in his complaint that in Cobb's theology, "the 'God the Father Almighty' confessed by the creeds is either replaced or reinterpreted by a deity who is strong on persuasion but weak on potency."[62]

CHAPTER EIGHT

Hope in the Midst
of Suffering
Jürgen Moltmann

In 1945, the advancing British armed forces captured a young German soldier. For him, the next three years meant prisoner-of-war camps in Belgium and then in Britain. Yet this incarceration proved to be a turning point in his life, triggering a crisis of faith that determined the direction he would follow from then on. Reflecting later on the importance of this time, the former prisoner wrote:

> In the camps in Belgium and Scotland I experienced both the collapse of those things that had been certainties for me and a new hope to live by, provided by the Christian faith. I probably owe to this hope, not only my mental and moral but physical survival as well, for it was what saved me from despairing and giving up. I came back a Christian, with a new "personal goal" of studying theology, so that I might understand the power of hope to which I owed my life.[1]

The German soldier—Jürgen Moltmann—went on to become one of the most widely read theologians of the late twentieth century.

━━━━━━━━━━━━━━━━━━━━━━━ ◆ ━━━━━━━━━━━━━━━━━━━━━━━

From Hope to Theology

Jürgen Moltmann was born in Hamburg, Germany, in 1926. His upbringing included a greater exposure to the German poets and philosophers than to the Christian faith.[2] Yet his boyhood experiences set the stage for the direction his theology would later take. In the 1970s he mused publicly about his youth and its influence on his thinking:

> With the eye of memory I see myself as a boy gazing out of the window of his parents' home upon the forests which cross the distant horizon of northern Germany. There the flatlands are wide and the heavens broad. There the horizon is a boundary which does not confine but rather invites one to go on beyond. That boy was filled with curiosity about what was on the other side of the horizon.

For Moltmann this boyhood memory evidenced a religious truth: "God is the one who accompanies us and beckons us to set out. And it is God who, so to speak, waits for us around the next corner."[3]

The spark of hope that flickered during his youth was fanned into flames in the crucible of suffering Moltmann encountered in the Allied war prisons:

> As I continue to look back I see a young prisoner of war interned in an English camp. His horizon there is the barbed wire, even though the war had been over for some time. . . . hope rubbed itself raw on the barbed wire! A man cannot live without hope! I saw men in the camp who lost hope. They simply lay down,

took ill, and died. When life's hopes flounder and crack up, a sadness beyond comforting sets in. But on the other hand, hope disturbs and makes one restless. One can no longer be content with his situation, with the way things are.[4]

Although as a conscripted soldier his chosen literary companions had been Goethe and Nietzsche, in the camp in Belgium an American chaplain gave him a Bible. For the first time, he read the Christian Scriptures, and it changed the direction of his life. In the years since then, Moltmann's theological writings have consistently retained a sense of newness and exploration. In 1994—thirty-six years after his release from the prisoner-of-war camps—he testified to the remarkable newness that theological studies always held for him: "Right down to the present day, theology has continued to be for me a tremendous adventure, a journey of discovery into a, for me, unknown country, a voyage without the certainty of a return, a path into the unknown with many surprises and not without disappointments. If I have a theological virtue at all, then it is one that has never hitherto been recognized as such: curiosity."[5]

Filled with resolve born from a hope for "a new, more humane Germany, and for a liberated, liberating church of Christ," upon his release from the war camps the future theologian returned to his home country and entered theological studies in Göttingen. The new crop of students Moltmann typified brought with them new questions requiring new answers: "The survivors of my generation came into the lecture halls from hospitals and prisoner of war camps inwardly shattered, their flesh bearing all the marks of war. A liberal, bourgeois theology would never have gotten through to us."[6]

The Göttingen faculty rose to the occasion. The influence of the theology of the Confessing Church inspired by Karl Barth was strong. Consequently, Moltmann was imbued with a fervent Christological focus. As he reports, "we learned the origin of the Christian faith in the suffering of him who was crucified and in the liberating power of the risen Christ."[7] This powerful commitment to the cross and resurrection provided the driving foundation for Moltmann's entire theological project.

Upon receiving his doctoral degree in theology in 1952, Moltmann headed for the pastorate. The young minister served a small Reformed church until 1957, when he launched his academic career. Moltmann taught briefly at the theological seminary (*kirkliche Hochschule*) in Wuppertal, where he came into contact with another budding young thinker who would later attain great status in theological circles, Wolfhart Pannenberg. A short tenure at the University of Bonn opened the way for Moltmann to accept the prestigious position of professor of systematic theology at the University of Tübingen in 1963. He held this post until his retirement in 1994.

Publication of his widely read *Theology of Hope*, printed in English in 1967, catapulted Moltmann into the theological limelight. Since then he has attained worldwide recognition, in part due to his prolific literary output. In contrast to many others in his field, however, the Tübingen theologian has shied away from producing a *summa,* an all-embracing summary of Christian doctrine, or even a multivolume systematic theology. Near the end of his career he explained this hesitancy:

> I have never done theology in the form of a defence of ancient doctrines or ecclesiastical dogmas. It has always been a journey of exploration. Consequently my way of thinking is experimental— an adventure of ideas—and my style of communication is to suggest. . . . So I write without any built-in safeguards, recklessly as some people think. My own propositions are intended to be a challenge to other people to think for themselves.[8]

Therefore, after the publication of a trio of books he now sees as preparatory studies,[9] beginning in 1980 Moltmann's project crystalized—in a somewhat unplanned way—into a series of loosely related writings that he refers to simply as "systematic contributions to theology."[10] Together these works reveal Moltmann's keen attempt to reconstruct the central Christian doctrines in the light of God's promises for the future.

Despite what may seem as a somewhat haphazard literary trajectory, from first to last in different, yet clear ways Moltmann's writings all speak about hope in the midst of suffering. Yet the theme we suggest is even more foundational. While readily visible in his early books, this theme remains evident as well in his recently published eschatology.[11] This hope is born from the promise of God's future, is based on the cross and resurrection of Jesus Christ, and comes to us in our present historical reality through the work of the Holy Spirit.

◆

A Hope-Filled Theology

Moltmann often keeps a specific picture on his desk when he engages in his writing projects. As he composed his eschatology, *The Coming of God* (which appeared thirty years after the publication of his first book, *Theology of Hope*), the picture that stood before him was Simone Martini's painting, *The Angel of the Annunciation*. Moltmann offers a telling description of the fourteenth-century work of art: "This angel of the future is gazing with great eyes towards the messianic Child of the coming God, and with the green branches in his hair and in Mary's hand proclaims the Child's birth. The tempest of the divine Spirit is blowing in the angel's garments and wings, as if it had blown him into history. And its meaning is the birth of the future from the Spirit of promise."[12]

As this description indicates, from beginning to end Moltmann's writings have been about hope. The focus on hope marks his conscious move beyond his theological mentor Karl Barth. In highlighting the hope that Christians share, Moltmann augments his Swiss forebear's strict Christological focus with an equally important emphasis on the future and consequently on the historical nature of reality.[13] Moltmann is convinced that because the Christian hope about which he speaks is grounded in history and experience, it answers the deepest aspirations not only of religious, but also of secular people. His basic insight seemed to be confirmed by the broad reception of his *Theology of Hope* in the midst of the turmoil and confusion of the 1960s. Nor was his suggestion merely a passing fad, as is evidenced by the continued interest sparked by Moltmann's subsequent works.

The focus on hope has given Moltmann a voice beyond strictly academic circles. He has been involved in ecumenical dialogues with Roman Catholics, Eastern Orthodox Christians, and Jews. Perhaps even more important was Moltmann's participation in the Christian-Marxist dialogues of the late 1960s, in which he took the lead in building bridges between Christians and revisionist Marxists. This provided him with a foundation from which to influence the revolutionary and political theologies that emerged during the 1960s and 1970s.

But what is the hope that Moltmann claims lies at the center of the Christian faith? For him, Christian hope is above all hope for the coming of God's "Kingdom of Glory." It is the eager expectation of the full freedom and community of humans, together with the liberation of all creation from bondage to decay. In short, Christian hope is eschatological—it is directed toward the ultimate fulfillment of the divinely given promises found in Scripture.

Moltmann, therefore, offers a thoroughgoing eschatological theology, a theology that centers on the present expectation of a glorious future. Indeed, he maintains that eschatology has too often been ignored, dismissed, or demoted to being a useless appendage to theology. Moltmann, in contrast, wants to give eschatology the place it deserves at the very heart of theology. He writes, "From first to last, and not merely in the epilogue, Christianity is eschatology, is hope, forward looking and forward moving, and therefore also revolutionizing and transforming the present."[14] The "theologian of hope" is convinced that a reorientation toward the future is both biblically sound and theologically necessary. He believes that an eschatological approach provides the way out of the impasse that plagues contemporary theology,[15] including the modern conflict between classical theism and atheism. In addition, he is convinced that by providing a "critical theory of God" that has direct social application, the focus on hope can overcome the destructive separation between theory and practice.

◆

The Philosophical Foundation

As a *Christian* theologian, Moltmann naturally draws heavily from biblical themes, especially the all-pervasive eschatological orientation of Scripture as discovered by his teachers at Göttingen. But the specifically philosophical foundation for the theology of hope arose out of Moltmann's critical engagement with another Tübingen professor, the revisionist Marxist philosopher Ernst Bloch.

In the 1930s, Bloch blended Jewish-Christian eschatology and Marxist scientific social analysis into a massive philosophical treatise bearing the evocative title *The Principle of Hope*. According to Bloch, humans are instinctively hopeful. That is, we are all driven by the quest to overcome the alienation we sense and to find our true sense of self. This quest drives history through revolutionary change in an attempt to attain the hoped-for utopia. Bloch declared that this as-yet-unrealized utopia, this "not-yet-being," exerts power over the present and even the past.[16]

Moltmann borrows much from Bloch, while rejecting the philosopher's atheism. According to Moltmann, Bloch's suggestion that humans can face the future in hope without appealing to God is an illusion. He writes, "A historical future without heaven cannot be a forecourt of hope and the motivation for any historical movement." On the contrary, Bloch's proposal "turns infinity into indefinite endlessness and makes the striving for fulfillment merely an 'on and on.'"[17]

Upon Bloch's fundamental insight Moltmann constructs a specifically Christian vision. He attempts to show that Christian hope is the only way to overcome the groundless, shallow variety Bloch offers. Against the Marxist philosopher, Moltmann maintains—to cite the description offered by one observer—

> that Christian hope is in fact not an abstract utopia but a passion for the future that has become "really possible" thanks to the resurrection of Christ. By entering into history the resurrection of Christ introduces a *novum* [a new reality] which gives substance to hope and opens up to it a definitive horizon (an *ultimum*) that does not signal the end of history but is rather a real possibility for human life and for history itself.[18]

In this manner, as several commentators have observed, Barth and Bloch become the "odd couple" lying behind Moltmann's program. Barth's Christ-centered approach provides the theological raw material, whereas Bloch's insight that to be human means to be a hopeful creature provides the philosophical orientation for Moltmann's interpretation of Christianity.[19]

◆

Hope and Promise

Moltmann's self-declared goal is to carve out a theology that is "biblically founded, eschatologically oriented, and politically responsible." As a result, he is less concerned with developing a systematic theology—"correct doctrine" or "pure theory"—as with what he calls "concrete doctrine" or "practical theory." The task of theology, in his estimation, is not so much to provide an interpretation of the world as to change the world in the light of the Christian hope for its ultimate transformation by God.[20] Yet throughout his books lies a scarlet metaphysical thread, namely, the "eschatological ontology" that characterizes all the theologies of hope, as well as the theology of Wolfhart Pannenberg. According to Moltmann, reality is not a predetermined or self-contained system of cause and effect. The future is not completely inherent in the present.[21] On the contrary, rather than being determined by the present, the future determines the present. In this manner, the future is "ontologically prior" to the present and the past. It does not rise from the present, but comes to it. The future draws the present forward into totally new forms of reality.

This outlook is appropriately illustrated in Moltmann's understanding of the nature of theological statements. Viewed from the perspective of the priority of the future, "theological concepts become not judgments which nail reality down to what it is, but anticipations which show reality its prospects and its future possibilities."[22]

In a sense, Moltmann follows a pattern somewhat similar to what we noted in our discussion of Paul Tillich. Analogous to Tillich's method of correlation, Moltmann's theology fulfills a type of answering function. He too believes that theology can speak relevantly to secular people because revelation provides answers to their needs and questions.[23] Reminiscent of Tillich, Moltmann declares, "If it is correct to say that the Bible is essentially a witness to the promissory history of God, then the role of Christian theology is to bring these remembrances of the future to bear on the hopes and anxieties of the present."[24]

Like Tillich, therefore, Moltmann's concern is to meet the questions of the present with answers drawn from revelation. But what is "revelation?" Here the Tübingen theologian's reading of Scripture leads him to interject the word "promise." He declares that both Israel and the early church regarded the primary form of God's presence among them as promise for the future.[25] According to Moltmann's characterization, Israel experienced God through a history of promise and faithfulness to promise. This experience of revelation led ancient Israel to see history as linear, as "moving on, leaving things behind and striking out towards new horizons as yet unseen."[26] And it gave rise to the prophetic voice, with its constant call for ever greater righteousness in the light of God's promises of a glorious future kingdom.

As a result of this view of history and revelation, the New Testament church viewed Christ, especially his death and resurrection, as God's promise of the future kingdom, and the early believers spoke of the Holy Spirit as the "earnest" of the promised future of Christ.[27] As they lived in the light of these promises, the early church became a people of hope who knew the faithfulness of God but remained continually restless for the coming of God's reign.

This focus on promise produces Moltmann's intriguing understanding of revelation. Rather than a supernatural incursion into history from beyond, revelation is the message of promise, the anticipation in the present of the totally new and unexpected events that are coming in the future. Even historical fulfillments of past promises do not exhaust the message. Instead, in Moltmann's words, "in every fulfillment the promise, and what is still contained in it, does not yet become wholly congruent with reality and thus there always remains an overspill." Such promissory revelation contradicts the present and opens it to a new reality that is not inherent in it.[28] Promissory revelation points to the future Kingdom of Glory, which, although it does not yet exist, is nevertheless "present" in its effects on the here and now. Concerning this present impact of the future kingdom, Moltmann declares, "As compared with what can now be experienced, it brings something new. Yet it is not for that reason totally separate from the reality which we can now experience and have now to live in, but, as the future that is really outstanding, it works upon the present by awaking hopes and establishing resistance."[29]

According to Moltmann, promissory revelation engenders a kind of knowledge, namely, the knowledge of things hoped for. But this knowledge is above all a perspective. Hopeful knowledge is anticipatory, provisional, fragmentary knowledge that always remains open and constantly strains beyond itself. Revelation, therefore, is not the unveiling of already existing truth, but—to cite Moltmann's own description—the "apocalypse of the promised future of the truth." Such knowledge "knows the future in striving to bring out the tendencies and latencies of the Christ event of the crucifixion and resurrection, and in seeking to estimate the possibilities opened up by this event."[30]

Hence, more than imparting "facts," revelation kindles faith and nurtures hope. As a consequence, Christians proclaim a hope borne from God's revealed promises for the future, which in turn respond to creation's sighs and groanings for redemption. Such hope, Moltmann declares, has a far-reaching impact on Christians in the here and now. Such hope "makes us ready to bear the 'cross of the present.' And it can hold to what is dead, and hope for the unexpected."[31]

The narratives of God's promises and human responses to these promises are found in the Bible, which witnesses to the promissory history of God. The primary value of the biblical narrative does not lie in the recounting of the past, however, but in pointing to God's coming reign. Moltmann writes, "In these accounts of the past we encounter the promissory history of the future of God. We find the future in the past, see the future revealed and anticipated in the past, and find ourselves taken up into this history of liberation."[32]

◆

The Suffering God of Hope

The innovative connection Moltmann forges between revelation and promise relates directly to his understanding of God.

Simply stated, like Pannenberg and other theologians of hope, Moltmann sees a link between God and the future Kingdom of Glory, in which God will be fully present and revealed in the world. Hence, Moltmann declares, "God is not 'beyond us' or 'in us,' but ahead of us in the horizons of the future opened to us in his promises." So intimate is this bond that he concludes that "the future must be considered as mode of God's being."[33]

But why this intense desire to associate God with the future? Perhaps the background for Moltmann's bold move lies in his own life experiences, especially his face-to-face encounter with evil during and after the Second World War. The former war prisoner seems convinced that the evil we see in history undercuts any conception of God as fully existing already—as the sovereign God "above us," for example. Instead of being the ground of this world, filled as it is with evil and suffering, God is the one whose coming kingdom contradicts and negates the world. This God transforms the world by drawing it into the Kingdom of Glory. Moltmann doesn't deny that God is present in our world. But he finds God's presence primarily in the power of suffering, which is most clearly evident in Jesus' cross and resurrection and in the sending of the Holy Spirit.

Moltmann's claim that God is present in the world draws us toward his understanding of God as triune. Indeed, the doctrine of the Trinity dominates Moltmann's later work, if not his entire career. He develops a concept of the Trinity as arising from the mutual, *perichoretic* ("interpenetrating") relationships of the three divine persons. This in turn forms the foundation for understanding the reciprocal, perichoretic relationships between God and the world.[34]

In this enterprise Moltmann attempts carve out an interpretation that lies between traditional Christian theism and process theology. The initial impetus for this attempt arises from one of Moltmann's most innovative proposals, namely, his use of the cross of Christ as the basis for an exploration of the doctrine of the Trinity. According to Moltmann, the cross not only effects human reconciliation, but also is the occasion in which God constitutes himself as triune within history.

"Trinity," in other words, is shorthand for the passion narrative of Christ. In a widely quoted and poignant statement in *The Crucified God,* Moltmann professor declares, "What happened on the cross was an event between God and God. It was a deep division in God himself, in so far as God abandoned God and contradicted himself, and at the same time a unity in God, in so far as God was at one with God and corresponded to himself."[35] Hence, the basis of the Trinity is the separation-in-unity that God experienced in this event. Because it is bound up with the event of the cross, God's triunity is historical—it is constituted in and through suffering and conflict. The cross opens God to the world so that what happens in history happens "in God," and in this manner the cross meets suffering with the voluntary suffering of love.

Moltmann is fully aware of the far-reaching implications of his position. He writes, "This means that God's being is historical and that he exists in history. The 'story of God' then is the story of the history of man." Moltmann then offers an explanation: "If one conceives of the Trinity as an event of love in the suffering and the death of Jesus—and that is something which faith must do—then the Trinity is no self-contained group in heaven, but an eschatological process open for men on earth, which stems from the cross of Christ."[36]

We dare not too quickly pass over the radical nature of Moltmann's proposal. His point is that the cross is not extrinsic to God's own being. Or, conversely, Moltmann is denying that God would be exactly who and what God is without the cross. Instead, through the dialectic of the separation and unity between Father and Son, the cross constitutes God's being as triune. This assertion marks a sharp break from classical theism.

It means that God is not the immutable, impassable deity of much of Christian theology. For Moltmann, God not only affects the world. God is also affected by the world.

———————————————◆———————————————

Hope or Process?

At first glance Moltmann's willingness to bring the triune God into history appears hardly dissimilar from the process conception of God. If events such as Christ's cross and resurrection and the sending of the Spirit actually constitute God's being as the triune one,[37] then isn't God dependent on the world to be who God is? Indeed, Moltmann's "trinitarian history of the cross" naturally raises a crucial question: Would God be triune apart from the events of world history? Is involvement with the world *necessary* for God's own being?

Nevertheless, Moltmann believes that his thesis differs sharply from the process theology of thinkers like John Cobb, Jr., whom we reviewed in chapter 7. In contrast to the process model, Moltmann rejects any idea that God's experiences of conflict, pain, and suffering in history are due to some inherent interdependence between God and the world. Instead, Moltmann adamantly assigns the historicity of God to an act of God's free and gracious choice. Instead of being Whitehead's process deity, the "fellow sufferer who understands," Moltmann's God is none other than the Father of Jesus Christ who "has decided from eternity for seeking love." And only "in his decision to go outside of himself lies the conditions for the possibility of this experience."[38]

Moltmann's appeal to "seeking love" provides the key to his attempt to carve out a middle position between classical theism and process theology. God's compassionate involvement with the world, he argues, is the expression of God's overflowing love. Consequently, in God "necessity" and "freedom" are transcended by God's own nature—love.[39] This means that although God is not compelled to relate to the world in the way that God does, this relationship is the natural outworking of divine love, which is God's nature. In other words, Moltmann is asking us to hold together two seemingly contradictory truths: God does not feel any compulsion to love; yet "the self-communication of his goodness in love to his creation is not a matter of his free will. It is the self-evident operation of his eternal nature." Or stating the point more succinctly: "The essential activity of God *is* the eternal resolve of his will, and the eternal resolve of his will *is* his essential activity."[40]

Lying behind Moltmann's appeal to the divine love is a novel understanding of what it means for God to create the world. Specifically, Moltmann speaks of creation as an act of divine self-limitation. "In order to create a world 'outside' himself, the infinite God must have made room beforehand for a finitude in himself." Hence, Moltmann envisions God "creating" within the infinite divine reality a finite "space" and "time" in which the world could exist—"creating" such a "space" by "withdrawing" from that space and hence limiting himself over against it. To designate this view, Moltmann coined a new term—"trinitarian panentheism."[41]

Moltmann's poignant image goes farther. Because God "withdrew" in order to give place to creation, the "space" that marks the world is "Godforsaken" space. Now the glorious truth of Christianity is that to redeem the Godforsaken world, God enters the godless "space" created through this divine self-limitation—an entrance into the world that involves suffering. But through such suffering God brings the world into the divine life. Moltmann explains: "By entering into the Godforsakenness of sin and death (which is Nothingness), God overcomes it and makes it part of his eternal life."[42] This, then, is the trinitarian history of the cross, which entails the suffering and death through which God constitutes himself as the triune one.

◆

The Trinitarian History of the World

In *The Crucified God* Moltmann focuses almost exclusively on the cross as the defining moment in the divine life. Later, however, in *The Trinity and the Kingdom of God,* he moves to a more elaborate analysis. Now he looks to what he sees as the various stages of the histories of both the Son and the Spirit at work in the world in bringing about the glorification of the Father. To this end Moltmann sets alongside the cross both the resurrection and the sending of the Spirit. These events indicate that the kingdom of God develops as one trinitarian member hands the task over to the next. Hence, rather than being the only active subject in the process of bringing about the kingdom, the Father is actually dependent upon the sending, surrender, and glorification of the Son as well as the Spirit. As the focus of activity is passed from one divine person to the next, the "history" of God comes to be marked by shifting patterns of relationship among the three trinitarian persons. This process finally leads to the eschaton, the ultimate future when the divine activity comes to its goal in the kingdom of God.

This change carries significant implications for Moltmann's conception of God. Whereas his earlier focus on the cross locates the unity of the triune God in that past historical event, Moltmann's shift to the eschaton transports the perfect divine unity to the future. In this manner, the unity of the three persons becomes one of *goal,* not *origin.* To describe this unity, Moltmann draws from the idea of *perichoresis*—a traditional theological doctrine that, as we have seen, speaks about the working together and "interpenetration" of the three persons. Building from this older doctrine, he speaks of the eschatological unity of the triune God in language that borders on the poetic: "The trinitarian persons form their unity by themselves in the circulation of the divine life."[43]

As we noted earlier, Moltmann's attempt to carve out a middle way between classical theism and process theology raises a serious theological question: Would God be the triune one—and therefore God—without the world? In struggling with this question, Moltmann joined a host of twentieth-century theologians who have, however, tended to pose it in a somewhat different manner. These thinkers have sought to determine the connection between what many refer to as the "immanent Trinity"—the divine life as Father, Son, and Spirit in eternity and apart from the world—and the "economic Trinity"—God as active in the flow of history, especially through the incarnation of the Son and the sending of the Spirit. Hence, the theological question becomes, What is the link between the triune God in God's own eternal reality apart from the world and the triune God as active in the flow of history?

By emphasizing God as existing in triune heavenly perfection from all eternity prior to divine self-expression in history, classical Christian theism tends to elevate the immanent or ontological Trinity over the economic Trinity, and hence to elevate eternity over time. But in the mid-twentieth century the Roman Catholic theologian Karl Rahner set the stage for a revisiting of the matter when he declared that the economic Trinity *is* the immanent Trinity, and the immanent Trinity *is* the economic Trinity.[44]

In *The Crucified God,* with its focus on the cross as the central event in the life of God, Moltmann appears to elevate the economic Trinity, even to the point of losing the immanent Trinity entirely. He seems to leave no room for any talk about an eternal triune life apart from the event of the cross. In his words, "Anyone who really talks of the Trinity talks of the cross of Jesus and does not speculate in heavenly riddles."[45] Beginning with *The Trinity and the Kingdom*, however, Moltmann offers a more carefully nuanced interpretation of the immanent Trinity and the economic Trinity that acknowledges an interdependence between the two. He now acknowledges some type of inner trinitarian life distinct from the constitution of the Trinity in history. Nevertheless, he remains adamant that the trinitarian life is indelibly stamped by salvation history. More specifically, the cross of the Son and the joy of love in glorification through the Spirit mark the inner life of the triune God from eternity to eternity.[46] And for Moltmann the immanent Trinity ultimately comes to completion only when the history of salvation comes to its eschatological goal: "When everything is 'in God' and 'God is all in all,' then the economic Trinity is raised into and transcended in the immanent Trinity."[47]

◆

Hope in the Midst of Suffering

But of what possible importance is this entire matter of God's presence in history? Moltmann is convinced that connecting God's own being with history is of grave consequence, above all for human social and political interaction.

Like many other late twentieth-century theologians, Moltmann is critical of structures of power and hierarchy, preferring instead to emphasize fellowship, equality, and interdependence. Viewed in this light, the future Kingdom of Glory cannot be the universal monarchy of the Lord of creation, but a harmonious fellowship of liberated nature and humans with God. This kingdom is God's "Sabbath." Hence, Moltmann declares, "the resting God begins to 'experience' the beings he has created. The God who rests in the face of his creation does not dominate the world on this day; he 'feels' the world; he allows himself to be affected, to be touched by each of his creatures. He adopts the community of creation as his own milieu." Moltmann describes the relationship humans then have with God as neither servants nor children but as friends, and "in friendship the distance enjoined by sovereignty ceases to exist."[48]

As these statements indicate, Moltmann seems to suggest that hierarchy and power are intrinsically evil. In his estimation, it is at precisely this point that the traditional doctrine of the Trinity proves problematic. It provides a justification for political and ecclesiastical totalitarianism: "The notion of a divine monarchy in heaven and on earth, for its part, generally provides the justification for earthly domination—religious, moral, patriarchal or political domination—and makes it a hierarchy, a 'holy rule.'"[49]

At the root of this problem is what Moltmann calls "political and clerical monotheism," which emerges whenever the doctrine of the Trinity disintegrates into "abstract monotheism."[50] For this reason, he criticizes all interpretations of God as trinity that reduce the three persons to modes of a single subjectivity, because this inevitably sets God over against the world and implies a hierarchical, monarchical relation between them.

How can this difficulty be avoided? Moltmann believes that a renewed understanding of the doctrine of the Trinity is the key, for this doctrine is a "critical principle" for theology in its mission of transforming the world. Societies, he explains, reflect their fundamental theological outlook, their fundamental understanding of God or the gods, in the way they organize themselves. Consequently, Christian cultures must rediscover the biblical concept of God's triunity as the community and fellowship among three equal persons, rather than a monarchy of one person over the others and the world. This is best facilitated, he believes, by an emphasis on the interplay of the three subjects within the trinitarian history of God, for this understanding links God intimately with the world and its history. This, then, is why he is so adamant in speaking about the distinct subjectivities of Father, Son, and Holy Spirit.

Moltmann is convinced that only in this manner can we construct a doctrine of God that focuses on mutuality rather than lordship. The perichoretic relationships of the trinitarian persons provides the foundation for a "cosmic *perichoresis,*" that is, "a mutual in dwelling of the world in God and God in the world."[51] In the end, this constitutes Moltmann's mature eschatological vision.[52]

◆

A Dependent God?

So what should we make of all of this? Moltmann has been hailed for his challenging explorations of the implications of eschatology and of the cross of Christ for the being of God. Furthermore, taking his cue from Bonhoeffer's cry that "only the suffering God can help," Moltmann opened up a new chapter in theology, making the dictum that God is the suffering one a new "orthodoxy."

But a gnawing question remains: In the end does Moltmann's doctrine of the trinity owe more to social and political considerations than to biblical and theological insight? If so, is it ultimately merely another example of a theologian recreating God in the image of a personal ideal? Moltmann succeeds in his goal of forging an intimate link between God's being and historical events. But at what cost?

Perhaps the most dogged criticism of Moltmann's theology has been the charge that it compromises the divine freedom and makes history the process by which God realizes God's own self.[53] Indeed one of Moltmann's sympathetic interpreters offers this telling appraisal: "World history is taken up into the inner-divine history in such a way that the deity of God is made ontologically dependent upon world history and God only truly comes to himself through the completion of world history."[54]

Moltmann has taken pains to separate himself from such charges.[55] Consequently, in the end his theology must be judged on the basis of his own concern. His desire is to show that—in the words of Richard Bauckham—"the goal of the trinitarian history of God is the uniting of all things with God and in

God." In short, he seeks to set forth "a trinitarian and eschatological panentheism."[56] Moltmann offers an intriguing understanding of a God who offers hope in the midst of suffering. But does his characterization reflect the God of the biblical narrative?

CHAPTER NINE

Reason and Hope
Wolfhart Pannenberg

One late winter afternoon, in the mid-1940s, a German teenager was walking home from his piano lesson. Following his normal pattern, he made his way through the woods as the sun was sinking into the horizon. Suddenly, however, the routine was broken. The young man noticed a light in the distance. He rushed to the spot. As he approached it, he found himself flooded—even elevated—by a sea of light. Reflecting later on what he had come to see as the "single most important experience"[1] of his life, Wolfhart Pannenberg concluded that Jesus Christ had in this experience claimed him for his own, even though he was not yet a Christian.

In response to the Christ who met him incognito that day, Pannenberg would later commit himself to the theological task. As a result, he would become the most forceful voice for the great tradition of theological reflection in the second half of the twentieth century.

◆

The Making of a Theologian

Wolfhart Pannenberg was born in 1928 in a part of northeast Germany that now belongs to Poland. Although baptized a Lutheran as an infant, during his early years he had almost no contact with the church. This did not, however, prohibit him from experiencing what he now sees as the grace of God in his life. Rather, a series of such experiences not only led him to faith, but also brought him to theology as his life's pursuit.[2]

At about the same time as his "light experience" occurred, young Pannenberg was browsing through the public library. A book by the atheist philosopher Friedrich Nietzsche caught his eye. Thinking it was a work on music, the budding pianist pulled the volume off the shelf. Nietzsche's work sparked in him an unrelenting interest in the deeper issues that philosophers explore.

Reading Nietzsche had another impact as well. The philosopher convinced his young reader that the influence of Christianity was responsible for the disastrous shape the world was in. This conviction, however, was short-lived. During his final years of high school (the German *Gymnasium*), Pannenberg encountered a literature teacher who had been a member of the Confessing Church during the Third Reich. This teacher's life contradicted Pannenberg's earlier conclusion about Christianity. In fact, as a result of this teacher's influence, the German youth—now in the midst of a quest to come to terms with the deeper meaning of reality—concluded that he needed to look more closely at the Christian faith. To this end, he inaugurated a study of theology and philosophy. His inquiry led Pannenberg to conclude that Christianity is the best philosophy. And this realization launched his life both as a devout Christian and as a theologian.

Pannenberg's theological interests soon took him to Berlin. Initially, the university student was fascinated with Marxism. But he soon discarded it when he determined that it simply couldn't stand up to rigorous intellectual scrutiny. More significantly, his exposure to the evils of Nazi Germany and Stalinist Eastern Europe led Pannenberg to realize that no human political system can ever give rise to the perfect human social structure. Instead, the ideal is a divine gift belonging to God's glorious future kingdom.[3]

Having rejected the Marxist alternative, Pannenberg was attracted to Karl Barth's attempt to establish God's sovereignty and to claim all reality for the God of the Bible. Therefore, in 1950, the fledgling theology student went to Basel to study with Barth. While there, Pannenberg grew steadily more uneasy with his mentor's method of pursuing this goal. Specifically, he objected to the radical distinction the great theologian drew between natural knowledge and divine revelation in Christ. In contrast to Barth, Pannenberg saw a much closer connection between creation and redemption. Later, he would build his own theological program from the realization that God's revelatory work is the completion of creation, rather than a stark contradiction to the world as we know it.[4] Pannenberg would seek the religious implications inherent in all human experience.[5]

Working with Barth had sharpened Pannenberg's perspective. But his own theological focus had not yet emerged. This would require a move. So in 1951 the future theologian switched to the university at Heidelberg, where he studied under some of the leading scholars of the day.[6] During these years, a group of students from various disciplines (who came to be known as "the Pannenberg circle") met regularly for what became a lively theological discussion. In this fertile context, Pannenberg's understanding of the nature of revelation finally gelled. The foundational conclusion that would drive his entire academic output became evident in the title of the volume that formed the literary deposit of the work of "the Pannenberg circle," *Revelation As History.*[7]

After completing his academic training in 1955, Pannenberg launched his theological career. Initially he taught at the Lutheran church seminary in Wuppertal (1958–61), before moving to the University of Mainz (1961–68). Then in 1968 he was invited to join the fledgling Protestant faculty at the University of Munich. Pannenberg remained in this post until his retirement in 1993.

◆

The Quest for a Reasonable Faith

"Perhaps if you have heard anything about my work," Pannenberg declared to a group of students in Denver, Colorado, "you have learned that I am accused of being a rationalist by some people. Others call me a fundamentalist.... But ... there is one thing I am certainly not; I am certainly not a pietist."[8] In this seemingly enigmatic remark, the theologian indicated his diagnosis of the illness of modern theology, as well as his prescription for its cure. The current malaise, he believes, is the result of the "privatization" of religious belief in general, and of Christian theology in particular, that characterizes Western culture. From his perspective, theology has lost its public voice and has contented itself with speaking about the realm of private beliefs.

According to Pannenberg, the roots of the evacuation of theology from the public sphere lie in the Enlightenment—when thinkers elevated universal human reason as the way of overcoming the divisions in European society after the polarization of the Church into rival Catholic and Protestant factions. This radical shift in culture precipitated a crisis in theology. Before the Enlightenment, theologians looked to God's saving events in history as providing the foundation for faith. Christian thinkers accepted these events on the basis of what they believed to be God's own authoritative witness to the events of salvation history. According to classical teaching, this witness came to us either directly through Scripture, seen as the product of the divine inspiration of the prophets and apostles (the Reformation position), or indirectly through Scripture as interpreted by the teaching office of the church (the Roman Catholic view).

The Enlightenment outlook, however, set aside the idea of a divine, authoritative testimony to historical events. In its place thinkers subjected sacred history to the standards of the scientific method. In the minds of many, the introduction of the critical tools of scientific inquiry into the realm of biblical history had a disconcerting effect on the Christian faith. It called into question the biblical accounts of the salvation historical events and thereby undercut the historical basis for the faith.

The post-Enlightenment theologians were quick to rise to the challenge. If the canons of scientific inquiry undercut the certainty of a faith that rests on historical events, they reasoned, then why not provide a new foundation for faith and thereby free it from the shifting sands of historical research? The alternative the post-Enlightenment theologians lit upon was the conversion experience. These thinkers proposed that rather than looking to historical events, with all their uncertainties, the experience of conversion—which they believed provides its own certainty—could provide the foundation for faith.

The effect of this move was monumental. It opened the door to a far-reaching shift away from the classical approach, which began with a rational appeal to historical fact, to the modern approach, which builds from the subjective experience of the believer and the personal decision of faith.[9] It is this modern view that Pannenberg vehemently rejected as "pietism" in his disclaimer to the students in Denver.

Actually, the German theologian differentiates between two distinct, yet equally erroneous pietistic alternatives. The one, the position of the radical pietists in whose ranks Pannenberg includes Rudolf Bultmann, dismisses the historical content of the Christian tradition as irrelevant. The other, which Pannenberg labels "conservative pietism," grounds the plausibility of the historical aspects of the faith in the experience of faith. For example, because of their own experience of personal conversion, conservative pietists are certain that Jesus performed miracles and rose from the dead. Hence, they dutifully sing, "You ask me how I know He lives? He lives within my heart."[10]

In either case, the effect is the same. For his part, Pannenberg refuses to tread the pathway charted by either type of pietist theology in the ill-fated attempt to overcome the problem posed by the Enlightenment. But wherein lies an alternative? To answer this question, Pannenberg goes back behind the Enlightenment to the Reformation—to the great German reformer, Martin Luther. Luther declared that by nature faith cannot be derived from itself (as the pietists claimed), but only from beyond itself. And this "beyond itself" is nothing else but "in Christ," that is, in what Christ has done for us. Borrowing from Luther, Pannenberg boldly declares that faith is dependent on a historical basis, specifically, the historical activity of God. Otherwise, faith is simply not trust in God; it is only trust in faith itself.[11]

Pannenberg, therefore, is convinced that no nonrational decision of faith can meet the philosophical and historical challenges to the Christian claim to knowledge of God. This leads directly to theology. If faith is to be valid, actual truth must lie beneath it.[12] The task of theology is to pursue the truth and thereby to place Christian faith on firm intellectual footing.

In this way, Pannenberg returns to the classical model of theology. Reminiscent of older thinkers, he sees theology as a public discipline related to the quest for universal truth. And the question of truth, in turn, must be answered in the process of theological reflection. For this reason, he adamantly opposes any attempt to shield the truth content of the Christian tradition from rational inquiry. Theological affirmations, he insists, must be subjected to the rigor of critical inquiry into the historical reality on which they are based. Theology, in other words, must be evaluated on the basis of critical canons, just as the other sciences are, for they all deal with truth. Thus the truth of the Christian faith must be measured in accordance with how it fits together with—even illumines—all human knowledge.[13]

But Pannenberg doesn't advocate a simple return to the pre-Enlightenment situation. On the contrary, at one crucial point he parts company with the older view and proposes a truly innovative answer to the Enlightenment critique. For Pannenberg, truth is not found in the unchanging essences lying behind the flow of time. Our quest is not directed toward the discovery of a set of timeless truths or Platonic Forms. Instead, truth is historically conditioned and ultimately eschatological.[14] This means that until the final day (the eschaton), truth will by its own nature always remain partial, and all the truth claims we make will remain debatable. Therefore, theology, like all human knowledge, has a certain provisionality about it. We must treat all our theological statements as hypotheses that we test by how well they fit with other knowledge.

For Pannenberg, this conclusion is not merely dictated by the discoveries of the Enlightenment, however. Instead it arises from the Bible itself. He is convinced that the Scriptures indicate that only at the end of history is the deity of God unquestionably open to all.[15] Until that great day, we see only dimly.

◆

Reasonable Hope and Hopeful Reasoning

As is readily evident in Pannenberg's alternative to pietism, his is a theology of reason. That is, he believes that theology is above all a rational discipline. But his understanding of truth as being ultimately eschatological suggests that his theology also focuses on hope. For this reason, those who watched his meteoric rise to prominence in the 1960s placed him together with Jürgen Moltmann and other German thinkers as an architect of what was then labeled "theology of hope."[16]

Indeed, Pannenberg's is a theology of hope insofar as his understanding of truth results in a theology that bears a thoroughgoing eschatological orientation. The hopeful note arises likewise from his focus on the reign of God. He does not, however, follow nineteenth-century theology in understanding this reign to be an ethical community. He draws, rather, from more recent exegetical discoveries, which find the source of the concept in the apocalyptic movement and the teaching of Jesus.[17] On this basis, he concludes that God's reign consists in the eschatological sovereign dominion of God, which has already broken into history in the appearance of Jesus.

Pannenberg believes that as a result of Jesus' coming, the Christian community is to be a people of hope. We live in hopeful expectation of the final consummation of God's rule over the entire world. But such hopeful living does not detach us from the world. As a people of hope, whose eyes are directed to the future consummation of God's reign, the Christian community cannot simply retreat into a privatized ghetto of individual or familial piety. Rather, the calling of the church is to remain in the world, for this is where the struggle for truth occurs. In this public sphere, the church engages in theology, which is a public and rational endeavor because it is linked with the quest for ultimate truth—the truth of God! And the purpose of such a theology is to give a "rational account of the truth of faith."[18]

---◆---

Theology as the Study of God

Pannenberg follows the classical tradition at another point as well. As is implicit in the very name "theology" (which means literally "the teaching about God"), he sees the enterprise as

closely bound up with the explication of the Christian conception of God. In fact, he declares that even though theological
reflection moves beyond the doctrine of God to include other
central topics (e.g., anthropology, ecclesiology, eschatology), theology's all-inclusive object is God.[19]

Although he follows the classical conception of theology,
Pannenberg's rationale for this understanding is anything but
classical. Reminiscent of the reformers' focus on God as the sovereign one, Pannenberg defines God as "the power on which
all finite reality depends" or "the power that determines everything."[20] From this basic definition, however, Pannenberg constructs a quite innovative thesis: God's divine status is bound
up with God's demonstration of lordship over creation.[21]

This observation gives shape to Pannenberg's entire enterprise. In his estimation, the connection between God's deity
and the divine manifestation of lordship over creation means
that it is "only in the event of final salvation that the reality of
God will be definitively established." Consequently, the entire
process of history climaxing in the consummation entails "a
self-demonstration of God's existence."[22]

But what about the "meantime"? To answer this question,
Pannenberg again draws from his fundamental thesis. The connection between God's deity and the demonstration of God's
reign means that if the idea of God corresponds to an actual
reality, it must be able to illumine human existence, as well as
our experience of the world as a whole. In Pannenberg's words,
"It must be made plausible that all finite reality depends on
him, not only human beings and the course of their history, but
also the world of nature." The role of theology lies precisely
here. For Pannenberg, the overarching task of systematic theology is to demonstrate the illuminating power of the Christian
conception of God. Theology accomplishes this task by present-
ing "a coherent model of the world as God's creation."[23] That
is why the doctrine of God encompasses the entire traditional
theological corpus from anthropology to eschatology.

◆

The Triune God

If the central task of theology is to show the power of the Christian conception of God to illumine all human experience, then it is not surprising that the doctrine of the Trinity would emerge as the heart of Pannenberg's systematic theology.[24] Indeed, God as triune lies at the center of the Christian conception of God.

While this may once again suggest a classical orientation to Pannenberg's program, in fact at this point he parts company with theological practice since the Middle Ages. Unlike his predecessors, Pannenberg doesn't begin with God's unity and then ask how God can likewise be three persons. Pannenberg rejects this tactic as riddled with potential problems. Above all, this approach views God as primarily a single acting subject, rather than the cooperative working of three persons. To avoid such dangers, his systematic presentation starts with the doctrine of the Trinity and only then moves to discuss God's unity and the divine attributes.[25]

Opting for this approach places Pannenberg squarely in the middle of the contemporary theological debate over the connection between the *immanent* Trinity—the triune God in God's own eternal essence—and the *economic* Trinity—the triune God as active in salvation history.[26] His desire to ground all theology in what is implicit in God's own self-disclosure provides the foundation for his solution to this grave theological problem. Simply stated, Pannenberg seeks to derive his understanding of the doctrine of the Trinity from the manner in which the Father, Son, and Spirit appear in the primary event of revelation—the life and message of Jesus. Consequently, whatever can be said about the immanent Trinity must flow out of our understanding of the economic Trinity, that is, out of the activity of the triune God in the divine economy.

Crucial to Pannenberg's development of the doctrine of the Trinity is his concept of self-differentiation.[27] In his view, the essence of "person" is to give oneself to the counterpart. This means that to be a person entails being dependent. Defining "person" in terms of dependency offers Pannenberg a way to overcome the traditional emphasis on subordination within the Triune God—specifically, the assertion that the Son and the Spirit are subordinate to the Father—which in his estimation has been detrimental to theology. By extension from his definition, all three Trinitarian persons are dependent. That is, they are mutually dependent on each other.

Pannenberg sees this mutual dependency operative in salvation history. In sending the Son into the world with the message of the reign of God, the Father has made his rulership over creation—and hence his deity—dependent on the Son's completion of his mission. In the pouring out of the Spirit into the world the divine goal is now dependent on the Spirit's eschatological completion of the process of salvation history. But this means, Pannenberg boldly asserts, that only at the consummation, when God is "all in all," will the unity of the divine being be demonstrated once and for all.

◆

The Christological Focus

In Pannenberg's estimation, the doctrine of the Trinity lies at the heart of theology. But because the coming of Jesus clearly marks the heart of the Christian narrative, in many respects Christian theology rises or falls with Christology—the study of the person and work of Christ.

Like many theologians, Pannenberg has always been concerned with issues of Christology. In fact, English readers were first introduced to his work through the tome *Jesus — God and Man*. Because it contains his articulate defense of the historicity of Jesus' resurrection, this volume won for Pannenberg—at least initially—the accolades of his more conservative readership. Perhaps more significant, however, was the actual theological use to which he put this historical event. According to Pannenberg, the resurrection comprises God's confirmation of Jesus' appearance and mission, for this event marked the inauguration of the general resurrection that the apocalyptic preachers believed would mark God's eschatological in-breaking into human history to assert divine sovereignty.

Pannenberg has characterized his monograph as an attempt to do Christology "from below." That is, he wanted to begin with Jesus as a human being and then ask how this human person—Jesus of Nazareth—could likewise be the revelation of God. But Pannenberg believes that a strict Christology from below is inappropriate when one is engaging in *systematic* theology. For this reason, the Christology section of his three-volume *Systematic Theology* begins with the classical theological concept of *logos* (or Word). Traditionally, theologians have understood this Christological term as declaring that Jesus is the principle of the unity of the world. Pannenberg, however, adds an interesting twist to this traditional idea. He declares that the term *logos* represents the order of the world as history. Consequently, Jesus is not the logos as some cosmic abstract principle, but in his human life as Israel's Messiah and as the one who reveals the proper relationship we creatures ought to have with our Creator.

This latter dimension motivates an additional innovative feature of Pannenberg's Christology. Classical theologians have generally envisioned a direct connection between Jesus and God, which led them to focus on Jesus' person. Jesus, they argued, is the product of the act of incarnation whereby the pre-existent Word took to himself our humanness. Pannenberg, in contrast, argues for an indirect connection that arises from Jesus' relationship to the Father as it unfolds in Jesus' own history.[28] As the one who was obedient to the Father to the point of death, Jesus revealed to us that the way to participation in life lies in humbly placing oneself in God's service. For this reason, Jesus is the eternal Son, the Word.

Pannenberg's Christology is equally innovative in its presentation of Jesus' work. Like classical theology in general, Pannenberg declares that in his crucifixion, Jesus acted as our substitute. But in contrast to the "exclusive substitution" that Pannenberg finds in so much traditional Christology, following his German colleague Dorothee Sölle he understands Jesus' death as an "inclusive substitution." Jesus didn't die so that we can avoid death. Instead, in tasting death for us he has radically altered it. No longer do we need to be terrified by death. On the contrary, because we participate through faith in the new life brought by Christ, we look forward as well to participating in God's eternal life beyond death.[29]

———————————————◆———————————————

The Centrality of the Spirit

Pannenberg's Christology provided English readers with their initial introduction to his work. But in his *Systematic Theology* pneumatology, the doctrine of the Spirit, emerges as the central dimension. In fact, Pannenberg sees his entire three-volume work as an attempt to develop a new pneumatology. His goal in doing so is to combat what he decries as the unfortunate tendency in theology to reduce the role of the Spirit to that of providing the solution for phenomena that lie beyond rational explanation.

The key point in Pannenberg's pneumatology is the concept of "field." Although field theory played an important role in nineteenth-century science, Pannenberg draws from a much earlier source, namely, the doctrine of a physical *pneuma*, or "spirit," developed by the ancient Stoic philosophers.[30] The early Christian theologians had rejected this doctrine in favor of the conception of God as "mind," and Pannenberg finds this patristic view problematic, because it is susceptible to the atheistic criticism articulated in the nineteenth century. Like the atheist critics, he concludes that the classical understanding of God as reason and will (that is, mind) is merely a human projection. Instead of the classical conception, Pannenberg conceives of the divine essence as an "incomprehensible field," which, following the Stoics, he speaks of as dynamic spirit. This divine essence or spirit likewise comes forth as the third person of the Trinity, the Holy Spirit.[31]

Not only does field or spirit characterize the divine life, according to Pannenberg, the Spirit also forms an all-pervasive presence in creation and in human life. In advancing this postulate, Pannenberg consciously connects the Christian confession that the Spirit is the source of life in creation with the discovery in modern biology that "life is essentially ecstatic."[32] Biologists declare that each organism lives in an environment that nurtures it. At the same time, each organism is oriented by its own drives beyond its immediate environment toward its future and the future of its species. Viewing this through theological eyes leads Pannenberg to see that in this sense creatures participate in God through the Spirit. As a result, he speaks of the Spirit as the environmental network or "field" in which and from which creatures live.

For Pannenberg the Spirit's role is not limited to the purely biological realm. Rather the dynamic field is also operative in human identity formation. Pannenberg argues that the human person is not to be defined as an "I" that exists prior to experiencing the world. Rather, we develop our identity as we gain an immediate perception of the totality of our personal existence. Pannenberg speaks of this perception as "feeling"[33] or the field in which a person lives.

Unlike the modern scientist, however, Pannenberg views biological life and the psychology of identity formation through theological eyes. Thus, he draws these various strands together in the Spirit's salvific role. In so doing, Pannenberg indicates how the same Spirit who is divine essence is likewise both the principle of the relation of God to creation and the principle of the participation of creation in the divine life.[34] The same "force" that lifts creatures above their environment and orients them toward the future ultimately leads to the self-transcendence that characterizes the human person and forms the basis for what the Bible describes as the believer's existence "in Christ." On this basis, Pannenberg describes sin, in turn, as "self-love." The root of sin is the "I" fixating on its own finiteness, rather than finding its identity from its true source, namely, existence "in Christ."[35]

One other piece must be added to complete Pannenberg's theological puzzle. His understanding of the connection between the divine Spirit and creation draws from a specific interpretation of space and time. According to Pannenberg, our perception of space and time as composed of individual parts presupposes an undivided whole that forms the background or context for the segments we perceive. These intuitions of infinite space and of time as an interconnected whole point to God as the omnipresent and eternal one.[36]

In short, then, as Spirit, God is the field in whom creation and history exist. Pannenberg offers this description: "The presence of God's Spirit in his creation can be described as a field of creative presence, a comprehensive field of force that releases event after event into finite existence."[37] This God is both immanent in the world and transcendent over it. God is immanent in that all creation and all events live from their environment, that is, from the divine field, the source of life who also raises creatures beyond themselves to participate in some measure in the divine life. Yet God is more than the chain of finite parts of time and space, and the divine life is more than the sum of the lives of finite creatures. Hence, God is transcendent.

More importantly, however, Pannenberg derives God's transcendence from the future orientation inherent in the relation between God and the world. As Spirit, God is the whole that provides meaning to each finite event of history. Rather than arising from the present, however, this meaning is ultimately future, for the meaning of history and the connection between each event and that meaning emerge only in the future. This future *telos* ("end") or meaning of history transcends each moment within history as that glorious future reality toward which all history is moving. In the same manner, God's transcendence is a transcendence of the future over the present.

◆

A Theology for the Church

Despite its seemingly heavy intellectual tone, Pannenberg's work has sought to carve out what is in fact a theology for the church. Perhaps better stated, he has sought to be a theologian both of the church and for the public sphere.[38] Indeed, Pannenberg would protest any suggestion that these are two distinct pursuits. Instead, the expressed goal of his work is the unity of the church, not as an end in itself but as a necessary condition for its mission in and to a secularized world.

For this reason, Pannenberg has devoted much energy to ecumenical endeavors. Through his work on the Faith and Order Commission of the World Council of Churches, he has sought to facilitate the establishment of eucharistic fellowship among the churches. He believes that this kind of Christian unity is the only way the church's voice can speak with credibility in contemporary secular society.[39]

This conviction forms the basis for Pannenberg's ecclesiology, or doctrine of the church. According to Pannenberg, the church is to be a witness to the temporality of all human institutions prior to the coming of the reign of God. As it gives expression to fellowship among humans and between humans and God—especially in the Eucharist—the church becomes the sign of God's eschatological kingdom.[40] This divine reign alone is the hope of the world. To be a servant to this task by setting forth Christian truth has always been Pannenberg's driving passion.

◆

A Relevant Theology?

The theology that Pannenberg carved out during his career charted a course between two opposing tendencies in contemporary theology. It provided a way to move beyond the existentialist bent that dominated German theology throughout much of the twentieth century. At the same time, Pannenberg offered an innovative proposal that took seriously the Enlightenment challenge to theology while steadfastly refusing to capitulate to the contemporary tendency in American theological thinking to give up on the classical quest for ultimate truth.

These features of Pannenberg's theology have won him a prominent place in the contemporary theological scene. But they have also triggered a wholesale dismissal of his theology by those who—rightly or wrongly—think it is simply not relevant to their context. William Placher, for example, reviewing the initial volume of Pannenberg's monumental *Systematic Theology*, offered this concluding appraisal:

> Reading Pannenberg, one admires his erudition and one learns from his insights. This volume has plenty of both. But he seems to live in a world where some significant paradigms can be assumed: a world where Western tradition as a whole remains essentially unproblematic, where people generally seem to know what counts as a reasoned argument, and where theologians

know what counts as "the theological tradition." One may envy that world or hate it, feel nostalgia for it, dream of restoring it or dismiss it as good riddance. But many of us trying to write theology in this country find it to be a world in which we do not live.[41]

Perhaps Pannenberg's work and Placher's response indicate just how wide the theological North Atlantic Ocean has become over the last fifty years.

CHAPTER TEN

Liberating Praxis
Gustavo Gutiérrez

In 1968 a group of church leaders gathered in the city of Medellín, Colombia. This event marked the second meeting of the Episcopal Council of Latin America (CELAM), the bishops of the Roman Catholic Church in the region. But this meeting, often called CELAM II, would make history. For the first time, Catholic clergy condemned the Church's traditional alliance with the ruling powers of Latin America, and they publicly articulated a theme that would reverberate around the world— "liberation"—that is, liberation from oppression and social injustice.

Three years later, in 1971, the perspective that informed CELAM II appeared in the form of a book bearing the challenging title *A Theology of Liberation* (published in English in 1973). The author of the volume was a Peruvian priest, theologian, and activist who had served as a member of the theological advisory team at CELAM II, Gustavo Gutiérrez. A powerful theological movement, "liberation theology," was born.

◆

The Struggles of an
Activist Theologian

What triggered the new theological thinking that emerged at CELAM II? On February 15, 1966, two years before the bishops met in Medellín, the Colombian military ambushed and killed the leader of a group of guerrillas—but not just any revolutionary leader. This man, Camilo Torres, was a Roman Catholic priest who six months earlier had, in his words, "left the rights and privileges of the clergy." In explaining his actions, he wrote, "I have stopped saying Mass in order to bring about love for neighbor in the temporary sphere, economic and social. When my neighbor has nothing against me, when I have brought about the Revolution, I will offer Mass again if God permits."[1] Since graduate school, Torres had been a friend of Gustavo Gutiérrez.

Although the death of Torres was a "decisive influence"— to cite Gutiérrez' own characterization—it was but the culmination of many factors that led the Peruvian priest to develop an understanding that we now know as "liberation theology." Gutiérrez was born in Lima, Peru, in 1928. Osteomyelitis confined young Gustavo to bed for six years. To this day a limp forms a permanent physical reminder of his boyhood illness. Yet disease could not prevent Gutiérrez from gaining an education. So he studied—first medicine and later theology. Preparation for the priesthood took him to Catholic educational institutions in Europe—Louvain, Lyon, and Nymegen—culminating in a doctorate in theology.[2]

With degree in hand, Gutiérrez returned to his homeland to teach theology at the University of Lima and work with a parish situated among the poor of the city. But his plans changed. Like others before him, including Karl Barth and Reinhold

Niebuhr, the young clergyman discovered that the theology of his training paled in the face of the needs of people around him—in Gutiérrez' case, the poor in the slums of the capital city. What he found especially distressing was the attitude of the Roman Catholic Church, which throughout the history of its presence in Latin America had favored the powerful and wealthy—the elite upper class—rather than taking up the cause of the poor.

Although Gutiérrez' fame spread quickly in North America, his message was not always welcomed in Roman Catholic circles. In 1979 the Latin American bishops met in Puebla, Mexico, for CELAM III. The Church leaders intended that this gathering repudiate the radical positions taken at the Medellín gathering. To this end, they excluded Gutiérrez from the meeting. Undaunted, he and a group of sympathetic theologians rented a nearby house from where they could still exercise influence over the deliberations. In the end, the hopes of the leadership were dashed. The bishops endorsed the liberationist idea of God's "preferential option for the poor," criticized the military dictatorships of Latin America, and praised the "base communities," the grassroots groups of Christians that had sprung up across Latin America.

Soon the alarm over liberation theology drew a response from the Vatican itself. In September 1984 the Sacred Congregation for the Doctrine of the Faith, Rome's office for identifying and correcting heresy within the Church, released a document critical of liberation theology. The piece, entitled "Instruction on Certain Aspects of the 'Theology of Liberation,'" was the work of Joseph Cardinal Ratzinger, the conservative head of the Sacred Congregation. Ratzinger warned against the alleged defects inherent in liberation theology, especially its supposedly uncritical acceptance of concepts borrowed from Marxist thought.[3]

Then Cardinal Ratzinger and the Sacred Congregation "silenced" a leading Brazilian liberation theologian, Leonardo

Boff. The order meant that Boff could not lecture in public or publish anything for one year. In the meantime, Gutiérrez had not escaped notice. The Vatican launched an investigation into his orthodoxy. Although the matter cost the theologian precious time, in the end the commission was unable to find any basis for a charge of heresy.

Eventually, the Vatican's position began to soften. In April 1986 a second Ratzinger document emerged, the "Instruction on Christian Freedom and Liberation." While retaining the critical posture of the earlier piece, the overall tone had shifted somewhat, giving more comfort than concern to Latin American liberation theologians.[4]

◆

The Precursors of Liberation Theology

As the outcome of the papal investigation of Gutiérrez' orthodoxy suggests, what is most distinctive about liberation theology is not the doctrinal beliefs of its proponents, but the perspective from which they engage in theological reflection. Specifically, liberation theologians take as their point of departure the experience of the poor and the struggle of the marginalized for liberation. The beginning point of such reflection lies in the recognition that God is present in the attempts of the disenfranchised to throw off oppression. Consequently, to cite Gutiérrez' own words, "The theology of liberation is rooted in a revolutionary militancy."[5]

Viewed from this perspective, Gutiérrez is not the actual founder of liberation theology, even though he is often referred to as its "father." He himself suggests that the movement dates back to the Spanish conquest, specifically to the few brave Spanish priests in Latin America, such as Bartolomé de Las Casas, who defended the native peoples against the conquistadors. In contrast to the conquerors, who dismissed the Indians as non-humans, Las Casas reminded the emperor of Spain that the indigenous peoples were also created in God's image; therefore, they too deserved respect and justice. Anticipating the liberation theologians of the twentieth century, the sixteenth-century priest linked salvation to social justice. By treating the Indians unjustly, he warned, the Spaniards were placing their own salvation in jeopardy.[6]

As important as this historical forerunner may be, a more recent horizon holds greater direct significance. The actual foundation for liberation theology lies in developments in the 1950s and 1960s. One such factor was the emergence in Europe of a movement closely associated with Jürgen Moltmann's theology of hope known as "political theology." One proponent, Johannes Metz, a Roman Catholic colleague of Moltmann's at Tübingen, elevated political "praxis," or committed involvement, as the starting point of theological reflection.[7] Meanwhile, the Second Vatican Council, meeting in Rome (1962–1965), as well as Pope John XXIII's vision of the Church as a church of the poor, provided inspiration to reform-minded Catholics and opened the door to laity and clergy alike to engage in radical social and political involvement.[8]

By this time, the practical groundwork for liberation theology had been laid through the work of Paulo Freire, a Catholic educator in northeastern Brazil. The late 1950s and early 1960s witnessed an increasing disenchantment with economic development as the means for eliminating poverty in Latin America. Consequently, Freire looked to the poor themselves to take the first steps in dealing with their plight. He argued that they must liberate themselves from their "dominated-conditioned mentality" and free the rich from their "dominating-conditioned" mind-set. To this end, Freire engaged in what he termed *conscientização* ("making aware").[9]

During the next years, several particularly harsh regimes came to power in Latin America and sought to suppress the efforts of Freire and others. At the same time, the gap between rich and poor became a gaping chasm. In this situation, a growing number of voices began calling for what the Puebla bishops termed a "second violence" to meet such "institutionalized violence." That is, these Christian leaders called for revolution! Liberation theology emerged in this revolutionary situation. Its task was to reflect on the role that Christians and the Church should play in that situation.

◆

Theology as Contextual

We already noted that the starting point for liberation theology is the struggle of the marginalized. This observation is closely connected with a fundamental shift in the way theology is pursued. Implicit in liberation theology is the assumption that theology must be contextual. That is, by its very nature theological reflection is inescapably linked with a specific historical, social situation.

In making this claim, these thinkers are applying to theology a theory from the human sciences commonly called the "sociology of knowledge." Dermot A. Lane summarizes its central thesis: "Knowledge is not neutral or value-free. Instead all knowledge tends to embody the social circumstances and conditions of its time."[10] Theorists take the matter a step further. Because knowledge is socially conditioned, it tends to reflect the vested interests of the knower. And these vested interests vary from society to society, from culture to culture, and even from social class to social class.

From this insight arises the widely-evoked "hermeneutic of suspicion." At its foundation lies the assumption that in every claim to knowledge someone's vested interests are operating, generally those of the dominant and powerful in society. If this is the case, then we must be suspicious of all knowledge claims. We must come to see how they reflect and serve the interests of the powerful while victimizing the marginalized. Liberationists apply this theory to the struggle of Latin America's poor classes against their oppressors. The dominant "knowledge" in the region is in fact conditioned by the dominant class, and thereby it serves as an "ideology" perpetuating the status quo. This ideology of the oppressor must be countered by another, namely, the critical knowledge that arises among those who stand against the oppressive upper class. And the critical knowledge that can bring the church into the struggle is a specific theology, a theology of liberation.

In this manner, liberation theology becomes a contextualized theology par excellence. It is a theology exclusively by and for the poor in their struggle for liberation. Hence, Gutiérrez is seeking to set forth a truly indigenous Latin American theology, which arises out of involvement in the unique sociopolitical realities of that region. This theology differs radically from the dominant theology of the Church. The Peruvian activist explains: "Here faith is lived by the poor of this world. Here the theological reflection seeking self-expression has no intention of being a palliative for these sufferings and refuses integration into the dominant theology. Here theology is ever more conscious of what separates it from the dominant theologies, conservative or progressive."[11]

As these words indicate, Gutiérrez believes that the contextualized nature of theology accounts for the differences between Latin American theology and its European and North American counterparts. More specifically, whether liberal or conservative, North Atlantic theologies seek to address the situation posed by modern, Western nonbelievers. As a result, these theologies address the question, How can we to speak about God in a secular world? But, Gutiérrez adds, this is simply not the Latin American reality. The Latin American situation is not conditioned by the question of the nonbeliever—nearly everyone there is a Christian. Instead, it demands a response to the question of the "nonperson," that is, "the human being who is not considered human by the present social order—the exploited classes, marginalized ethnic groups, and despised cultures." For this reason, "our question," Gutiérrez explains, "is how to tell the nonperson, the nonhuman, that God is love, and that this love makes us all brothers and sisters." This is the driving force behind liberation theology.[12]

It was this dimension of liberation theology—its assumption that theology is contextual—that triggered the concern of Rome. Because the unity of the Church, including its unity in doctrine, has always been a pillar of Roman Catholic teaching, Church leaders could not avoid becoming alarmed by a movement that called for the construction of "local" theologies. Such a call appeared to open the door to schism. Nevertheless, despite the initial opposition voiced from many quarters, this aspect of Gutiérrez' program has prevailed. Nearly everyone today agrees that theology is in some sense always contextual and hence that the Latin American situation ought somehow to color the theology that arises within that region.

◆

A Theology of the Poor

But what exactly is significant about the Latin American context? Liberation theologians maintain that the single most significant feature of Latin American society is poverty—not just poverty in general, but a specific type of poverty. In contrast to the poverty present in Europe or North America, Latin American poverty is endemic, pervasive, and imposed. It is the result of sinful social structures that work on behalf of the extreme wealth of a small minority and impoverish the vast majority.

Such systemic poverty, Gutiérrez maintains, works to crush the humanity of the masses.

Liberation theologians point out that throughout Latin America poverty has reached catastrophic levels. As the poor of Latin America grow poorer, the rich prosper more than ever. Many who dare to protest this situation are mysteriously killed or simply disappear. One such case that gained world wide attention was the death of Archbishop Oscar Romero of El Salvador. This Church leader was assassinated by a death squad while saying Mass one day after he publicly called for Salvadoran soldiers to refuse orders to shoot their fellow citizens.[13]

In the midst of such disparities, the majority of people in Latin America—rich and poor, powerful and powerless—remain professing Christians, and the Catholic church is either officially established or tremendously influential throughout the region. But far from being "neutral," the Church has traditionally taken the side of the oppressors. No wonder Gutiérrez speaks harshly to a Church that "has contributed, and continues to contribute to supporting the established order."[14]

◆

The Marxist Connection

One of the most controversial aspects of liberation theology is its analysis of the causes of Latin American poverty, especially its use of Marxist social analysis to understand both the situation and its solution. Gutiérrez and others claim that the problem emerges as economic dependence imposed *externally* by European and North American multinational corporations is combined with institutionalized violence against the poor perpetuated *internally* by ruling oligarchies and military regimes, which cooperate with the multinational corporations in return for their support. These regimes rule with an iron fist, ignoring human rights, civil liberties, and basic human dignity—all in the name of "national security." This unholy alliance, Gutiérrez theorizes, accounts for the economic marginalization of the majority of Latin Americans. The Peruvian activist describes the context in which he labors:

> What we are faced with is a situation that takes no account of the dignity of human beings, or their most elemental needs, that does not provide for their biological survival, or their basic right to be free and autonomous. Poverty, injustice, alienation, and the exploitation of human beings by other human beings combine to form a situation that the Medellín conference did not hesitate to condemn as "institutionalized violence."[15]

But haven't North Atlantic nations assisted Latin America through various "development" projects? Liberation theologians offer a resounding "No." Coming as it has "with strings attached," development aid has served only to deepen the situation of domination and dependence.

According to liberation theologians, loosing the vise grip under which the people of the region groan requires drastic action, a radical break with the status quo. Gutiérrez, for example, asserts that "there can be authentic development for Latin America only if there is liberation from the domination exercised by the great capitalist countries, and especially by the most powerful, the United States of America."[16] This quotation reveals the basic political-economic orientation that characterizes not only the Peruvian activist but most of his associates as well. The nearly unanimous opinion among liberation theologians is that capitalism is inherently evil. According to Gutiérrez, replacing the present system with a new socialist society is the best way to fulfill Jesus' command to offer a cup of cold water in his name. He explains that "to offer food or drink in our day is a political action; it means the transformation of a society structured to benefit a few who appropriate to themselves the value of the work of others. This transformation ought to be directed toward a radical change in the foundation of society, that is, the private ownership of the means of production."[17]

Lying behind this statement is Marxist social analysis. According to Marx, labor is part of a person's essential human identity. For this reason, when people are forced to sell the fruits of their labor for less than full value, they are both exploited and dehumanized. Such a situation arises whenever those who own the means of production take away the "surplus value" of the workers' labor. Exploitation and alienation eventually ignite a struggle between the classes, climaxing in revolution.

Liberation theologians claim that this Marxist analysis pinpoints the forces currently at work in Latin America. Theirs is a situation in which—to cite Gutiérrez' poetic description—a "broad and deep aspiration for liberation inflames the history of humankind in our day, liberation from all that limits or keeps human beings from self-fulfillment, liberation from all impediments to the exercise of freedom."[18] In such a context, whether or not the Church should get involved is no longer relevant. The only crucial question is whose side will it take. For Gutiérrez, there can be only one answer. And to find it we need only consider where God stands in this struggle. The Peruvian theologian is convinced that God is the God of the poor.

In speaking about the "preferential option for the poor," liberation theologians are not saying that the economically marginalized automatically stand in right relationship with God. Rather, preference for the poor means that the God who loves all people identifies with the poor and sides with the poor against every oppressor who would exploit or dehumanize them. Consequently, in the present revolutionary situation the Church must cast its lot with the oppressed. Such "liberating praxis," in turn, becomes the starting point for all genuine theology.

◆

Theology as Critical
Reflection on Praxis

This perspective of solidarity with the poor leads to the methodological innovation of liberation theology. Traditionally, theologians generally placed the mission of the church and Christian ethics after reflection. We first get our theology straight, they surmised, and we then seek to understand what it means to live out our basic beliefs. According to Gutiérrez, however, the order is exactly opposite. Theology, he writes in an often quoted description, is "a critical reflection on Christian praxis in light of the word of God."[19]

With this statement, Gutiérrez is relegating theoretical reflection to second place in the "hermeneutical circle." It is the "second act" following on the heels of the Church's "first act," namely, praxis, or engagement in God's liberating work in the world. In other words, theological reflection involves bringing the word of God to bear on Christian involvement with and for the poor so as to orient and guide such action, while at the same time providing an appropriate language for speaking about the God who is active in liberation.[20] This reversal has far-reaching implications for our understanding of theology. It means that theological reflection can never be merely detached, theoretical, or objective.

But is there warrant for such a radical shift? Liberation theologians claim that such a reversal in theological method is demanded by both philosophical and theological considerations. As we noted earlier, Gutiérrez and his colleagues build from the conclusions of the sociology of knowledge, namely, that rather than being simply a detached, objective grasp of truth in itself, all human knowledge arises out of our engagement within some specific social context. This means that we don't find truth by thinking instead of acting; we discover it as we reflect on our acting. As in all forms of knowledge so also in theology, acting is the first act, which is then followed by reflection.

The theological consideration flows out of another point we made earlier. Liberation theologians believe that we come to know God as we obediently engage in God's own work in the world, and this work is fundamentally that of liberation. In Gutiérrez' poignant words, "To know God is to work for justice. There is no other path to reach God." But how do we know that God is engaging in the work of liberating the poor? Here Gutiérrez appeals to Scripture, which he sees as the primary and normative record of the revelatory liberating experiences of God's people. Repeatedly the biblical narrative presents God as acting in history to liberate the weak and abused from bondage and oppression. Such activity cannot be restricted to the distant past. Instead, God's liberating work continues in the present.[21]

◆

Salvation as Liberation

Gutiérrez' reading of Scripture leads him—like many other Christians—to conclude that salvation is the central theme of the Christian faith. But here he calls traditional Catholic theologians to task. They err, he asserts, in viewing salvation as exclusively "quantitative," that is, as "guaranteeing heaven" for the greatest number. In contemporary Latin America, in contrast, the pressing need is to reinterpret salvation in qualitative terms, for this alone will lead to commitment to social transformation. In keeping with this conclusion, Gutiérrez presents liberation theology as a reconstruction of the doctrine of salvation.[22]

A careful reading of his work reveals that Gutiérrez doesn't simply equate salvation with economic liberation. On the contrary, he takes pains to explain that there are in fact three different levels of liberation in Christ, namely, the traditional understandings of personal transformation and liberation from sin, as well as liberation from social oppression and marginalization.[23] Nevertheless, Gutiérrez senses that the situation in Latin America demands that we zero in on the social aspect. Viewed from this perspective, salvation occurs as God and humans work together within history to bring about the full humanization of all people, according to God's own good intention for humankind. Gutiérrez, therefore, calls on Christians in Latin America to become "sisters and brothers,"[24] that is, to abolish unjust social systems that oppress, exploit, and alienate people.

In this task, the Church has a crucial role to play. In essence, our Christian mission is liberating praxis. That is, our task is to engage in the transformation of society along the lines of God's own kingdom. To this end, the Church must be converted to the poor—join them in the struggle to throw off oppression. Gutiérrez realizes, of course, that total liberation is ultimately a gift that God alone can and will give at the end of time, when God's kingdom comes in its fullness. But in the meantime, the Church is to work toward building a just society. According to Gutiérrez, all actions that advance this goal are in some sense salvific. He explains: "Any effort to build a just society is liberating. And it has an indirect but effective impact on the fundamental alienation. It is a salvific work, although it is not all of salvation." Above all, the Church must direct its efforts toward and on behalf of the poor. By being properly involved in the world of the poor, "the church finds its full identity as a sign of the reign of God to which all human beings are called but in which the lowly and the 'unimportant' have a privileged place."[25]

Gutiérrez reluctantly admits that efforts to build a just society might include violence. Although not the ideal, such violence may be the only way to counteract the "institutionalized violence" of oppressive regimes. He offers this telling apologetic: "We cannot say that violence is all right when the oppressor uses it to maintain or preserve 'order,' but wrong when the oppressed use it to overthrow this same order."[26]

But Gutiérrez prefers that the Church focus its efforts on the main tools of its mission, such as the prophetic denunciation of oppressive structures of society, the annunciation of God's will for total liberation from all that dehumanizes people, and direct involvement with the poor. Above all, he desires that the Church be an "authentic church of the poor," that is, one that suffers with the marginalized even to the point of martyrdom.[27]

◆

A Theology for All Seasons?

As we have noted already, from the beginning liberation theology has been controversial. Questions concerning his orthodoxy have continually plagued Gutiérrez, as well as others in the movement. But his appraisal of the causes of poverty in Latin America has been equally contested. Critics refuse to place the blame for the plight of masses entirely at the feet of North Atlantic governments and corporations and their Latin American cronies. Rather, they wonder if some responsibility might also rest with the economic policies of Latin American governments themselves.[28]

Similarly Gutiérrez' alleged Marxism has engendered scathing criticism. Critics warn that using Marxist social analysis leads inevitably to an embracing of its attendant atheistic ideology. For example, they argue that the Marxist perspective on the economic causes of human alienation is inseparable from the belief that the human person is not a creature of God but rather the product of one's own self-creation through work.[29]

Gutiérrez has been challenged on biblical and theological grounds as well. Some critics aren't convinced that we can truly say that God "favors" the poor. Others question whether theology can really be made secondary to praxis. And they fear that the focus on praxis will displace Scripture as our ultimate norm, thereby opening the door for the church to become captivated by—and even taken captive to—a human ideology. "Right praxis," such critics retort, "ultimately depends on right theory."[30]

Finally, critics are concerned that Gutiérrez' focus on the presence of God in this world and in human history does not give sufficient place to the transcendent. If God is encountered and known only through engaging in liberating action within history, where does that leave the transcendent dimensions of grace and the eschatological kingdom of God, which form such powerful motifs in the writings of theologians such as Moltmann and Pannenberg?

Liberation theologians have been reticent to engage in intellectual sparring contests with their detractors. Rather than focusing so intently on whether or not it is intellectually persuasive, Gutiérrez suggests that this theology ought to be appraised by its fruits.[31] And it has borne good fruit. The Peruvian activist and his friends have opened the eyes of Christians to see the plight of the suffering poor, not only in Latin America but also around the world and even in their own backyards. Similarly, the movement has voiced a crucial reminder of the social significance of the gospel in a world of increasing disparity between the "haves" and the "have nots."

Despite positive contributions such as these, since the demise of Marxist regimes in the late 1980s and early 1990s, the influence of liberation theology as such has waned. Even its original architects have fine-tuned their theological understandings, altered their approach, or developed other interests. In 1988, while writing a new introduction for the fifteenth-anniversary edition of *A Theology of Liberation,* Gutiérrez hinted at the changes that had occurred in his own thinking since the early 1970s. He concluded his lengthy reappraisal by suggesting that he himself no longer holds to everything he had written in the original volume. But then he quickly added that such rethinking of his position does not lessen the book's importance as his gift to God:

> Allow me to end with a personal story. Some years ago, a journalist asked whether I would write *A Theology of Liberation* today as I had two decades earlier. In answer I said that though the years passed by, the book remained the same, whereas I was alive and therefore changing and moving forward thanks to experiences, to observation made on the book, and to lectures and discussions. When he persisted, I asked whether in a love letter to his wife today he would use the same language he used twenty years ago; he said he would not, but he acknowledged that his love perdured. My book is a love letter to God, to the church, and to the people to which I belong. Love remains alive, but it grows deeper and changes its manner of expression.[32]

Here Gutiérrez stands as a role model for us all. As his theology changes, develops, and grows, one thing remains constant. In all he says and does, he seeks to serve the God he loves and the people to whom God has called him to minister.

CHAPTER ELEVEN

Theology of Women's Experience
Rosemary Radford Ruether

"The more one becomes a feminist the more difficult it becomes to go to church."[1] This remark by a leading Christian theologian capsulizes the feelings—and the pain—of many women. Some of these women, including the speaker herself, have set themselves to the task of devising an alternative to the hopelessly patriarchal traditional church: "women-church."

Participants in women-church gather in homes and living rooms to share personal stories of how they have experienced oppression in a society and in churches in which males dominate. Rather than invoking only the classical language of "God the Father," they also pray to and worship the Mother Goddess. In one important ritual within women-church, the Exorcism of Patriarchal Texts, a worship leader reads passages from the Bible which the participants believe oppress women and the group responds in liturgical fashion, "Out, demons, out!" Then one of the participants proclaims, "These texts and all oppressive texts have lost their power over our lives. We no longer need to apologize for them or try to interpret them as words of truth, but we cast out their oppressive message as expressions of evil and justifications of evil."[2]

One theologian from whom women-church derives its theological impetus is Rosemary Radford Ruether.

◆

The Journey to Feminist Theology

Born in 1936, Rosemary Radford grew up in what she describes as "a relatively privileged, patriotic, and pious family." Young Rosemary's father died when she was twelve. Thereafter, the chief influence in her life became her mother—a devout Catholic, avid ecumenist, and committed feminist in the tradition of the late-nineteenth- and early-twentieth-century movement—as well as several of her mother's friends. The "family background of strong, independent, and intellectual women" cultivated in Ruether at an early age a keen sense of autonomy and self-confidence as a woman.[3]

After her basic education in Catholic private schools, in 1954 Ruether entered Scripps College in Claremont, California, with the goal of studying fine arts and becoming an artist. But she underwent a shift in focus. Ruether explains:

> My interest was soon attracted into the humanities and history curriculum. I became fascinated with Christian origins. I wanted to find out how a somewhat unlikely Jewish messianic movement of the first century had managed to conquer the Mediterranean world and fall heir to all the going ideas of late Greco-Roman civilization. I began to explore the intellectual and social history of late antiquity and patristic Christianity and ended up doing a doctor's degree in that area at the Claremont Graduate School.[4]

Events beyond the classroom, however, became even more formative for her thinking. Ruether found herself living in the context of a changing society and a changing church. As old patterns of racial relationships were being challenged in 1960s America, Ruether, like many other "privileged" college students, was drawn to the civil rights movement. Her interests took her to Mississippi in the summer of 1965, where she worked as a volunteer with the Mississippi Child Development Group. This experience was transformative. "Here, for the first time," she later wrote, "I learned to look at America from the Black side; to see safety in the Black community and danger in nightriding whites or white officers of the law."[5]

Then with doctoral degree in hand,[6] Ruether—together with her husband, a political science major she had married while at Scripps—set out for Washington, D.C., to teach at the School of Religion at Howard University (1965–1976). Her presence on the faculty of an African American divinity school not only strengthened her ties to the civil rights movement, but also introduced her to the fledgling Black theology that was beginning to reshape the curriculum of the school. More importantly, it put her at the center of the peace movement. The activist scholar participated in numerous "sing-ins" and "pray-ins," which won for her more than one night in jail. Since then, Ruether has been continually concerned about social justice.

At the same time, another debilitating problem attracted her attention—sexism, above all the long history of sexism within Christianity. But the Roman Catholic Church of which she was a part was showing signs of change in at least one respect. The Second Vatican Council had created a climate of freedom which fostered critical thinking by its adherents. Initially Ruether's critical posture focused on difficult question that had emerged in the early 1960s, the Church's opposition to contraception. But visiting professorships at Harvard (1972–1973) and Yale (1973–1974) provided a context for her to engage with the broader task of developing a feminist theological method.

The die was now cast. Ruether, who soon moved to Garrett-Evangelical Theological Seminary near Chicago, would become the most widely-read and influential articulator of the emerging feminist movement in theology. But her feminism would remain only one dimension of a much larger program, namely, an unflinching opposition to what she sees as oppression in its many forms. Hence, for Ruether the purpose of theology is not limited to developing a specifically feminist consciousness, but to fostering compassionate commitment to liberation from all forms of bondage.[7] This is evident in her recent attempt to blend feminism and environmentalism into what Ruether and others term "ecofeminism."[8] Despite this wider agenda, her work as a feminist theologian on behalf of women remains her most significant contribution.

◆

A Theology of and for Women

Ruether is, of course, only one of a growing number of thinkers who share a concern about the oppression of women. Many of these thinkers look to her as mentor and pioneer.[9] According to one participant in the movement, feminist theologians agree on several fundamental points: Traditional Christian theology is patriarchal (done by men and for men). Traditional theology has either simply ignored or falsely caricatured women and women's experience. The patriarchal nature of traditional theology has had deleterious consequences for women. Women must now take their place as equal shapers of the theological enterprise.[10]

As this summary suggests, the driving force of feminist theology as well as its primary source and norm is women's experience—or, we should say, women's experience as defined by feminists themselves. And according to Ruether, the fundamental experience that all women share, whether or not they are aware of it, is that of being oppressed by a sexist or patriarchal social system.

In this aspect, the feminist impulse resembles the liberation theology we noted in our study of Gustavo Gutiérrez. Like him, feminist theologians begin with a specific life situation, namely, oppression and the struggle for liberation from oppression. Thus, feminists agree with Gutiérrez that theology is in some sense critical reflection on praxis, that is, reflection on the experience of oppressed persons freeing themselves from domination. And like Gutiérrez, feminists prefer to draw more from sociological than from philosophical categories to provide the foundation for their appraisal. As a result, they too speak of sin and salvation in sociopolitical terms.

The difference between feminist theologians and their Latin American colleagues lies in their estimation of exactly who are the oppressed. Gutiérrez is chiefly concerned with persons suffering from enforced poverty, and consequently the experience of the poor in Latin America provides the foundation for his theology. Ruether, in contrast, argues that the oldest and most basic oppression is sexism and its social expression: patriarchy, the domination of women by men.

Beneath the surface of Ruether's approach is Paul Tillich's method of correlation. As we noted in chapter 4, Tillich views theology as the attempt to correlate the questions of contemporary culture with the answers of revelation, so that the cultural setting determines the form of the answers. In good Tillichian fashion, Ruether appeals to women's unique experience of oppression and of liberation from oppression as providing the form for her theological formulations. This in turn leads to what she views as the "feminist critical principle," namely, "the promotion of the full humanity of women."[11]

But should the experience of either men or women determine our theology? Should we not instead search for what is universally human, rather than gender specific? To this question Ruether offers a powerful response. She argues that there is no such thing as a universal, objective theology. Rather than being gender neutral, the supposedly universal theology of the

Christian tradition has in fact been male-oriented and male-dominated. Not only has men's experience colored theology, it has determined theology's content and form. In such a situation, the elevation of women's experience provides a sorely needed antidote: "The use of women's experience in feminist theology, therefore, explodes as a critical force, exposing classical theology, including its codified traditions, as based on *male* experience rather than on universal human experience. Feminist theology makes the sociology of theological knowledge visible, no longer hidden behind mystifications of objectified divine and universal authority."[12]

In the face of the patriarchal character of traditional theology, Ruether calls for a new method that can produce a theology of and for women. This method proceeds through three steps.[13] First, feminist theology begins critically. The theologian recalls how women have been oppressed not only by a male patriarchal society, but more importantly by an oppressive male-dominated church. Such critical engagement brings to light the sexism of traditional theology. Next the feminist theologian seeks to recover alternative biblical and extrabiblical traditions that present women in a positive light. Such traditions support "women's personhood, her equality in the image of God, her equal redeemability, her participation in prophecy, teaching, and leadership." On the basis of such alternative traditions, the theologian then recasts traditional Christian categories, symbols, and doctrines with a view toward the full personhood of women. These three "moments" of theological reflection provide the dialectical process lying at the heart of Ruether's program.[14]

◆

The Patriarchal Past

According to Ruether, one reason oppression is so pernicious is that it is embedded in the fundamental ideology supporting an oppressive society. She explains: "The existing social hierarchy and system of power are justified and sacralized by defining them as the order of creation and the will of God."[15] And were this not enough, the ideology of domination also claims that the subjugation of the dominated persons is justified as the punishment for some primordial sin the victims had supposedly committed.

Ruether sees just such a victimizing ideology at work in the most noxious oppression in the history of humankind, the dominance of men over women. For her, the entire history of the Judeo-Christian tradition (which she differentiates from the Jewish tradition[16]) is marked by the subjugation of women as well as their invisibility and enforced domination by men. This history has denied women not only their equality with men, but also their very humanity.

The litany of biblical materials that come under Ruether's feminist scalpel is almost endless: Old Testament references to female "uncleanness" after childbirth and during menstruation, New Testament strictures against women speaking in church, and texts scattered throughout the Bible that suggest the subordination of women to men in some sort of ontological "chain of being." To these texts could be added the writings of the major figures of church history. Ruether chastises Augustine for identifying maleness with the image of God, Thomas Aquinas for regarding females as "misbegotten males," the reformers for doing nothing to change the status of women in the church, and even Karl Barth for placing woman second to man in the covenants of nature and grace.[17]

For Ruether, all such writings drip with androcentrism—a view of reality that elevates the male as the norm and suggests that women are inferior, defective, and less than fully human. The feminist thinker finds that androcentrism does not merely lie at the fringes of the Christian tradition; it is deeply imbedded in the very fabric of Christianity: "Starting with the basic assumption that the male is the normative human person and, therefore, also the normative image of God, all symbols, from God-language and Christology to church and ministry, are shaped by the pervasive pattern of the male as center, the female as subordinate and auxiliary."[18]

According to Ruether, the social manifestation of andro-centrism is patriarchy. But unlike the somewhat narrow focus many people give to this term (that is, the subordination of fe-males to males), she understands patriarchy in a broad manner. Patriarchy is operative wherever the principle of domination and submission is at work; it is present wherever we find hierarchies of power and control. Indeed, patriarchy includes "the whole structure of Father-ruled society: aristocracy over serfs, masters over slaves, king over subjects, racial overlords over colonized people."[19] Every element in the Christian tradition that embodies or affirms patriarchy, she adds, must be challenged!

Ruether readily admits that coming to realize the pervasive presence of patriarchy in the Christian tradition may at first be painful, even for women who have been victimized by that tradition. When they come to see the androcentrism of Chris-tianity, "An entire social and symbolic universe crumbles within and outside them. They recognize in the familiar the deeply alien."[20] Yet this consciousness-raising is necessary, if women are to gain the sense of personhood that they ought to have.

◆

Recovering Women's Lost Memory

Ruether's goal is nothing less than a total revolution against a society structured along the lines of patriarchy. She writes, "Culturally, sexism defines the whole system of reality, from 'matter' to 'God.' One cannot challenge sexism without the de-thronement of the cultural universe as an authentic and good model of life."[21] But taken alone, this negative first step in the feminist theological method is insufficient. If women are to gain their sense of personhood, the first aspect must lead to a second, positive moment—the recovery of the lost memory of women.

Ruether agrees with other feminists that this enterprise involves uncovering the stories of great women of faith and courage in the tradition. Such recovery provides a powerful means of overcoming the patriarchal cast of the dominant tradition. But in this task Ruether is not content to appeal solely to what has traditionally served as orthodox Christianity. Instead, she makes use of numerous additional sources: non-Christian pagan religions; marginal, even "heretical" movements within Christianity; philosophies such as liberalism, romanticism, and Marxism; and contemporary stories of women's oppression and liberation. In all of these, she seeks to give voice to elements that are regularly silenced by the dominant male culture.[22]

At the same time, Ruether continues to see herself as a Christian,[23] even as one who appeals to Scripture. Of course her foundation is not the Bible in its entirety, but what she terms the "prophetic-liberating tradition" of Scripture. This tradition provides the impetus for Ruether's engagement in theology from the "underside" of society: "The prophetic tradition creates a shift in the social location of religion. Instead of religion being socially located on the side of the ruling class, race, and gender, justifying their power as divinely ordained, the prophetic tradition speaks through prophets, male and female, located on the side of the poor and marginalized people of the society."[24] More significantly, however, this tradition gives rise to the "feminist critical principle" so central in Ruether's approach. The feminist theologian finds in the prophetic-liberating tradition the vision of a completely nonhierarchical and "earth-friendly" society in which patterns of domination and submission are replaced by "compassionate solidarity." Obviously, such a vision leads directly to an explicit critique of patriarchy and to the inclusion of what was formerly excluded—women.[25]

The feminist concern to bring to speech previously silenced voices carries important implications for Ruether's understanding of revelation. The activist Catholic, Ruether, elevates the feminist critical principle as the ultimate hermeneutical norm for detecting the revelatory Word in the past, including within the biblical tradition itself. Indeed, because the Bible is thoroughly permeated by patriarchy, Scripture alone or Scripture in its entirety is simply not our final authority. On the contrary, she appeals to Scripture against Scripture: "Feminist readings of the Bible can discern a norm within Biblical faith by which the Biblical texts themselves can be criticized. . . . On this basis many aspects of the Bible are to be frankly set aside and rejected."[26]

Nor can revelation be restricted to the past, even if certain historical events, including Jesus, remain paradigmatic for all revelation. The feminist theologian also recognizes women's experience as in some sense revelatory. In fact, she argues that such "revelation" must shape and mold Christian theology if women and liberated men are to find theology credible.

But to what extent? Some observers surmise that Ruether goes so far as to elevate experience over the biblical revelation. They claim, in the words of William Oddie, that "'feminist consciousness' is the channel for the primary revelation, by which all others are to be judged."[27]

Reconstructing the Vision

Despite its importance, the task of recovering women's lost memory does not yet bring Ruether to her ultimate goal. Instead, feminist theological reflection reaches its climax only as it engages in a thoroughgoing revision of traditional Christian symbols. Placing her program within the broader category of liberation theology, Ruether explains:

Liberation theology today consists not only in a discovery of this prophetic, transformative side of the tradition but also its recontextualization or restatement for today. Speaking a prophetic word of God is not simply an exegesis of past texts but the midrashic retelling of the story of liberation in the contemporary context. The Holy Spirit is a present, not simply a past, revelatory power. Thus liberation theologies are not simply confined to what they can "find" in past tradition. They are empowered to restate the vision in new dimensions, not imagined or only hinted at and undeveloped in the past.[28]

It comes as no surprise that the central symbol standing in need of transformation is the Christian understanding of God. Above all others, this aspect of Christianity has been held captive by androcentrism and distorted by the influence of patriarchy. Consequently, it is precisely here that a feminist theology— arising as it does out of women's experience—can provide a crucial corrective. Ruether explains: "The patriarchal distortion of all tradition throws feminist theology back upon the primary intuitions of religious experience itself: namely, the belief in a divine foundation of reality which is ultimately good, which does not wish evil or create evil, but affirms and upholds our autonomous personhood as women, in whose image we are made."[29]

According to Ruether, patriarchy has done its diabolical work by importing dualism into our idea of God. The feminist theologian characterizes as *dualistic* any perspective that divides what belongs inextricably together. What makes dualistic thinking so malicious is our tendency automatically to contrast the two items in the dualism to each other and to rank them according to some arbitrary scale. Hence, every dualism tends to set in opposition what it divides and to establish hierarchies of good and evil, domination and subordination.

Ruether then takes the matter a step farther. She claims that dualism is a characteristically male way of envisioning reality.

Men display a marked tendency to construct dualisms in a manner that women do not. Traditional theology, she adds, plagued as it has been by male-oriented thinking, has been markedly dualistic. It regularly imports into its frame of reference dualisms: nature versus spirit, transcendence versus immanence, soul versus body, redemption versus creation, good versus evil, and of course male versus female.[30]

According to Ruether, this dualistic approach has served to subjugate and dehumanize women. Male dualists have identified women with the "lower nature" and males with the "higher nature." They have correlated women with matter, body, creation, immanence, and evil, in contrast to maleness, which dualists link to spirit, soul or reason, transcendence, redemption, and good. The end result is alienation, especially the alienation of women.[31] Ruether is convinced that because dualistic thinking leads to the oppression of women, it must be rooted out of Christian theology. And a good place to start is with the doctrine of God. But how? And to what extent?

Feminist theologians are in agreement that the traditional imagery of God as male is oppressive and hence must be replaced. Hence, Ruether asserts, "God is both male and female and neither male nor female," and inclusiveness can only occur if we speak of the deity by employing female as well as male metaphors. But the feminist theologian takes this critique of the Father-image of God a step farther. *Any* parent image of God, she argues, is patriarchal. *Any* such image involves an inherent, oppressive dualism that destroys personal autonomy: "Patriarchal theology uses the parent image for God to prolong spiritual infantilism as virtue and to make autonomy and assertion of free will a sin."[32]

The solution, therefore, lies in discovering a *nondualistic* model of God. To accomplish this task, Ruether turns to the concept of the divine developed by Paul Tillich. However, she offers a twist on Tillich's nomenclature, giving it a more feminine cast. Hence, Tillich's "Ground of Being" becomes Ruether's "primal Matrix" or, to cite her more widely-known term, "God/ ess." Rather than the personal God of classical Christian theism, God/ess is the "transcendent matrix of Being that underlies and supports both our own existence and our continual potential for new being."[33]

Ruether's chief concern, however, is not to replace the personal God of the Christian tradition. Instead, she hopes by dialectical thinking to provide an image of the divine that overcomes the dualism inherent in the traditional image. Hence, Ruether cautions against identifying God/ess with *either* side of the classical dualisms of Western thought. The divine reality is not bound up with spirit, transcendence, maleness, or even humankind. But neither is God/ess simply to be equated with matter, immanence, femaleness, or nature. On the contrary, God/ess embraces all such dualities in a higher dynamic unity. And because everything is linked with God/ess, rather than forming a "great chain of being" with the divine at the top and inanimate nature at the bottom, all aspects of reality are radically equal.[34]

Critics repeatedly find in such talk overtones of monism, the belief that everything is interconnected and part of an all-embracing divine All. Indeed, Ruether's God/ess comes dangerously close to the concept of the great Mother Goddess advanced by more radical, "post-Christian" or even pagan feminists, whose veneration of this primordial figure often verges on the worship of the earth and even themselves as the repository of the divine. Indeed, Ruether herself identifies God/ess with the liberated self of the feminist woman: "The liberating encounter with God/ess is always an encounter with our authentic selves resurrected from underneath the alienated self."[35]

Of course, Ruether's intention is not to fall into pure monism. Instead, she sees herself as providing a dialectical theology that affirms the dynamic unity of all reality. In this dialectic she desires to affirm both God and "Gaia," the earth goddess popularized by many of the "new pagans" who comprise one of the more radical branches of the ecology movement. For Ruether "Gaia" represents the immanent voice of the divine, "the personal center of the universal process," whereas "God" symbolizes the masculine, transcendent voice of the divine.[36] But as Ruether's project indicates, in its attempt to avoid dualism, any such dialectical thinking risks running aground on a subtle form of monism.

A second candidate for Ruether's feminist reconstruction of Christian symbols is Christology. The person of Jesus Christ is, of course, an obvious choice if for no other reason than: any *Christian* feminist theology must cope with a male savior. In contrast to the "post-Christian" feminists who find no place for Jesus, Ruether thinks the central figure of Christianity is salvageable, but only if certain theological barnacles are eliminated: "Once the mythology about Jesus as Messiah or divine *Logos*, with its traditional masculine imagery is stripped off the Jesus of the synoptic Gospels can be recognized as a figure remarkably compatible with feminism." This means of course that the Chalcedonian Christology of Christian orthodoxy must be discarded.[37]

Like most Christian feminists, Ruether regards Jesus as a paradigm of the true humanity. Once again Paul Tillich's ideas, specifically his designation of Jesus as the New Being, lie behind Ruether's musings. In her account, Jesus of Nazareth was a liberator who denounced the structures of power and status that defined privilege in Jewish society. Jesus' message pointed beyond himself to the new humanity to come—the redemptive, radically egalitarian humanity free of dualisms and hierarchies. And in his life he showed what it means to live freed from patriarchal attitudes and behavior patterns.

According to Ruether, it is this new humanity—and not Jesus as such—that is fundamentally the Christ. Jesus was the Christ insofar as he represented and served as the forerunner of the new humanity. This means obviously that "Christ" is much larger than Jesus. She explains: "Christ, as redemptive person and Word of God, is not to be encapsulated 'once-for-all' in the historical Jesus. The Christian community continues Christ's identity."[38]

But what about the cross? What did Jesus accomplish? What are we to make of sin and salvation? Here Ruether steers clear of individualistic and other-worldly conceptions. Rather than being lodged in human finitude or the outworking of some primordial transgression, sin is fundamentally the distortion of relationship or even "wrong relationship." In sin, we absolutize our own rights to life and power, rather than seeing our fundamental interrelatedness with others. We misuse our freedom so as "to exploit other humans and the earth and thus to violate the basic relations that sustain life." This leads to the cycle of violence and the construction of systems of control. Consequently, salvation does not involve recapturing a supposedly lost immortality, but the fullness of life within our finite limits. Viewed in this context, Ruether describes the meaning of Jesus' crucifixion, which for her is "not a deterministic 'self-sacrifice' for individual 'sins,' but a political assassination on the cross of collective apostasy by the political and religious institutions that claim authority over our lives."[39]

Ruether's revisionist understanding of the "atonement" lies behind the intriguing "Feminist Midrash" or interpretive story with which she begins her highly acclaimed book *Sexism and God-Talk*. The story offers an imaginative account of salvation history involving a female deity, "the Queen of Heaven," and a figure who appeared to Mary Magdalene after Jesus' resurrection. This figure, who is "taller and more majestic [than Jesus] ... regal and yet somehow familiar, a woman like [Mary] herself," informs Mary that she is now the "continuing presence of Christ" who will "continue the redemption of the world." As the midrash closes, Ruether discloses the meaning of the cross in a manner that borrows from the older theme of the death of God: "With Jesus' death, God, the heavenly Ruler, has left the heavens and has been poured out upon the earth with his blood.

A new God is being born in our hearts to teach us to level the heavens and exalt the earth and create a new world without masters and slaves, rulers and subjects."[40]

For her part, Mary now comes to a deep understanding of the entire drama: "Mary felt a clear, calm center within herself. 'So this is why he had to die. . . . As long as he was here among us, we wanted him to take power. . . . But our ideas of God's rule were still based on domination and subjugation. . . . we must make ourselves and our relationships with each other anew. This is the beginning of the new world.'"[41] Ruether hopes that the reader might share Mary's "aha" experience.

◆

But Is It Christian?

Ruether has done a great service by steadfastly pointing out that the evils of androcentrism and patriarchy are not limited to society, but have also invaded the church. Critics, however, are concerned that in her attempt to address these errors by revising Christian symbols, Ruether has simply gone too far. Some critics focus on Ruether's specific reformulations, such as her conception of God/ess. Elizabeth Achtemeier, for example, finds in this image an unmistakable loss of divine transcendence as well as a dangerous linking of God to creation. Achtemeier is concerned that the feminist model is a far cry from Christianity:

> No religion in the world is so old as is this immanentist identification of God with creation. It forms the basis of every nonbiblical religion, except Islam; and if the church uses language that obscures God's holy otherness from creation, it opens the door to corruption of the biblical faith in that transcendent God who works in creation only by his Word and Spirit. Worshippers of a

Mother Goddess ultimately worship the creation and themselves, rather than the Creator.[42]

But the problem goes deeper. The heart of the debate over feminist theology lies in its appeal to the feminist consciousness as its highest authority, as well as the use of women's experience to determine what is and what is not normative in Scripture and the Christian tradition. Critics fear that if we draw our "critical principle" solely from the consciousness of a particular group—such as women—we have effectively eliminated any other criterion for engaging in self-criticism. As a result, feminist theologians run the risk of merely replacing an old ideology with a new one.[43]

An equally grave danger has been noted by persons within the movement itself. Pamela Dickey Young, for example, worries about what might eventually emerge if feminists allow a principle from outside the Christian tradition, such as women's experience, to determine what is truly "Christian." She fears that the feminist theological method might ultimately allow a person to label "Christian" whatever he or she wishes. In such a situation, an anti-feminist could use the Christian tradition in "less liberating ways."[44]

The application of this critique to Ruether's theology is obvious. Even though she wants to retain some type of appeal to Jesus, when she elevates her understanding of women's experience to be the controlling norm that determines what in the Christian tradition—including Jesus' own teachings—is normative and what is not, the feminist thinker risks moving theology into the realm of sheer ideology.

Young adds yet another worry. She fears that the feminist approach may lead into a new relativism: "If one appeals only to a member's self-identification as a criterion for deciding what is or what is not part of a given religious tradition, one is left with a relativism that must accept all without judgment or discernment."[45] In other words, without some type of norm lying

beyond the self-consciousness of participants within the community—whoever they may be—Christianity degenerates into
whatever any individual or group says it is.

In short, Ruether's theology of women's experience raises
the question of primacy. Is Christianity one of several ideolog-
ical tools that serve the struggle to create a society in which
women—as well as all other marginalized and oppressed elements, including even the environment itself—receive their
just due? Or is the creation of the new society an aspect of a
more encompassing Christian vision?

CHAPTER TWELVE

Global Theology
John Hick

As we have seen throughout these chapters, it is usually the case that a problem or perspective in recent and contemporary theology may be associated with a single thinker. Certainly, many may be involved in the discussion of such a problem or the development of such a perspective, but it is often one person that towers over the others as making the most decisive or vivid contribution. In the discussion of religious pluralism, the towering figure has been John Hick.

Like those of many others, Hick's story, as he himself tells it, is the tale of someone starting out as a young person on a fundamentalist track and ending up on a quite liberal one.[1] Born in 1922 in England, as a child Hick was taken to the local Anglican church services, which he later described as "a matter of infinite boredom."[2] A law student at the University of Hull and influenced by the Inter-Varsity Christian Fellowship there, he experienced a religious conversion to a fundamentalist brand of Christianity, as he describes it. Intending to enter the ministry, he joined the Presbyterian Church of England. During the

Second World War he was a conscientious objector. By the time he had received his undergraduate degree at Edinburgh University and his doctorate in philosophy at Oxford and had been through his ministerial training and served for a few years as a Presbyterian minister, he was leaving behind what he perceived as his former theological narrowness. He taught at Cornell University, Princeton Theological Seminary, Cambridge University, the University of Birmingham, England, and the Claremont Graduate School in California. (Upon his arrival at Princeton, there was a stir among American Presbyterians over whether Hick's ministerial status should be honored.)

During these years he made important contributions to "analytic" philosophy and produced many influential volumes including: *Faith and Knowledge, Evil and the God of Love,* and *Eternal Life.* It was already in Birmingham, however, with its large communities of Muslims, Sikhs, Hindus, and Jews, that he had begun to be opened to the larger world of religion. This experience, followed by extensive world travels and the study of world religions, led eventually to his culminating contribution—many discussions and books in defense of religious pluralism, most notably *An Interpretation of Religion: Human Responses to the Transcendent.*

Upon his retirement from the Claremont Graduate School, he returned to Birmingham England, where is he is a Fellow of the Institute for Advanced Research in the Humanities at the University of Birmingham.

◆

What's the Problem?

One of the most pressing issues at the turn of the millennium—and it will only get worse—is the question of religious pluralism. In recent years the spectacular and rather sudden advances in transportation and communication have made the world very small and our awareness of other cultures very large. Perhaps the most obvious consequence of this increased cosmopolitan consciousness, as we might call it, is our growing awareness specifically of the great variety of world religions, with their varying conceptions and stories about the divine, creation, revelation, salvation, the future life, and the like. This in turn has thrown into the sharpest relief an age-old issue that, until now, has largely lain dormant: religious exclusivism vs. religious pluralism.

So our world has gotten smaller and our awareness of other cultures—and other religious traditions—has gotten bigger. What's the problem? The problem is that many of these traditions have claimed exclusive authority for their teaching— claiming that their teaching is true, and the others, where they conflict with it, are false. More specifically, such traditions maintain that they and they alone provide the means of salvation. Certainly this is the case with the Western traditions of Judaism, Islam, and Christianity—at least in their original and traditional versions. Christianity, for example, has insisted in one way or another throughout its history that *extra Christum nulla salus,* "outside of Christ there is no salvation."[3] No wonder that such a perspective is called religious exclusivism.[4]

Of course, in the case of traditional Christianity, as well as other exclusivist perspectives, such a claim could mean various things. It could mean "hard" exclusivism, the doctrine that there is no salvation apart from a knowledge of and conscious commitment to Christ. Or it could mean "soft" exclusivism, sometimes called "inclusivism," the idea that it is only through Christ that God has effected salvation, though this may include many who have never heard the gospel. And, of course, there are exclusivists who are at the same time universalists—believing that salvation is possible only through Christ, though God will, in fact, save all. In time we will have to come back to these distinctions.

It would seem that, whatever problems may arise, Christian exclusivism is firmly rooted in the biblical teaching. It is, undeniably, part of the very fabric of original and traditional Christianity. There are, in fact, several well-known and explicit exclusivistic pronouncements in the New Testament. The two best-known examples of these are: the statement attributed to Jesus in John 14:6, "I am the way, and the truth, and the life. No one comes to the Father except through me," and the statement from Peter's sermon in Acts 4:12, "There is salvation in no one else, for there is no other name under heaven given among mortals by which we must be saved." There are many more such claims that directly or indirectly affirm that Christ and Christ alone is the divinely appointed means of salvation. But it is not a matter of toting up a number of biblical passages. As we said above, this is so much a part of the biblical-Christian teaching and vision that it is hardly deniable by anyone reading the text with honesty. However, it is one thing to grant that exclusivism is present in the text, and another thing to grant that it is true. Some, who even call themselves Christian theologians, do *not* grant that it is true.

Why not? For many, religious exclusivism in any form, with its perceived egocentrism, intolerance, and arrogance, is at best jarring and distasteful—especially so for those enamored with "political correctness"—and should drive us to a more accommodating view, such as *religious pluralism*. Negatively speaking, religious pluralism is the denial that any one religious tradition has a monopoly on salvific truth. Positively, it is the affirmation that the great religions of the world represent, under the guise of different cultural expressions, essentially the same religious truth and teaching about salvation. As the well-worn image has it: one hand, many fingers.

The pluralistic hypothesis is propelled, largely, by two observations. First, it is incontrovertible that nearly all of us experience the world as we do, and believe as we do, because of the accidents of birth. Think how different your life and outlook would be if you had been born at a very different time or place. Imagine yourself, for example, having been born in the 1500s in a radically different culture. None of us chose the circumstances that have shaped and molded our fundamental beliefs and practices—including religious beliefs and practices. Whether that is good or bad, it is surely a fact of life. Moreover, reflection on this fact may tend to relativize for us our own particular beliefs and practices. The second observation is more controversial. It is the claim that at the center of the world's great religions is found a common or universal core. Those who believe this usually (even predictably) identify this core of authentic religion as an experience with a universal, transcendent reality and a consequent cultivation of selflessness. According to the pluralist hypothesis, this is what all great religions are really about. If that doesn't square with, say, the Bible, then the Bible will just have to be deculturalized or otherwise adapted to our wider and more cosmopolitan awareness.

The conflict of exclusivism vs. pluralism is seen by many, and rightfully so, as cutting to the heart of Christianity, at least as it is biblically and traditionally conceived. Further, it is one of the issues that today divides Christians concerned with what a contemporary version of Christianity should look like. Spearheading one proposed version is John Hick.

◆

Hick's Pluralist Hypothesis

We have already seen that Hick has contributed in many ways to contemporary philosophical, theological, and religious thought. We have also seen that his major—one might even say culminating—contribution lies in his case for religious pluralism. Though the thesis of religious pluralism is very old, Hick has given it a renewed and forceful statement commensurate with the global consciousness that is forcing itself upon us. Hick himself likens his version of religious pluralism to a "Copernican revolution" in theology. He makes this case in numerous writings, including *God and the Universe of Faiths* and a more popular book with the suggestive title *God Has Many Names*. Far and away the most important, however, is already mentioned *An Interpretation of Religion: Human Responses to the Transcendent*.[5]

Several general points need to be made at the outset. First, Hick hits head-on the culture-centeredness of most religious beliefs—the fact that such beliefs are largely, if not completely, determined by upbringing and cultural environment. According to Hick, we should entertain no illusions about that. He argues that this recognition is the first step towards shedding a religious provincialism that insulates us from the contributions of the wider religious world. "The only reason for treating one's tradition differently from others is the very human, but not very cogent, reason that it is one's own! . . . let us avoid the implausibly arbitrary dogma that religious experience is all delusory with the single exception of the particular form enjoyed by the one who is speaking."[6] Even more pointedly, Hick asks:

> Is it compatible with limitless divine love that God should have decreed that only a minority of human beings, those who have happened to be born in a Christian part of the world, should have the opportunity of eternal life? . . . there is nothing to fear in a greater openness to God's presence within the religious life of all humankind; on the contrary, there is a release from an artificially restricted vision into a greater intellectual honesty and realism and a more mature Christian faith.[7]

Second, we have already used expressions such as "authentic religion" in connection with the pluralist hypothesis. Hick, too, is adamant that not just any old thing that goes under the name of "religion" is worthy of that name. We are confronted on every side by "religions" that thrive on the bizarre or are just plain wacko. These are rejected immediately by the serious religious pluralists, such as Hick. What they have in view, rather, are the great world religions, the religious traditions that for so many centuries have, undeniably, contributed so much to the shaping of religious awareness and the instilling of moral ideals.

Third, Hick thinks that the origins of the world's great religions was not quite accidental. Rather, there is an identifiable period of human history marked by a kind of concentration or deepening of religious awareness. It's as if a giant step had been taken on the religious front, more or less at the same time and in different cultures. Hick calls this "the axial age," signifying a kind of pivot or transition to something new in the religious consciousness.[8] "The axial age was an uniquely significant band of time. With certain qualifications we can say that in this period all the major religious options, constituting the major possible ways of conceiving the ultimate, were identified and established and that nothing of comparably novel significance has happened in the religious life of humanity since."[9]

The period in question extended roughly from 800 to 200 B.C.E. Associated with it is a panoply of great names, great movements, and great literature. It produced in China—Confucianism and Taoism; in India—Buddhism, the Hindu *Upanishads* and *Bhagavad Gita*; in Persia—Zoroastrianism; in Israel—the great Hebrew prophets and much of the Hebrew Scriptures; and in Greece—Pythagoras, Socrates, Plato, and Aristotle. Hick treats the rise of Christianity and Islam as developments within the prophetic tradition of Semitic religion and Mahayana Buddhism as a development of early Buddhism.

Still more to the point is Hick's observation that the axial religions represent a shift to soteriology, that is, a concern with personal salvation. Preaxial religions more or less accepted the world as it was. Axial religions realized that something is wrong in the world and recognized that it is our responsibility to fix it.

What is wrong in the world is human self-centeredness; what is called for is a shift—a personal transformation—from a self-centered or egocentric life to a Reality-centered life. This, says Hick, is what all the great world religions are really about at their core. They all express, in different ways: (1) the recognition of a transcultural and transcendent Reality and Source of all things; and (2) the need to identify oneself with this Reality, to become transparent to it, to be inspired and uplifted by it, and thereby to attain a degree of selflessness or genuine saintliness. The production of saintliness—understood as selflessness or "generous goodwill, love, and compassion"—is, says Hick, the criterion by which we should judge the adequacy and authenticity of a religion.[10] This transformative experience is characteristically wrought over a period of considerable time, requiring the utmost spiritual concentration and self-discipline. In this respect, our models should be the great religious teachers such as the Buddha, Jesus, and other Great-Souled Ones. As for the ultimate end of each of us, Hick advocates universalism, the idea that everyone will eventually be saved, though this may involve a future purgative process and possibly numerous reincarnations.[11]

The transcendent Reality and this transformative experience are, understandably, expressed differently by the great religious traditions. In the attempt to get at the unity-in-diversity of this experience, Hick employs the awkward but instructive expression, "salvation/liberation/ultimate fulfillment." Such an expression attempts, of course, to draw upon the language of several traditions at once and to suggest that they all come to the same thing. In a remarkably concise way he summarizes his whole project:

> I want to explore the pluralistic hypothesis that the great world faiths embody different perceptions and conceptions of, and correspondingly different responses to, the Real from within the major variant ways of being human; and that within each of them the transformation of human existence from self-centeredness to Reality-centredness is taking place. These traditions are accordingly to be regarded as alternative soteriological "spaces" within

which, or "ways" along which, men and women can find salvation/liberation/ultimate fulfillment.[12]

◆

One God, Many Faces

It is to be expected, it is natural, and in fact it is inevitable that the world religions' representations of the Real and their experiences of salvation/liberation/ultimate fulfillment will differ. We are talking about representations of the Real, for example, that have been molded at the hands of radically different cultures. Surely the most striking difference is between the Real conceived as a personal being and the Real conceived as impersonal. Even here we have variations on both sides. Hick thus uses the plural forms to characterize these as "the *personae* of the Real" and "the *impersonae* of the Real." In this he is reflecting the language of the ancient Roman theater in which the Latin *persona* meant the mask worn by a performer to indicate his or her role.

Hick examines first the almost universal need or propensity to think-and-experience the Real as *personal*, that is, as existing as "a center of consciousness." Clearly, the religious traditions that we are most familiar with do precisely this. We have only to think of Krishna, Vishnu, and Brahma of the Hindus; or Allah of the Islamic tradition; or Yahweh of the Hebrews; or the Heavenly Father taught by Jesus. These are not to be thought of as mere psychological projections, but rather as points at which the Real interfaces different cultural situations. Hick cites Krishna and Yahweh as good examples of how the Real is apprehended as two distinctly different divine personae, each operating in independent cycles of stories. Just as these personae are genuinely rooted in the Real, so the stories that tell of them and of their deeds are to be distinguished from fantasies and fairy tales. Rather, "the myths of a religious tradition are stories by which the story-telling community lives and in terms of which it understands its existence in the world."[13]

Likewise with the *impersonal* conceptions of the Real. We encounter these, for example, in the Brahman of the Vedanta Hindu tradition, the Sunyata of the Mahayana Buddhist tradition, and the Tao of Chinese religion. Brahman, for instance, is seen as the primordial Reality, the undifferentiated Unity, the "One without a second," of which everything—including us— is a part. The idea is to overcome the illusion of duality and multiplicity to attain Brahman consciousness. Such impersonal conceptions of the Real, says Hick, are no less stamped by a cultural experience and conceptuality than are the personal ones. In either case there is no such thing as, in Hick's words, "an unmediated mystical experience of the Real."[14] More important, whether it be the devout Jew, Christian, Muslim, or theistic Hindu, the Pure Land, Mahayana, Theravada, or Zen Buddhist, what is experienced is a salvific recreation, the dissolution of the ego-boundaries, a liberating transformation. As Hick expresses it:

> The spiritual disciplines and the inner resolves and actions through which theists and non-theists change, and the interpretive frameworks in terms of which they understand their own transformation, are very different. And yet the transformation undergone within these diverse forms of the life and systems of self-understanding is recognisably the same. It is this common soteriological process that suggests that the gods and the absolutes that produce it are different modes of presence of the same ultimate transcendent Reality.[15]

Throughout Hick's development of his pluralist hypothesis and especially here, in his focus on the variety of religious ex-

pression, the influence of three western philosophers is apparent. First, he is fond of citing the line from the scholastic philosopher Thomas Aquinas: "Things known are in the knower
according to the mode of the knower."[16] That is, any understanding of any thing is going to be conditioned by and bear
the marks of the cognitive faculties—along with their peculiar
features and limitations—by which that thing is apprehended.
Second, and certainly pervasive throughout Hick's approach,
is his debt to the eighteenth-century German philosopher Immanuel Kant. Kant's great contribution (whether one accepts it
or not) was to distinguish between reality as-it-is-in-itself (*an
sich*) and as-it-appears-to-us (*Erscheinung*). According to Kant,
any "theoretical" understanding necessarily takes shape in
terms of the intellectual conditions or structures of the intellect
that make that understanding possible.[17] Finally, Hick draws
upon the well-known insight of the twentieth-century German
philosopher Ludwig Wittgenstein: We all "see" and experience
things in a way dictated by what we bring to the seeing or experiencing; we are disposed to a certain perspective and interpretation.[18] Clearly all of this provides the philosophical ground for
Hick's pluralistic hypothesis.

◆

Hick vs. the Bible

Obviously, Hick has come a long way since his fundamentalist
days. Not surprisingly, his Christology—his understanding of
the person and work of Christ—has also undergone a radical
development.

There is hardly a place in Hick's global theology for the view
that Jesus Christ is the exclusive Son of God, a pre-existent one
who enters the world and, through his death and resurrection,
effects salvation for those who hear and believe. Hick is greatly

influenced by a rather severe employment of the historical-critical approach to the Bible, which yields a quite different picture of the historical Jesus from the traditional one. In this view, the New Testament portrait of Jesus is the result of early layers of theological development—expansion, embellishment, and strong doses of wishful thinking—superimposed on the historical reality of Jesus of Nazareth. The New Testament as we have it provides scant evidence for the divine nature of Jesus, a doctrine that is largely the offspring of early theological speculations and debates, expressed in such formulas and pronouncements as we encounter in the Nicene Creed of 325: "[He is] the only begotten Son of God, begotten from the Father before all time, Light from Light, true God from true God, begotten not created, as the same substance with the Father, through whom all things came into being."[19]

Such talk seemed like a good idea at the time, and Hick acknowledges that it did in fact serve a purpose. But he argues that it has now become embarrassing excess baggage. The doctrine of Christ's divinity, along with its exclusivistic corollary, ill-befits our present global awareness and should be discarded.

In 1977, Hick edited a controversial volume of essays by several prominent scholars called *The Myth of God Incarnate*. The title says it all. Hick holds that it is doubtful from a historiographical standpoint that Jesus ever claimed to be divine, and that such a claim is, at any rate, incoherent from an intellectual standpoint. Thus, it is a myth. But it is important to be clear about the word "myth." In his own contribution to the volume, "Jesus and the World Religions," Hick makes his meaning clear: "A myth is a story which is told but which is not literally true, or an idea or an image which is applied to someone or something but which does not literally apply, but which invites a particular attitude in its hearers."[20] Thus Jesus was, in truth, not even a divine *persona*. Like so many other great religious teachers, he was one who attained a transparency to the transcendent Reality and taught others to embark on the path of selflessness:

> I see the Nazarene . . . as intensely and overwhelmingly conscious of the reality of God. He was a man of God, living in the unseen presence of God, and addressing God as *abba,* father. His spirit was open to God and his life a continuous response to the divine love as both utterly gracious and utterly demanding. He was so powerfully God-conscious that his life vibrated, as it were, to the divine life; and as a result his hands could heal the sick, and the "poor in spirit" were kindled to new life in his presence.[21]

Jesus was, to say it succinctly, "our sufficient model of true humanity in a perfect relationship to God."[22] But just because he is our model doesn't mean that he is the only model.

◆

Questions, Doubts, and Resistance

The issue of exclusivism vs. pluralism is heating up as perhaps the most divisive debate of contemporary theology. Certainly the proposal of a global theology, such as Hick's, is meeting with fierce resistance. This is hardly surprising. It is seen by many of a conservative and traditionalist bent to be a direct assault on the substance of the Christian proclamation.

The conception of salvation advocated by Hick is, for example, quite different from the traditional Christian one. Talk about "enlightenment" and "liberation from ego-centeredness"—however high-minded and ennobling—is not what many have taken to be the stuff of Christian salvation. Especially for those in the Protestant tradition, salvation is a matter of sin, guilt, grace, and forgiveness. The idea of salvation as a struggle to attain saintliness and, thus, union with Transcendent Reality, appears alien to the New Testament image of standing before a forgiving God, "Just as I am, without one plea, but that thy blood was shed for me!" The charge is: Pluralism is, quite simply, a radically different idea of what reconciliation with God means and what has been required to bring it about.

Of course, the traditional view is the biblical view, and for someone like Hick that's just the problem. We have seen that Hick is greatly influenced by a style of New Testament scholarship that yields a very different picture of the historical Jesus from the one portrayed in those documents, namely, that the real Jesus, the Jesus of actual history, taught and exemplified ideas similar to those taught and exemplified by the great teachers of other world religions. It would be a mistake, however, to think that such a view has the general support of New Testament scholars. Even if the Jesus of history is different from the Jesus of the Gospels, according to the general perception he is not *that* different. More specifically, although *The Myth of God Incarnate* created quite a stir, it made nary a dent in the mainstream consensus about the historical Jesus, his messianic-self consciousness, and the like. Rather, biblical scholars went on believing pretty much as they had before. There are, in fact, good scholars on both sides of these issues, making for a good game of "pick your scholar." Hick has picked his.

Then there is the inevitable problem of competing truth-claims among the religions. Certainly it is true that the great religious traditions share many fundamental teachings. For example, it is well known that every tradition has its own formulation of the Golden Rule, "Do to others as you would have them do to you." Nonetheless, the complaint is that in its attempt to make the great world religions come out at the same point—to make them say, at their heart, the same thing—some very important differences must be overlooked. For instance, there is a key difference in respect to soteriology, the doctrine of salvation, in that the ideas of guilt and forgiveness, so central to Christian thought, are not central in Eastern religions. But aren't there many other differences? For one, is the Christian image of the resurrection of the body, judgment, and afterlife even remotely similar to ideas of transmigration of souls, innumerable reincarnations, and eventual absorption into an impersonal Reality? In Christianity are we not dealing with a religion that is, quite simply, a radically different total vision of things? Is not the texture and "feel" of Christianity quite simply different from that of the Eastern perspectives?

These are examples of rather obvious objections to global theology. Some others are suggested by the following questions:

(1) Does the pluralistic hypothesis demand or dictate the denial that Jesus was God-Incarnate, so that even if he was God-Incarnate the pluralistic hypothesizer could never recognize it? Is the rejection of such a conviction the result of scholarly assessments of history, texts, and so on, or is it simply ruled out of court at the start on the basis of the pluralist hypothesis itself?

(2) Given the relative and perspectival character of our representations of the Real, what assurance do we have that any of our representations are relevant? How can we speak of the nature or properties of the Real if, as Hick for example says, the Real is a propertyless "undifferentiated" Reality, devoid of everything that the mind projects upon it?

(3) Even though the production of saintliness is a goal of all great religious traditions, can this alone be taken as a criterion of the adequacy of their claims about God or the Real? Might not a religion be ethically uplifting but conceptually misguided?

(4) In spite of the claim to incorporate the insights of the several great religious traditions, is not pluralism almost always tilted in the direction of Eastern religions and heavily freighted with monistic and pantheistic features?

Of course, not all of these points are relevant to the work of John Hick himself, nor would he be surprised by any of them. In fact, in his *A Christian Theology of Religions,* written in an engaging dialogue style, he systematically considers what he sees as the standard criticisms of his "Copernicized Revolution in Religion."[23] His view of Jesus Christ has been treated in a Christological study, *The Metaphor of God Incarnate*.[24]

◆

Roman Catholics: Vatican II

The Roman Catholic tradition has surely been associated historically with the most extreme form of exclusivism. After all, in 1442 the Council of Florence did affirm Cyprian's assertion that "there is no salvation outside the Church," where "Church" had long since come to mean the Roman Catholic Church, and elaborated on its meaning:

> [The holy Roman Church] firmly believes, professes, and proclaims that those not living within the Catholic Church, not only pagans, but also Jews and heretics and schismatics, cannot become participants in eternal life, but will depart '"into everlasting fire which was prepared for the devil and his angels" [Matt. 25:41], unless before the end of life the same have been added to the flock.[25]

It may, therefore, be a surprise to some that in recent years Roman Catholicism has in some ways outstripped Protestant traditions in its attempt to be more accommodating of non-Christian religions.

One of the most influential theological events of the twentieth century was Pope John XXIII's convening of the Roman Catholic Church's Twenty-First Ecumenical Council, conducted from October 11, 1962, until December 8, 1965. Because it was the second Ecumenical Council to be held at the Vatican, it is known as "Vatican II." Some dramatic changes were to come out of Vatican II, not the least of which concerned the Church's stance on non-Christian religions.

The Council's "Declaration on the Relationship of the Church to Non-Christian Religions" asserts:

> The Catholic Church rejects nothing which is true and holy in these religions. She looks with sincere respect upon those ways of conduct and of life, those rules and teachings which, though differing in many particulars from what she holds and sets forth, nevertheless reflect a ray of that Truth which enlightens all men. . . . The Church therefore has this exhortation for her sons: prudently and lovingly, through dialogue and collaboration with the followers of other religions, and in witness of Christian faith and life, acknowledge, preserve, and promote the spiritual and moral goods found among these men, as well as the values in their society and culture.[26]

What is involved here is more than an encouragement to the Church and her traditional antagonists to forget past quarrels and to strive sincerely for mutual understanding and cooperation for the betterment of the world, though that is included: "On behalf of all mankind, let them make common cause of safeguarding and fostering social justice, moral values, peace, and freedom."[27] The Declaration quoted above includes language extolling the claims and practices of several non-Christian religions: Hinduism, with its fruitful mythology, philosophical inquiry, ascetic practices, and deep meditation; Buddhism, with its stress on the insufficiency of this shifting world and the attainment of supreme enlightenment though one's own efforts or with a higher assistance; Islam, which adores one God, merciful and creator, is associated with Abrahamic faith, reveres Jesus as a prophet, honors Mary, his mother, and anticipates the day of judgment; Judaism, in whose patriarchs, prophets, and Moses is found the beginnings of the Church's faith, in whose Exodus from Egypt the salvation of the Church was mystically foreshadowed, and from whom Christianity has received the revelation of the Old Testament.[28]

In none of this does the Roman Catholic Church minimize its own custodianship of salvific truth: "It is through Christ's Catholic Church alone, which is the all-embracing means of salvation, that the fullness of the means of salvation can be obtained."[29] Nevertheless, the opening up or broadening of the Church's recognition of what is going on in non-Christian religions is unmistakable.[30] And it is certainly a move in the direction of what we earlier called "soft" exclusivism, or what is sometimes called "inclusivism."

But of course the Declarations from Vatican II did not just fall out of the blue. The Church has been sensitive for some time to the fate of those who have never benefited from the Christian proclamation. A good example of this was the introduction, at the Council of Trent in the seventeenth century, of the doctrine of "baptism by desire."[31] The idea was to accommodate those pagans who, though never having heard the gospel, are conscientious in their moral and spiritual lives and thus implicitly desire baptism and union with the Church. They are Christians "in principle," as it were. Catholic theologian Paul Knitter calls this doctrine the shift from "outside the Church no salvation" to "without the church no salvation."[32]

◆

"Anonymous Christians"?

It is not really a big step from "baptism by desire" to the more recent and much-touted idea of "anonymous Christians." This idea stems from the work of Catholic theologian Karl Rahner (1904–84), for many years professor of theology at the University of Innsbruck, Austria, and author of *Foundations of the Faith* and the multivolume collection of essays *Theological Investigations*. (The latter was eight thousand pages long in the German edition; his writing was so thick and ponderous that his brother Hugo, a Jesuit theologian, promised some day to translate it into German!) Rahner was regarded by many as the most influential theologian of contemporary Catholicism, and certainly the most powerful theologian at Vatican II.

With his idea of anonymous Christianity, Rahner has probably done more for the shaping of progressive Catholic thought on the topic of non-Christian religions than anyone. Anonymous Christians are religious people who are Christians even though they don't know about Christianity expressly. In the essay "Christianity and the Non-Christian Religions," Rahner develops this idea in relation to four theses. First, Christianity is the "absolute" religion, universal and without equal. Second, until Christianity enters on a particular social-historical scene, a non-Christian religion may be a "lawful" religion, containing genuinely supernatural and gracious elements derived from Christ. Third, Christianity must not confront a member of a lawful non-Christian religion as a mere non-Christian, but as an "anonymous" Christian, someone touched by God's grace and truth. Fourth, the Church will regard itself not so much as an exclusive community, but as the "tangible vanguard" and "explicit expression" of what it hopes is a present though hidden reality outside the visible Church.[33]

All of this is intended to cultivate on the part of Christians a more "optimistic" view of the religious—even salvific—possibilities of non-Christian religions, without denying their distortions and inadequacies. It is intended also to redefine the Church's missionary enterprise away from proselytizing to informing those in other traditions about the meaning and fullness of their own salvation as revealed in Christ, its ultimate source. Rahner declares:

> It is possibly too much to hope, on the one hand, that the religious pluralism which exists in the concrete situation of Christians will disappear in the foreseeable future. On the other hand, it is nevertheless absolutely permissible for the Christian himself to interpret this non-Christianity as Christianity of an anonymous kind

which he does always still go out to meet as a missionary, seeing it as a world which is to be brought to the explicit consciousness of what already belongs to it as a divine offer or already pertains to it also over and above this as a divine gift of grace accepted unreflectedly and implicitly.[34]

Not everyone has greeted Rahner's proposal of "anonymous Christianity" with unmitigated approval. A significant example is another German-speaking Catholic theologian, the University of Tübingen professor Hans Küng. Like Rahner, Küng seeks to be thoroughly rational in his theological approach. But he goes much further in his advance beyond standard Catholic beliefs. This is evident from the fact that, after too many controversial (not to say heretical) claims, in 1979 his privilege of teaching Catholic ministerial students was denied; he ceased to be, officially, a Catholic theologian. Though originally enamored of Karl Barth, he was eventually characterized by Rahner as being more liberal than even liberal Protestants.

In his early and most influential book, *On Being a Christian,* Küng trenchantly remarks:

> It would be impossible to find anywhere in the world a sincere Jew, Muslim, or atheist who would not regard the assertion that he is an "anonymous Christian" as presumptuous. To bring the partner to the discussion into our own circle in this way closes the dialogue before it has even begun. This is a pseudo-solution which offers slight consolation. Is it possible to cure a society from a decline in membership by declaring that even non-members are "hidden" members? And what would Christians say if they were graciously recognized by Buddhists as "anonymous Buddhists."[35]

According to Küng, the rich variety of religious expression should not be addressed with a supercilious shrug of the shoulders—this shirks the responsibility of tough thinking about an urgent and difficult matter. Nor is it possible to flatten out the great religions to a least common denominator—the important differences must be frankly admitted. We have to bite the bullet and acknowledge that these religions are, in their own right, different but legitimate salvific paths.

For Küng, this means a shift from *ecclesiocentrism*—an emphasis on the centrality of the Church—to *theocentrism*—an emphasis on the centrality of God. Salvation is rooted in God, not the Church. It also means a shift from a patronizing accommodation of other religions to a recognition of the genuine insights to be found in non-Christian religions, and to a genuine dialogue that would be to the advantage of all honest truth-seekers, Christian and non-Christian alike.[36] But, for Küng, what this approach does *not* mean is an abandonment or even minimizing of Christian *uniqueness*. We have already mentioned some of the real differences among the great religions and thus the uniqueness of each. But for Küng there is a special uniqueness about Christianity. This is where Christology comes in. What is the role of Christ in all of this? Küng answers that Christ is not the "constitutive" but rather the "normative" mediator of salvation. This means that though salvation can come independently of Christ, he is nonetheless the model of salvation, for *everyone.* Jesus of Nazareth is "ultimately decisive, definitive, archetypal for man's relations with God, with his fellow man, with society."[37] In this respect, Küng has to concede that Christians have an edge.

It is really nothing new to insist, in one way or another, on the centrality, uniqueness, or normative character of Christianity, while at the same time acknowledging a means of salvation for those outside the geographical, historical, or social reach of the Christian gospel. Such a formula is nearly as old as Christianity itself. Neither is its present expression limited to current discussion within the Roman Catholic tradition. When Karl Rahner was writing, so was C. S. Lewis, an Anglican of somewhat conservative inclinations, who nonetheless entertained his own version of anonymous Christianity: "There are people in other religions who are being led by God's secret influence to concentrate on those parts of their religion which are in agreement with Christianity, and who thus belong to Christ without knowing it."[38]

---◆---

Intolerance or Arrogance?

We have seen that Christian exclusivism comes in two forms: what we have called "hard" exclusivism, which is the claim that those are excluded who have not heard the Christian gospel or who have heard it but rejected it; and "soft" exclusivism or "inclusivism"—the claim that even those who haven't heard may enjoy the salvation made possible in Jesus Christ. Many, however, would object to *any* form of exclusivism on the grounds that it is an arrogant, insensitive, chauvinistic, and intolerant stance.

But the exclusivist might respond in this way. Surely, just because religious exclusivism is out of step with some peoples' political sensibilities does not mean that it is therefore wrong. Furthermore, biblical Christianity has never been interested in accommodating the world's agenda, though it has claimed to stand in judgment on that agenda. In any event, doesn't the oft-repeated charge of intolerance misfire? There is nothing wrong with intolerance as such. We are all intolerant of many things, and rightfully so. Even the pluralist position is intolerant of the exclusivist position insofar as it judges it to be mistaken and to be repudiated. In fact, because the pluralist position rejects all religious claims except those that it espouses, it itself is just another example of religious exclusivism! People of any religious tradition must always be on guard against arrogance, insensitivity, and chauvinism. But intolerance—in the sense of evaluation, judgment, and rejection of ideas and practices perceived to be wrong—would always seem to be in order in any meaningful debate. The pluralist will have to do better than simply accuse the exclusivist of intolerance.

Further, one grows weary of the complaint that if we had been born and raised in a different cultural setting we would think entirely differently about things like religion. Surely that is true, but it is true for the pluralist too, whose pluralistic view is molded by circumstance, education, and so on. In this respect, should we not be glad for an upbringing that has taught us that $2 + 2 = 4$, that racial discrimination is wrong, and all sorts of other useful, important, and *true* things? Finally, no one is scandalized by the fact that only one (if any) of the many competing theories in science, politics, philosophy, and the like can be true. Why, then, do some pluralists exclude out of hand the possibility that one religious position may be true to the exclusion of the others? Is there something more, such as a strong dose of personal preference, than biblical studies, theology, and philosophy going on here?

Be that as it may, the question of the finality of Christ— whether Christ is the criterion of all religious and theological truth or but one criterion among many—will be a dominating question, and maybe *the* question, of Christian theology for a generation to come.

CHAPTER THIRTEEN

Theology in a Postliberal Age
George Lindbeck

In 1962, a thirty-nine-year-old Lutheran medievalist from Yale University was invited to represent the Lutheran World Federation at the Second Vatican Council, convened by the reform-minded Pope John XXIII. The Lutheran professor's selection to be one of the approximately sixty delegated observers from outside the Roman Catholic Church arose largely because of his work on medieval Catholic thought.

The experience of attending all four sessions of the Council changed the direction of this Lutheran professor's interests. From this point on, he devoted himself to questions of ecumenism, especially discussions between Lutherans and Catholics. During the next two decades, he participated in over a dozen official interchurch dialogues, serving as cochair of several. Such involvement led the ecumenical leader to realize how specific doctrines continued to pose roadblocks to church cooperation. And it sparked in him a concern to discover a new way of thinking about doctrine itself. He later explained how for a quarter century he had experienced a growing dissatisfaction with the usual ways of thinking about those norms of communal belief and action which are generally spoken of as the doctrines or dogmas of churches. It has become apparent to me, during twenty-five years of involvement in ecumenical discussions and in teaching about the history and present status of doctrines, that those of us who are engaged in these activities lack adequate categories for conceptualizing the problems that arise. We are often unable, for example, to specify the criteria we implicitly employ when we say that some changes are faithful to a doctrinal tradition and others unfaithful, or some doctrinal differences are church-dividing and others not. Doctrines, in other words, do not behave the way they should, given our customary suppositions about the kinds of things they are. We clearly need new and better ways of understanding their nature and function.[1]

This "growing dissatisfaction" gave birth to a new and creative way of understanding doctrine. And the ensuing book that flowed from the pen of this dissatisfied ecumenist, *The Nature of Doctrine: Religion and Theology in a Postliberal Age* (1984), became a rallying point for the fledgling postliberal movement. The author of the volume was George Lindbeck.

◆

From "Liberalism" to "Postliberalism"

The designation "postliberal" immediately raises a crucial question: What is the "liberalism" in connection to which, this development is "post"? That is, in what sense are postliberal thinkers "post"-liberal?

Today many people use the word "liberal" to refer to theologians who in the name of "relevance" are willing to jettison certain traditional doctrines, such as the virgin birth of Christ. Although some Christians wear the label as a badge of honor, like its opposite, "fundamentalist," "liberal" is generally used to cast aspersions upon those with whom one differs. When used in this manner the term is quite imprecise, being largely dependent on the exact theological commitments of the speaker. Hence, we often quip, "A 'liberal' is anyone to the 'left' of me and a 'fundamentalist' anyone to my 'right.'"

Technically, however, as we saw in chapters 1 and 2, "liberalism" designates a specific historical movement in Protestant theology whose heyday occurred around the turn of the twentieth century. This movement, often designated "classical Protestant liberalism," encompassed such theological luminaries as Albrecht Ritschl, Adolf von Harnack, and Walter Rauschenbusch, as well as the prominent preacher Harry Emerson Fosdick. Although a diverse group, liberal thinkers tended to hold several characteristics as common. Their ultimate goal was to reconstruct Christian belief in the light of modern knowledge. The liberals were convinced that Christian theology simply could not ignore recent developments in Western society. The survival of Christianity, they believed, depended on its ability to adapt to the emerging modern scientific and philosophical mind-set.[2]

But how could this reconstruction be accomplished, given the role of traditional authorities in the church? The liberal program involved the rejection of the unquestioned, absolute right of church tradition or church hierarchy to determine the pattern of theology. In their place, the liberals elevated the right of the individual to criticize and reconstruct traditional beliefs. This did not mean that the liberals were bent on dismantling willy-nilly classic Christian doctrine, only that they resolutely relegated to themselves the prerogative to reject traditional beliefs when they sensed the modern situation demanded it.

One traditional authority to which liberals no longer gave unswerving allegiance was Scripture. Throughout the nineteenth century, scholars had subjected the Bible to intense scrutiny. Research into the origins of the biblical documents had cast doubt on the accuracy of the Bible's depiction of historical events and had undermined the traditional claims about the identity of those who actually had written many of the canonical books. The liberals were convinced that such historical-critical scholarship had effectively destroyed the traditional dogma of the supernatural inspiration of Scripture.

The liberals did not simply throw out the Bible, of course. But rather than accepting everything taught in Scripture, they looked within its pages for the timeless core of truth that the acids of modern historical, scientific, and philosophical knowledge could not erode. Hence, they believed that a pure "kernel" of unchanging truth lay within the Bible, encased in a host of antiquated cultural ideas and expressions. In their estimation, the task of theology was to separate the essence of Christianity from the disposable husk. For many liberal theologians, this husk included miracles, supernatural beings (angels and demons), and apocalyptic events that heralded a catastrophic end of the world. Having concluded that the true gospel was practical or ethical in focus, they set forth a theology that they believed advanced the reign of God in the world.

In chapter 1 we indicated how Karl Barth and others launched a scathing attack against classical Protestant liberalism. Yet, rather than rolling over and dying, liberalism raised its head repeatedly throughout the subsequent century. Facets of the liberal program reemerged, especially among those theologians who had grown suspicious that Barth and company had gone too far in exorcizing the ghost of liberalism from the theological mansion.

Two theologians we surveyed in this volume serve as examples of how the concern to take seriously modern philosophical and scientific understandings resurfaced later in the twentieth century. Paul Tillich represents those who borrowed themes from the newer philosophies, such as existentialism. And John Cobb, Jr., is indicative of theologians who wanted to correlate theology with the emphasis on change and evolution that typify both science and culture. To these, we could add other names and movements—such as the secular theology of the 1960s and the continuation of the liberal focus on the authority of the individual and on individual experience present in, for example, Ruether's feminist theology or John Hick's religious pluralism.

Beginning in the 1980s, however, a new critique of the liberal program emerged: *postliberalism*. Somewhat reminiscent of Barth's earlier call for a wholesale break with the liberalism of his day, the postliberals call for a move beyond the latent liberal program they found within much of twentieth-century theology. Yet perhaps in contrast to Barth, postliberals remain liberals in one important way. They do not advocate "abandoning modern developments and returning to some form of preliberal orthodoxy"—to cite the words of George Lindbeck.[3] Postliberals readily admit that there simply is no going back.

◆

From Medievalist to "Postliberal"[4]

Like John Cobb, Jr., George Lindbeck was born on the mission field during the third decade of the twentieth century (in 1923). The son of Swedish-American Lutheran missionaries, young George spent his childhood years in China and Korea. But as was typical for "missionary kids," higher education meant relocating to the United States. Lindbeck attended one of the most prominent Lutheran institutions in the land, Gustavus Adolphus College in Minnesota, where he received his bachelor's degree in 1943. Then it was on to Yale, where he would spend the rest of his academic life, first as a student and later as a professor.

In 1946 Yale Divinity School awarded Lindbeck the B.D., the standard ministerial degree of the day, which was followed nine years later by a Ph.D. from Yale University (1955). His initial academic interest focused on medieval philosophy and theology. Doctoral work in this area took Lindbeck beyond the walls of Yale to Toronto and Paris to study with two of the leading medieval scholars of the day, Étienne Gilson and Paul Vignaux. Meanwhile, in 1952, Lindbeck received an appointment to the Yale faculty, where he served as Pitkin Professor of Historical Theology until his retirement in 1993.

Historical theology, however, has not been the field in which Lindbeck has contributed most to theology. Although he has published in this area as well as in ecumenical studies, what has won him a place in the contemporary discussion is his new way of conceptualizing doctrine—a contribution that has marked an important move beyond the liberal understanding. Hence, in his lifetime Lindbeck has made the leap from medievalist to postliberal. But what exactly does he find problematic in the residual liberalism of his own theological heritage?

To answer this question, Lindbeck contrasts two widely held, but in his estimation insufficient, ways of conceptualizing what doctrine is all about, each of which presupposes a corresponding understanding of religion. The one that comes first historically is what he calls the "cognitive-propositionalist" approach. This view, which characterizes the older orthodoxy, assumes that theological statements, or doctrines, make "first-order" truth claims. That is, they assert that something is objectively true or false (for example, Jesus was born of a virgin). However, according to Lindbeck this view identifies religion too closely with its cognitive dimension, with the series of assertions it holds to be objectively true. And because propositionalists assume that such doctrines are either true or false, Lindbeck fears that within this framework ecumenical progress can come only at the expense of one church capitulating to the doctrinal positions of another.

In Lindbeck's reading, the liberal project has sought to overcome these difficulties by proposing a second approach—the "experiential-expressive" approach. According to liberalism, religion arises out of personal religious experience. Consequently, rather than having cognitive content, doctrines are the outward expressions of "inner feelings, attitudes or existential orienta-tions."[5] Lindbeck, however, is not convinced. Liberal theo-logians, he complains, erroneously assume that there is some identifiable core religious experience common to all Christian traditions or even to all world religions.

If liberalism's foundation in religious experience is problem-atic, what marks the way forward?

◆

The Move to Narrative

Lindbeck is not the first theologian who has attempted a move beyond liberalism. Others have sought to do so by building from a proposal generally known as "narrative theology." Nar-rative theologians are concerned to find a way to overcome the current crisis in Christian identity. At the heart of this crisis, they assert, is the silence of Scripture in the church, which nar-rative theologians argue is due in part to individualistic read-ings of the Bible. Coupled with this is the demise of a sense of theological tradition and the loss of the importance of theology for the personal and corporate life of Christians.[6]

Narrative theologians seek to meet this challenge by drawing from the contemporary observation that human beings are *story-tellers*. All tribes and peoples express their understanding of re-ality by telling stories. This is evidenced, for example, by the creation stories in the opening chapters of Genesis. Such narra-tives emerge from the human need to sense that the flow of time is not chaotic and insignificant. Narratives fulfill this need by linking the past and the future with the present, that is, by understanding the present in the light of the past and the future.[7]

One plank in the foundation for narrative theology was laid by Lindbeck's colleague at Yale, Hans Frei.[8] In his book, *The Eclipse of Biblical Narrative* (1974), Frei argues that theologians have erroneously attempted to salvage the biblical story in the face of modern criticism by detaching the story's meaning from its truth. Thereby they have created two separate and irreconcilable disciplines—biblical theology and historical criticism. Rather than attempting to salvage the significance of the discredited biblical stories by looking for some timeless kernel of universal truth within them, Frei proposes that theologians take seriously the narrative nature of the biblical stories.[9] At the same time, against conservatives he argues that the importance of these narratives lies not in their presentation of historically accurate information, but in their ability to show us a reflection of the actual (narrative) shape of reality.[10]

On the basis of Frei's proposal, narrative theologians seek to mine the deeper purpose of stories. By unfolding a plot and developing the characters within the story line, narratives are able to offer insight into the human condition, as well as the origins and goal of human life.[11] More specifically, narratives play a crucial role in the development of personal identity. Narrative theologian George Stroup, for example, explains that human identity develops as individuals interpret the whole of personal life from the perspective of certain events from the past and in accordance with an "interpretive scheme" that includes such intangibles as personal values, ideals, and goals. This interpretive framework, Stroup adds, arises within a social context or "tradition" that, by reciting an ongoing story, provides the categories through which people understand their own lives.[12]

Hence, narrative theologians are convinced that personal identity always has a *communal* element; it is shaped by the community of which the person is a participant. The members of any such community are held together by the narrative they share. In fact, to belong to a group means to share the community narrative—to recite the same stories and to allow them to shape one's identity.

Of greatest significance for Christian narrative thinkers, of course, is the Christian community, which appeals to the biblical narratives—above all the story of Jesus—as the foundational resource for constructing its identity and interpreting its world. This, in turn, provides the context for understanding biblical authority. This authority lies in the Bible's function in the life of the Christian community. The Bible narrates the events that form the focus around which the community gathers. Scripture provides the narratives and symbols to which the community continually returns in order to understand itself and its faith.[13] What is crucial about the Bible, therefore, is not so much the doctrines that it supposedly contains, but the story that it tells. In fact, for narrative thinkers, "doctrines . . . are not the upshot of the stories; they are not the meaning or heart of the stories. Rather they are tools . . . meant to help us tell the story better."[14]

◆

The Ethicist's Approach to Narrative

The author of the quotation above, the feisty Duke Divinity School ethicist Stanley Hauerwas, is often hailed as the premiere narrative thinker of our day.[15] Whether or not this is the case, Hauerwas is decidedly postliberal. When he set out to study theology at Yale, he simply assumed he would become a liberal theologian. Yet, throughout his writings he has consistently attempted to critique liberalism. As he bluntly declares, "I am not tying to save the liberal project, I am trying to save the church from the liberal project."[16]

Like Frei, Hauerwas believes that stories reflect how humans live and act in the world. He shares with other narrative theologians the idea that the human person is fundamentally a "narrative."[17] But Hauerwas is not content to produce a theory of narrative. Rather, he wants to move from theory to practice—to set forth the implications of the Christian story for *living* as the people of God in the world.[18] In this interest, he represents those thinkers who develop what we might call an "ethicist" approach to narrative theology.

Hauerwas is generally known for his defense of what many scholars term an "ethic of virtue." In so doing, he is consciously rejecting the modern focus on "action" and hence the modern attempt to construct an "ethic of doing."[19] For him the central ethical question is not "What constitutes a good action?" but "What constitutes a good person?" This leads Hauerwas to narrative theology.

Our personal character is never a static, given reality, he maintains, but develops "through our history." In describing this process Hauerwas employs three interrelated concepts—"character" (or virtue), "vision" and "narrative." "Character" refers to the cumulative source of human actions; it is "our deliberate disposition to use a certain range of reasons for our actions rather than others." At the same time, what we are becoming is a product of the basic manner in which we view the world and ourselves. It is affected by our "vision," by our tendency "to see the world in a certain way and then to become what we see." But this vision is not something we develop in isolation. Rather, because we view the world in accordance with story-related metaphors and symbols, our vision is formed and given content by the narrative context in which we live, by "the stories through which we have learned to form the story of our lives." Such paradigmatic narratives not only describe the world in the present but indicate how it ought to be changed.[20]

This understanding leads directly to the Christian community, the church, which Hauerwas elevates as the focal point of the development of Christians as a people of character. In fact, he is convinced that the church's most important social task is, "nothing less than to be a community capable of hearing the story of God we find in the scripture and living in a manner that is faithful to that story." This entails being "a community capable of forming people with virtues sufficient to witness to God's truth in the world." In the fulfillment of this task, the church draws from its own narrative, specifically from the stories of Israel and Jesus, which are to shape and form the lives of Christians.[21]

But why focus on biblical narratives? For Hauerwas the answer is readily at hand. Narrative is the form through which God has chosen to disclose God's own nature. Because of the narrative character of God's activity, as well as the narrative character of our own lives, biblical narratives speak to us about God and ourselves. Hence, the Bible is authoritative, because it contains the narratives through which we come to know the truth. We look to the Bible because it helps us remember the stories of God, which guide us as we seek to live as Christ's disciples. For Hauerwas, then, ethics does not follow after a systematic presentation of the Christian faith, as in most traditional presentations, but must come at the beginning of Christian theological reflection.[22]

◆

Doctrine, the Rules of the Community

Narrative theologians propose that the way forward in the contemporary situation lies in appropriating the role of the faith community in the formation of Christians as people of character. While this offers a helpful perspective, even proponents admit that narrative theology doesn't provide all the answers. Michael Goldberg, for example, outlines three critical issues any narrative theology must face: "(1) the relationship between stories and experience—the question of truth; (2) the hermeneutic involved for understanding stories rightly—the question of meaning; and (3) the charge of moral relativism—the question of rationality."[23] Considerations such as these lead Paul Nelson to conclude that "narrative is not a universal solvent for all theological problems or disagreements."[24]

The problems left unresolved by the turn to narrative provide an appropriate context in which to view Lindbeck's proposal. Like the narrative theologians, Lindbeck emphasizes the foundational importance of the biblical narrative.[25] He agrees that "to become a Christian involves learning the story of Israel and of Jesus well enough to interpret and experience oneself and one's world in its terms." He is also concerned that the church rediscover biblical narrative, so that—to paraphrase his lucid one-liner—the text might absorb the world, rather than the world the text.[26] To this end, Lindbeck calls the people of God to return to the "classic pattern of biblical interpretation" with its "consensus-and-community-building potential."[27]

Lindbeck is not only interested in the story the faith community tells, however. He also pays attention to "the grammar that informs the way the story is told and used."[28] This desire to find a place for church doctrine in contemporary theological method marks the step Lindbeck takes beyond his narrative colleagues. The place Lindbeck creates for doctrine, together with the understanding of religion that corresponds to this view of doctrine, capsulizes his move beyond his liberal forebears. In place of the outmoded cognitive-propositionalist approach of the older orthodoxy and the experiential-expressivist alternative lying at the foundation of liberalism, Lindbeck offers a third view, which he calls the "cultural-linguistic" approach. He believes that this proposal provides the key for the construction of a truly postliberal theology.

To understand Lindbeck's suggestion we look to what is at work behind the scenes. His proposal is indebted to a specific assumption about what it means to be human. Similar to narrative theologians, Lindbeck believes that we are thoroughly social beings and that our cultural context gives shape to our experience of the world. In fact, he goes so far as to say that we cannot have an experience apart from the dynamic working of our social context. "We cannot identify, describe, or recognize experience qua experience," he explains, "without the use of signs and symbols." Lindbeck's thorough-going adherence to this theory is evident in what he says next: "These [signs and symbols] are necessary even for what the depth psychologist speaks of as 'unconscious' or 'subconscious' experiences, or for what the phenomenologist describes as prereflective ones. In short, it is necessary to have the means for expressing an experience in order to have it, and the richer our expressive or linguistic system, the more subtle, varied, and differentiated can be our experience."[29]

For Lindbeck, following contemporary thinking in the discipline known as the sociology of religion, religion is an integral dimension of our experience-shaping cultural context. Religions, he writes, are "comprehensive interpretive schemes, usually embodied in myths or narratives and heavily ritualized, which structure human experience and understanding of self and world."[30] In other words, the convictions or doctrinal system of any given religion provide its adherents with a comprehensive interpretation of reality. This overarching interpretive framework, in turn, allows them to experience the world the way they do. To cite an example that Lindbeck himself offers: "Luther did not invent his doctrine of justification by faith because he had a tower experience, but rather the tower experience was made possible by his discovering (or thinking he discovered) the doctrine in the Bible."[31]

This understanding of the experience-forming role of religious traditions stands in stark contrast to the older liberal assumption that religion is the *product* of experience. Lindbeck's view leads likewise to another crucial aspect of his radical break with the liberal understanding. He denies what he takes to be the foundational assumption of liberalism, namely, that some common experiential core lies beneath and gives unity to the various religious traditions. Rather than being the diverse products of what ultimately is an identical experience everyone shares, the various religions comprise quite different ways of

viewing the world. "Adherents of different religions," Lindbeck demurs, "do not diversely thematize the same experience;
rather they have different experiences." Again an example he
offers indicates the extent to which he is willing to apply this
point: "Buddhist compassion, Christian love and—if I may cite
a quasi-religious phenomenon—French Revolutionary *frater-
nité* are not diverse modifications of a single fundamental human awareness, emotion, attitude, or sentiment, but are radically (i.e., from the root) distinct ways of experiencing and being
oriented toward self, neighbor, and cosmos."[32]

But what does all this have to say about Christian doctrine?
In developing his response Lindbeck draws from contemporary
linguistic theory, especially the thought of the German philosopher Ludwig Wittgenstein.[33] We might summarize the under-
lying idea by reminding ourselves that every language has rules
that those who would speak the language must use in their
speaking. For example, to speak French requires that a person
learn, accept, and act upon rules of French grammar.

In a similar manner, Lindbeck declares that doctrines constitute what we might call the rules of discourse of the believing
community. Doctrines act as norms that instruct adherents
within the community how to think about and live in the
world. Hence, like rules of grammar, church doctrine has a
"regulative" function. In Lindbeck's words, doctrines function
as "community authoritative rules of discourse, attitude, and
action." They are "teachings regarding beliefs and practices that
are considered essential to the identity or welfare of the group
in question." As such, "they indicate what constitutes faithful
adherence to a community."[34] To borrow an image from Wittgenstein, doctrines establish the ground rules for the "game" of
Christian thinking, speaking, and living.

Lindbeck is convinced that this regulative understanding of
doctrine provides a way to overcome the impasse that develops
whenever theologians debate whether a specific doctrine is objectively true, as classical orthodoxy argues, or false, as liberals

often suggest. This debate, he argues, erroneously assumes that doctrinal statements make first-order truth claims, that is, that they purport to assert something objective about reality. Instead, like rules of grammar, such statements are second-order assertions. They make "intrasystematic" truth-claims. Their truth or falsity can only be discussed in connection with their place within the totality of Christian doctrines. And the truth or falsity of any one doctrine is dependent upon whether or not it coheres with the other doctrines in the Christian belief system. Lindbeck offers an example: "For a Christian, 'God is Three and One,' or 'Christ is Lord' are true only as parts of a total pattern of speaking, thinking, feeling, and acting."[35]

Here again, the analogy from language is helpful. Although rules of grammar are stated in the form of propositions, it would be improper to ask whether any one of them is objectively "true" or "false." Raising such a question involves a fundamental misunderstanding of the type of proposition the rule in fact is. The question of objective truth requires ripping the proposition out of its context, treating it apart from its regulative role within the language itself.

The application to doctrines is obvious. According to Lindbeck, church doctrines function primarily as rules for speech about God, rather than as actual assertions concerning God. He writes, "Just as grammar by itself affirms nothing either true or false regarding the world in which language is used, but only about language, so theology and doctrine, to the extent that they are second-order activities, assert nothing either true or false about God and his relation to creatures, but only speak about such assertions."[36]

Where does this leave theology? Lindbeck's answer once again moves him beyond liberalism. In contrast to the liberal program of "translating Scripture into extrascriptural categories," he calls for an "intratextual theology," which "redescribes reality within the scriptural framework" and aims at "imaginatively incorporating all being into a Christ-centered world." This theology draws from the text, centered as it is on the biblical narrative, to explore what it means to articulate and live out the community's vision within a specific time and place.[37]

To this end, the theologian expounds the doctrinal core or framework of the Christian faith, determines that it coheres within itself, and indicates how doctrine illumines human existence. On this basis, the theologian engages with the statements and practices of the church, "explaining, defending, analyzing, and regulating the liturgical, kerygmatic, and ethical modes of speech and action."[38] In this manner, the theologian seeks to determine the extent to which all such beliefs and practices cohere with the Christ-centered world depicted in Scripture.

◆

But Is It Sufficient?

Lindbeck's postliberal proposal has caused quite a ripple on the contemporary theological pond. Together with narrative theology, it has won the support of theologians from a variety of backgrounds. Its adherents laud the narrative approach as providing a way to affirm the normative role of Scripture in the life of the church, while taking seriously the problems and challenges that led to the collapse of the older orthodoxy.

In addition, Lindbeck has been applauded specifically for carving out a place for doctrine that avoids the ahistorical propositionalism which initially triggered the sharp reaction that launched the ill-fated liberal program. In so doing, Lindbeck has reintroduced an easily overlooked role of doctrine. Indeed, church doctrine ought to function in a regulative manner in the faith community.

More common than uncritical embrace (or unqualified rejection for that matter[39]) has been cautious appropriation of Lindbeck's proposal. Many thinkers go away with the impression that although Lindbeck has moved theology in the right direction, much further work remains to be done. Perhaps the most crucial area that cries out for additional reflection is the whole matter of ontological truth claims. Lindbeck's close linking of doctrine with the construction of a coherent vision of the world and the forming of personal and communal identity seems to beg the sticky question as to whether or not such a coherent vision and thus the identity it produces somehow reflect a reality beyond itself. Obviously, a proposal that appears to bypass objective truth claims raises the eyebrows of anyone who is concerned to maintain some sense in which church doctrines are first-order assertions.[40]

But Lindbeck's view has also ignited concern over a different potential implication. Some theologians wonder whether his program, as well as that of Hauerwas,[41] leads to a "sectarian" view of the church, one in which the church no longer assumes any role or has any voice in the public realm.[42]

Clark Pinnock spoke for many in offering this telling appraisal:

> Perhaps it would be wise for Lindbeck to come right out and admit that doctrines do all three things: They make truth claims, they express inner experience, *and* they serve as rules for God's people. What he is actually doing here is emphasizing and exploring the third function as something that has been neglected. In this respect he surely has a point.[43]

If Pinnock is right, the way forward entails delineating exactly how doctrines function in all three ways and doing so in a manner that does not collapse the three functions into either the first, as in the older orthodoxy, or the second, as was the error of liberalism. Any explanation that does less would mark a retreat behind, rather than a move beyond Lindbeck's postliberal proposal.

Notes

CHAPTER I

1. Karl Barth, quoted in Eberhard Busch, *Karl Barth: His Life from Letters and Autobiographical Texts,* trans. John Bowden (Philadelphia: Fortress Press, 1976), 20.

2. Barth's humor is reflected in the story of the man who, having been introduced to him, asked him if he knew the famous theologian of the same name. Barth's reply: "Know him! Why, I shave him every morning!"

3. It was almost an accident that the book was published at all. The lectures were delivered extemporaneously to a popular audience of about six hundred people. Someone had taken them down in shorthand and, at the conclusion of the lectures, presented a transcription to the surprised professor. That the lectures were immediately published in an English translation says something about their impact.

4. Adolf Harnack, *What Is Christianity?,* 3rd ed., trans. Thomas Bailey Saunders (London: Williams & Norgate, 1904), 13–4.

5. Ibid., 128, 145

6. James C. Livingston, *Modern Christian Thought: From the Enlightenment to Vatican II* (New York: Macmillan, 1971), 262.

7. Karl Barth, quoted in Busch, 81.

8. Ibid., 81.

9. Later, Barth told of covering the distance, involving high ridges and valleys, in two and a half hours by foot, and, of course, faster on his "trusty bicycle"—he was one of the first pastors in his canton to own one (Ibid., 73).

10. Eduard Thurneysen, quoted ibid., 97.

11. The second edition was a complete rewrite of the first, and the subsequent editions were reissues of the second, with minor adjustments, and with new and often significant prefaces.

12. Jean-Paul Sartre, "Existentialism," in *Existentialism and Human Emotions,* trans. Bernard Frechtman and Hazel E. Barnes (New York: Citadel Press, n.d.), 13.

13. For example, Søren Kierkegaard, *The Sickness unto Death: A Christian Psychological Exposition for Upbuilding and Awakening,* ed. and trans. How-

ard V. Hong and Edna H. Hong (Princeton, N.J.: Princeton University Press, 1980), 126.

14. Unlike pseudonyms in the usual sense, Kierkegaard's involved the creation of whole and differing personalities. This device was part of his attempt at "indirect communication," by which he attempted to get the reader to see the point for himself or herself, apart from Kierkegaard's own apprehension of it.

15. Kierkegaard ("Johannes Climacus") makes this claim, in one way or another, everywhere in *Concluding Unscientific Postscript to the "Philosophical Fragments,"* ed. and trans. Howard V. Hong and Edna H. Hong (Princeton, N.J.: Princeton University Press, 1997), but especially in pt. 2, sect. 2, ch. 2.

16. Ibid., see especially 210ff.

17. Ibid., 326–7.

18. This study and related lectures (issued eventually in English as *Fides Quaerens Intellectum: Anselm's Proof of the Existence of God in the Context of his Theological Scheme*, tr. Ian W. Robertson [Richmond, Va.: John Knox Press, 1960]) Barth regarded as his most important, though least read, book.

19. He was greatly aided in this by a discovery of Heinrich Heppe's *Reformed Dogmatics: Set Out and Illustrated from the Sources,* ed. Ernst Bizer, and with a foreword by Barth himself, eventually translated by G. T. Thomson (London: Allen and Unwin, 1950).

20. Karl Barth, *Church Dogmatics,* I/1, trans G. T. Thomson, et al. (Edinburgh: T & T Clark, 1936–77), ix. (In referencing Barth's *Dogmatics* it is customary to cite the relevant volume and then its subvolume.)

21. The prize was awarded for significant contribution to European culture. Barth thought himself in odd company with previous recipients: Winston Churchill, Albert Schweitzer, Igor Stravinski, and Niels Bohr. It involved a considerable sum of money. He contributed most of it to various Swiss charities and used the rest to pay off his mortgage. (Karl Barth, *Fragments Grave and Gay,* ed. Martin Rumscheidt, trans. Eric Mosbacher [London: Collins, 1971], 95.)

22. Ibid., 100–1.

23. Ibid., 99.

24. Cited in Arthur C. Cochrane, *The Church's Confession Under Hitler* (Philadelphia: Westminster Press, 1962), 22–3.

25. John H. Leith, ed., *Creeds of the Churches: A Reader in Christian Doctrine from the Bible to the Present,* 3rd ed. (Atlanta: John Knox Press, 1982), 520–21.

26. Barth, *Church Dogmatics,* I/1:ix.

27. Ibid., II/2:105–6.

28. Ibid., II/2:94–145.

29. Ibid., II/1:257–321.

30. Barth was fond of pointing out that in his study hung a picture of Calvin, but next to it and at the same level hung a picture of Mozart. Directly above his desk was a print of the famous Grünewald *Crucifixion*— Barth likened himself to John the Baptist, who is represented as pointing to the crucified One. All of this may still be seen in the Barth house in Bruderholz, a few miles from Basel.

31. Barth, *Church Dogmatics,* I/1:98–140.

32. Karl Barth, *Against the Stream* (New York: Philosophical Library, 1954), 223.

33. Barth, *Church Dogmatics,* II/1:124ff.

34. Emil Brunner, "Nature and Grace," in *Natural Theology: Comprising "Nature and Grace" and the Reply "No!" by Dr. Karl Barth,* trans. Peter Fraenkel (London: Bless, 1946), 32–3.

35. Ibid., 53–60.

36. Ibid., 59.

37. Karl Barth, "No!," in *Natural Theology: Comprising "Nature and Grace" and the Reply "No!" by Dr. Karl Barth,* trans. Peter Fraenkel (London: Bless, 1946), 93, 94–109, and passim.

38. Barth, *Church Dogmatics,* I/1:xiii.

39. Barth, Ibid., I/1:223, 243–4. Brunner complained that Barth's use of this expression for his own purpose was maverick inasmuch it had always been used with a quite different sense, namely, that difficult passages of Scripture should be interpreted in light of the Creed (Emil Brunner, *Dogmatics,* vol. 2, *The Christian Doctrine of Creation and Redemption,* trans. Olive Wyon [Philadelphia: Westminster Press, 1952], 44).

40. Brunner, *Dogmatics,* 2:45.

41. Karl Barth, quoted in Busch, *Karl Barth,* 476–7.

42. Reported by James Luther Adams, *Dimensions of Faith: Contemporary Prophetic Protestant Theology,* ed. William Kimmel and Geoffrey Clive (New York: Twayne, 1960), 7.

43. John Godsey, ed., *Karl Barth, How I Changed My Mind* (Richmond, Va.: John Knox Press, 1966), 9.

CHAPTER 2

1. Walter Rauschenbusch, *Christianity and the Social Crisis* (New York: Association Press, 1907), 65.

2. H. Richard Niebuhr, *The Kingdom of God in America* (Chicago: Willet, Clark & Co., 1937), 193.

3. Reinhold Niebuhr, *Leaves from the Notebook of a Tamed Cynic* (Cleveland: World, 1927), 181.

4. This work was the published version of the prestigious Gifford Lectures, which Niebuhr (like Barth) was invited to deliver in 1939.

5. Reinhold Niebuhr, *The Nature and Destiny of Man*, 2 vols. (New York: Scribner, 1941), 18.

6. Reinhold Niebuhr, *Man's Nature and His Communities: Essays on the Dynamics and Enigmas of Man's Personal and Social Existence* (New York: Scribner, 1965), 24.

7. Niebuhr, *The Nature and Destiny of Man*, 1, 222.

8. Ibid., 1:223.

9. Reinhold Niebuhr, "Christian Faith and Social Action," in *Christian Faith and Social Action*, ed. J. A. Hutchison (New York: Scribner, 1953), 241.

10. Niebuhr, *The Nature and Destiny of Man*, 2:287.

11. Ibid., 298.

12. Ibid., 289–98.

13. Ibid., 288.

14. The prayer is found at the beginning of Reinhold Niebuhr, *Justice and Mercy*, ed. Ursala M. Niebuhr (New York: Harper & Row, 1974).

CHAPTER 3

1. It is unfortunate that the distinction between the German *Historie* and *Geschichte*, so central in theological discussion, can hardly be rendered in English. "History" and "historic" is perhaps the best that can be done.

2. Rudolf Bultmann, *Jesus and the Word*, trans. Louise Pettibone Smith and Erminie Huntress Lantero (New York: Scribner, 1934), 6.

3. Rudolf Bultmann, "New Testament and Mythology," in *Kerygma and Myth*, ed. Hans Werner Bartsch, trans. Reginald H. Fuller (New York: Harper & Row, 1961), 4.

4. Ibid., 122.

5. Rudolf Bultmann, *Jesus Christ and Mythology* (New York: Scribner, 1958), 18.

6. Bultmann, "New Testament and Mythology," 16.

7. Rudolf Bultmann, "Autobiographical Reflections," in *Existence and Faith: Shorter Writings of Rudolf Bultmann*, ed. Schubert M. Ogden (Cleveland: World, 1960), 288.

8. Bultmann, *Jesus Christ and Mythology*, 55–6.

9. Bultmann, "New Testament and Mythology," 33ff.

10. Rudolf Bultmann, *Theology of the New Testament*, trans. Kendrick Grobel (New York: Scribner, 1951), II:3.

11. Oscar Cullmann, *Christ and Time: The Primitive Christian Conception of Time and History*, rev. ed., trans. Floyd V. Filson (Phildelphia: Westminster Press, 1951), 23.

12. Cullmann's battle image was inspired by the Battle of El Alamein in North Africa, which many regard as the turning point of World War II.

13. Oscar Cullmann, *Salvation in History*, trans. Sidney G. Sowers et al. (New York: Harper & Row, 1967), 12.

14. See Bultmann's long review and rejection of *Christ and Time* in *Existence and Faith: Shorter Writings of Rudolf Bultmann*, ed. Schubert M. Ogden (Cleveland: World, 1960), 226–40. Cullmann's "Introductory Chapter to the Third Edition" of *Christ and Time* attempted to answer what was by then many lines of criticism, most notably Bultmann's.

15. Ernst Käsemann, "The Problem of the Historical Jesus," in *Essays on New Testament Themes* (London: SCM Press, 1964). The paper was first presented in 1953 in Marburg at a gathering of former Bultmann students.

16. James M. Robinson, *A New Quest for the Historical Jesus* (Naperville, Ill.: Allenson, 1959).

17. Albert Schweitzer, *The Quest of the Historical Jesus: A Critical Study of Its Progress from Reimarus to Wrede*, trans. W. Montgomery (New York: Macmillan, 1968).

CHAPTER 4

1. Paul Tillich, *On the Boundary: An Autobiographical Sketch* (New York: Scribner, 1966), 18.

2. Paul Tillich, *Systematic Theology* (Chicago: University of Chicago Press, 1951–63), 1:3.

3. Ibid., 8, 60, 61.

4. Ibid., 1:3ff., 8ff., 60ff.; 2:13ff. One might ask, however, whether Tillich's imputation of the method of correlation to Calvin is justified. A careful reading of lines quoted from Calvin may reveal an un-Tillichian emphasis, and the following lines from the same context should be noted: "Yet, however the knowledge of God and of ourselves may be mutually connected, the order of right teaching requires that we discuss the former first, then, proceed afterward to treat the latter." John Calvin, *Institutes of the Christian Religion*, ed. John T. McNeill, trans. Ford Lewis Battles (Philadelphia: Westminster Press, 1960), 1/1:3.

5. For Tillich's existential treatment of the traditional theistic arguments, see *Systematic Theology*, 1:204ff. For his analysis of the ontological and cosmological approaches (not necessarily arguments) to God, and the superiority of the latter, see his important essay, "Two Types of Philosophy of Religion," in *Theology of Culture*, cited above.

6. Tillich, *Systematic Theology*, 2:6.

7. Paul Tillich, *Biblical Religion and the Search for Ultimate Reality* (Chicago: University of Chicago Press, 1955), 182–3.

8. Tillich, *Systematic Theology*, 1:237.

9. Ibid., 2:7.
10. Ibid., 7ff.
11. Ibid., 1:133.
12. Ibid., 2:165ff.
13. Rudolf Bultmann, *Jesus Christ and Mythology* (New York: Scribners, 1958), 84.
14. Paul Tillich, *The Courage To Be* (New Haven, Conn.: Yale University Press, 1952), 190.
15. D. MacKenzie Brown, ed., *Ultimate Concern: Tillich in Dialogue* (New York: Harper & Row, 1956), 88–9.
16. Paul Tillich, *Dynamics of Faith* (New York: Harper & Row, 1957), 1ff.
17. Ibid., 1ff., 41ff.; Paul Tillich, "Existential Analyses and Religious Symbols," in *Contemporary Problems in Religion,* ed. Harold A. Basilius (Detroit: Wayne State University Press, 1956), 42ff.
18. Tillich, *Dynamics of Faith,* 41 (slightly edited).
19. Tillich, *Systematic Theology,* 2:161.
20. Ibid., 1:13.
21. According to a well-known joke, the bones of Jesus were discovered, and the news was brought to the Pope, who responded: "Good heavens! This news would be devastating to the Church! It must be kept secret!" The news was then brought to Billy Graham, who responded: "Oh, no! This makes nonsense of all my preaching!" Finally, the news was brought to Paul Tillich, who responded: "Well, what do you know. He actually existed!"
22. The most famous and influential of these discussions was the debate between Antony Flew, R. M. Hare, and Basil Mitchell. See "Theology and Falsification," in *New Essays in Philosophical Theology,* ed. Antony Flew and Alasdair MacIntyre (London: SCM Press, 1955), 96–130. The other essays in this volume reflect further, but related, philosophical-theological concerns of the time.
23. Karl Barth, *Dogmatics in Outline,* trans. G. T. Thomson (London: SCM Press, 1949), 25. The concluding references are to the first verses of 1 John.

CHAPTER 5

1. Dietrich Bonhoeffer, *Letters and Papers from Prison,* rev. ed., ed. Eberhard Bethge, trans. Reginald Fuller (New York: Macmillan, 1965), 139, 168.
2. Harvey Cox, *The Secular City* (New York: Macmillan, 1965), 1.
3. Ibid., 2.
4. Ibid., 17ff.

5. Dietrich Bonhoeffer, *The Cost of Discipleship*, 2nd ed., trans. R. H. Fuller (New York: Macmillan, 1959), 35ff.

6. For example, Eberhard Bethge was Bonhoeffer's personal friend as well as editor of his works, including *Letters and Papers from Prison*, the most important source for the radical interpretation. The germs of Bonhoeffer's insights were already contained in his first works, *Sanctorum Cummunio* (published in 1930) and *Act and Being* (1931), and the essential continuity of Bonhoeffer's development is unmistakably reflected in Bethge's important biography *Dietrich Bonhoeffer*, ed. Edwin Robertson, trans. Erich Mosbacher et al. (New York: Harper & Row, 1970). It is encouraging that in the revised edition of *The Secular City*, Cox softened his earlier appropriation of Bonhoeffer. Cox, *The Secular City*, rev. ed. (New York: Macmillan, 1966), xii.

7. Bonhoeffer, *Letters and Papers from Prison*, 187.

8. Ibid., 188.

9. Ibid., 187–8.

10. Dietrich Bonhoeffer, *Ethics*, ed. Eberhard Bethge, trans. Neville Horton Smith (New York: Macmillan, 1965), 196ff.

11. Ibid., 83–4.

12. Bonhoeffer, *Letters and Papers from Prison*, 190–1.

13. Wayne Best, quoted in *Letters and Papers from Prison*, xxii.

14. Dietrich Bonhoeffer, quoted in Eberhard Bethge, *Costly Grace: An Illustrated Biography of Dietrich Bonhoeffer*, trans. Rosaleen Ockenden (San Francisco: Harper & Row, 1979), 98–9.

15. John A. T. Robinson, *Honest to God* (Philadelphia: Westminster Press, 1963), 22–3.

Chapter 6

1. Friedrich Nietzsche, *The Gay Science*, in *The Portable Nietzsche*, ed. and trans. Walter Kaufmann (New York: Viking Press, 1954), no. 125, 95–6.

2. Ibid., no. 343, 447.

3. William Hamilton, "The Death of God," *Playboy*, 13 (August 1966), 84.

4. William Hamilton with Thomas J. J. Altizer, *Radical Theology and the Death of God* (New York: Bobbs-Merrill, 1966), 28, 46–7. That Hamilton and Altizer dedicated their book to Paul Tillich should be considered in light of Rubenstein's observation, made in the mid-1960s: "Every one of today's radical theologians was either Tillich's student or was profoundly influenced by his writings. In the context of much of today's theological writing, Tillich seems almost conservative. Nevertheless, all radical theologians have elaborated on themes which are at least implicit in Tillich. After all, it was Tillich who asserted in *The Courage To Be* that the God whom

Nietzsche said was dead was transcended in a 'God above the God of theism.'" Richard L. Rubenstein, *After Auschwitz* (Indianapolis: Bobbs-Merrill, 1966), 243.

5. Hamilton, "The Death of God," 137.

6. Ibid.

7. Hamilton and Altizer, *Radical Theology and the Death of God,* 131–2.

8. Thomas J. J. Altizer, *The Gospel of Christian Atheism* (Philadelphia: Westminster Press, 1966), 154.

9. Rubenstein, *After Auschwitz,* 246.

CHAPTER 7

1. For this incident, see John B. Cobb, Jr., "To Pray or Not to Pray: A Confession," in *Prayer in My Life,* ed. Maxie Dunnam (Nashville: The Upper Room, 1974), 83–112.

2. For a helpful summary of Cobb's early life, see David Ray Griffin, "John B. Cobb, Jr.," in *A Handbook of Christian Theologians,* ed. Dean G. Peerman and Martin E. Marty, enlarged edition (Nashville: Abingdon, 1984), 691–6.

3. For an introduction to the thought of this important philosopher, see Alan Gragg, "Charles Hartshorne," in the *Makers of the Modern Theological Mind,* ed. Bob E. Patterson (Waco, Tex.: Word, 1973).

4. See Griffin, "Cobb," 702.

5. Ibid., 703; Marjorie Hewitt Suchocki, "John B. Cobb, Jr.," in *A New Handbook of Christian Theologians,* ed. David W. Musser and Joseph L. Price (Nashville: Abingdon, 1996), 107.

6. John B. Cobb, Jr., "A Critical View of Inherited Theology," in *Theologians in Transition,* ed. James M. Wall (New York: Crossroad, 1981), 74–75. See also, John B. Cobb, Jr., *Process Theology as Political Theology* (Philadelphia: Westminster, 1982), x–xi.

7. Cobb, "Critical View of Inherited Theology," 75.

8. See Suchocki, "Cobb," 107.

9. See Cobb, "Critical View of Inherited Theology," 77; John B. Cobb, Jr. and Herman E. Daly, *For the Common Good* (Boston: Beacon, 1989).

10. See, for example, John B. Cobb, Jr., *Beyond Dialogue: Towards a Mutual Transformation of Christianity and Buddhism* (Philadelphia: Fortress Press, 1982), ix.

11. John B. Cobb, Jr., and Charles Birch, *The Liberation of Life* (Cambridge: Cambridge University Press, 1981); Cobb, "Critical View of Inherited Theology," 77.

12. On this, see Griffin, "Cobb," 706.

13. John B. Cobb, Jr., *Grace and Responsibility: A Wesleyan Theology for Today* (Nashville: Abingdon, 1995).

14. William L. Reese, "Parmenides," in *Dictionary of Philosophy and Religion* (Atlantic Highlands, N.J.: Humanities, 1980), 412–3; Eduard Zeller, *Outlines of the History of Greek Philosophy*, 13th ed., rev. Wilhelm Nestle, trans. L. R. Palmer (New York: Meridian Books, 1957), 61. Some historians, however, have questioned this interpretation of Heraclitus. "Can Heraclitus really have thought that a rock or a bronze cauldron, for example, was invariably undergoing invisible changes of material?" ask G. S. Kirk and J. E. Raven, *The Presocratic Philosophers*, corrected reprint (Cambridge: Cambridge University Press, 1963), 197.

15. Heraclitus, as quoted in Rex Warner, *The Greek Philosophers* (New York: Mentor Books, 1958), 26. Warner's source is John Burnet, *Early Greek Philosophy*, 4th ed. (New York: Macmillan, 1930), 132–41.

16. See, for example, the discussion by Teilhard de Chardin's disciple, Eulalio R. Baltazar, *God within Process* (Paramus, N.J.: Newman, 1970), 1–23.

17. A succinct summarization of Whitehead's philosophy is offered by Rosemary T. Curran, "Whitehead's Notion of the Person and the Saving of the Past," *Scottish Journal of Theology* 36/3 (1983): 363–85.

18. Reese, "Whitehead," 622.

19. Alfred North Whitehead, *Adventures of Ideas* (New York: Mentor, 1955), 223. See also the discussion in Alfred North Whitehead, *Process and Reality* (New York: Harper & Row, 1960), 4–26.

20. Ibid., 43.

21. Ibid., 28, 35, 309.

22. Ibid., 130, 374.

23. Ibid., 30, 156ff; Whitehead, *Adventures of Ideas*, 204.

24. The immortality of every actual entity is required by Whitehead's "ontological principle," for "everything in the actual world is referable to some actual entity." God functions as the ontological principle that fulfills this necessity. Whitehead, *Process and Reality*, 373.

25. Whitehead writes, "God is not to be treated as an exception to all metaphysical principles, invoked to save their collapse. He is their chief exemplification." *Process and Reality*, 521.

26. The dipolar nature of God in relation to the world is delineated in *Process and Reality*, 519–33. Whitehead also referred to God as displaying a threefold character: primordial, consequent, and superject. Ibid., 134–5.

27. Ibid., 287. See also Reese, "Whitehead," 624.

28. Whether Whitehead thought of God as an unbounded society or an actual entity has been debated by subsequent process thinkers. See Gene

Reeves and Delwin Brown, "The Development of Process Theology," in *Process Philosophy and Christian Thought,* ed. Delwin Brown, Ralph E. James, Jr., and Gene Reeves (Indianapolis: Bobbs-Merrill, 1971), 39–40.

29. Whitehead writes, "the World's nature is a primordial datum for God; and God's nature is a primordial datum for the World." *Process and Reality,* 529.

30. Ibid., 525.

31. Lewis S. Ford, "Divine Persuasion and the Triumph of Good," *The Christian Scholar* 50/3 (Fall 1967), 235–50. Reprinted in Brown, James, and Reeves, *Process Philosophy,* 298.

32. Whitehead rejects the classical understanding of God as the divine despot, claiming that in this way, "the Church gave unto God the attributes which belonged exclusively to Caesar." *Process and Reality,* 520.

33. Ibid., 532.

34. For a summary of the development of process theology and the views of representative theologians, see Reeves and Brown, "Development of Process Theology," 21–64. For a representative recent attempt to delineate a statement of Christian doctrine from a process perspective, see Marjorie Hewitt Suchocki, *God-Christ-Church* (New York: Crossroad, 1984).

35. Actually, Cobb has come to see his context as the postmodern world. For this judgment, see Ted Peters, "John Cobb, Theologian in Process (1)" *Dialogue* 29 (1990): 210; David Ray Griffin, "Post-modern Theology for a New Christian Existence," in *John Cobb's Theology in Process,* ed. David Ray Griffin and Thomas J. J. Altizer (Philadelphia: Westminster, 1977), 15–7.

36. See especially John Cobb, Jr., *A Christian Natural Theology* (Philadelphia: Westminster, 1965). Not even all process thinkers agree with Cobb that it is proper to speak of a *Christian* natural theology. See, for example, Schubert M. Ogden, "A *Christian* Natural Theology?" from "A Review of John B. Cobb's New Book: *A Christian Natural Theology,*" *Christian Advocate* 9/18 (September 23, 1965): 11f. Reprinted in Brown, James, and Reeves, *Process Philosophy,* 111–6.

37. See, for example, Alfred North Whitehead, *Science and the Modern World* (New York: Mentor, 1948), 165.

38. Cobb, *Christian Natural Theology,* 104.

39. John B. Cobb, Jr., and David Ray Griffin, *Process Theology* (Philadelphia: Westminster, 1976), 8–9. See also Norman Pittinger, "Process Thought as a Conceptuality for Reinterpreting Christian Faith," *Encounter* 44/2 (1983): 113.

40. Other process theologians share this theme with Cobb. See, for example, Schubert Ogden, "Toward A New Theism," revised from "Love

Unbounded: The Doctrine of God," *The Perkins School of Theology Journal* 19/3 (Spring, 1966): 5–17. Reprinted in Brown, James, and Reeves, eds., *Process Philosophy,* 173–87.

41. John B. Cobb, Jr., *God and the World* (Philadelphia: Westminster, 1965), 42–66.

42. Whitehead, *Process Theology,* 41–62.

43. Cobb's Christology is summarized in Cobb and Griffin, *Process Theology,* 95–110. For a fuller treatment, see Cobb, *Christ in a Pluralistic Age* (Philadelphia: Westminster, 1975).

44. Cobb notes his indebtedness to Whitehead in the introduction to his volume on Christology. Cobb, *Christ in a Pluralistic Age,* 27.

45. Cobb and Griffin, *Process Theology,* 22.

46. Cobb, *Christ in a Pluralistic Age,* 65, 76.

47. Cobb and Griffin, *Process Theology,* 98–9; Cobb, *Christ in a Pluralistic Age,* 123.

48. Cobb, *Christ in a Pluralistic Age,* 142.

49. Griffin, "Cobb," 112.

50. Cobb and Griffin, *Process Theology,* 102; Ted Peters, "John Cobb, Theologian in Process (2)," *Dialogue* 29 (Autumn 1990): 292.

51. Cobb and Griffin, *Process Theology,* 113–4.

52. Cobb, *Christ in a Pluralistic Age,* 257–8.

53. Cobb also remains true to Whitehead here. See Cobb and Griffin, *Process Theology,* 117–8.

54. See, for example, Cobb, *Process Theology as Political Theology,* 79.

55. For this view, see Pittinger, "Process Thought as a Conceptuality," 117. While these are not Cobb's words, his position would be similar.

56. Cobb, *Christ in a Pluralistic Age,* 226.

57. A helpful interaction with several central difficulties of process theology from a sympathetic perspective is found in Bernard M. Loomer, "Christian Faith and Process Philosophy," *The Journal of Religion* 29/3 (July 1949), as reprinted in Brown, James, and Reeves, *Process Philosophy,* 70–98. For an earlier engagement with Cobb's theology, see the essays in Griffin and Altizer, *John Cobb's Theology in Process.*

58. Wolfhart Pannenberg, "A Liberal Logos Christology: The Christology of John Cobb " in Griffin and Altizer, *John Cobb's Theology in Process,* 142.

59. Note the discussion by Lewis S. Ford, "Divine Persuasion and the Triumph of Good," *The Christian Scholar* 50/3 (Fall 1967) as reprinted in Brown, James, and Reeves, eds., *Process Philosophy,* 294.

60. Joseph A. Bracken, "The Two Process Theologies: A Reappraisal," *Theological Studies* 46/1 (1985): 127.

61. For this critique, see Jürgen Moltmann, *God in Creation* (San Francisco: Harper & Row, 1985), 78; Peters, "John Cobb (1)," 215.

62. Peters, "John Cobb, Theologian in Process" (2), *Dialog* 29 (Autumn 1990): 298.

CHAPTER 8

1. Jürgen Moltmann, "An Autobiographical Note," in A. J. Conyers, *God, Hope, and History: Jurgen Moltmann and the Christian Concept of History* (Macon, Ga.: Mercer University Press, 1988), 203.

2. No biography of Moltmann exists, but the theologian's scattered autobiographical reflections provide some information about his life. See "Foreword,"in M. Douglas Meeks, *Origins of the Theology of Hope* (Philadelphia: Fortress, 1974), x–xii; "Why Am I a Christian?" in *Experiences of God* (Philadelphia: Fortress Press, 1980), 1–18; "Autobiographical Note," in Conyers, *God, Hope, and History,* 203–23; *The Coming of God: Christian Eschatology,* trans. Margaret Kohl (Minneapolis: Fortress Press, 1996), xiii.

3. Moltmann, "Forward," in Meeks, *Origins of the Theology of Hope,* x.

4. Ibid., x–xi.

5. Ibid., xiii–xiv.

6. Ibid., xi.

7. Ibid.

8. Moltmann, *Coming of God,* xiv.

9. These three are *Theology of Hope,* trans. James W. Leitsch (New York: Harper & Row, 1967); *The Crucified God,* trans. R. A. Wilson and John Bowden (New York: Harper & Row, 1974); and *The Church in the Power of the Spirit: A Contribution to Messianic Ecclesiology,* trans. Margaret Kohl (New York: Harper & Row, 1977). Moltmann's own evaluation is reported in Richard Bauckham, *The Theology of Jürgen Moltmann* (Edinburgh: T. & T. Clark, 1995), 3.

10. To date, the series includes *The Trinity and the Kingdom,* trans. Margaret Kohl (San Francisco: Harper & Row, 1981); *God in Creation: A New Theology of Creation and the Spirit of God* (San Francisco: Harper & Row 1985); *The Way of Jesus Christ: Christology in Messianic Dimensions,* trans. Margaret Kohl (San Francisco: HarperSanFrancisco, 1990); *The Spirit of Life: A Universal Affirmation,* trans. Margaret Kohl (Minneapolis: Fortress Press, 1992); and *The Coming of God: Christian Eschatology,* trans. Margaret Kohl (Minneapolis: Fortress, 1996). For his own statement about this series, see Moltmann, *Coming of God,* xii.

11. See Moltmann, *Coming of God,* 194, 200. Moltmann himself suggests that in the process of writing, a program emerged that points "first, to a trinitarian thinking about God; secondly to an ecological thinking about the

community of creation; and thirdly, to an eschatological thinking about the dwellings of God in his people, in his Christ, and in our hearts through his life-giving Spirit." To these three the Tübingen theologian would add a fourth: God coming "to his 'dwelling' in his creation, the home of his identity in the world, and in it to his 'rest', his perfected, eternal joy." (Moltmann, *Coming of God*, xii, xiii.)

12. Ibid., xvii.

13. For a definitive study of Moltmann's reception of and reaction to Barth, see Meeks, *Origins of the Theology of Hope*, 15–53.

14. Moltmann, *Theology of Hope*, 16.

15. Jürgen Moltmann, "Theology as Eschatology" in *The Future of Hope, Theology as Eschatology*, ed., Frederick Herzog (New York: Herder and Herder, 1970), 9.

16. Marcel Neusch, *The Sources of Modern Atheism: One Hundred Years of Debate Over God*, trans. Matthew J. O'Connell (New York: Paulist Press, 1982), 189.

17. Jürgen Moltmann, *God in Creation: A New Theology of Creation and the Spirit of God*, trans. Margaret Kohl (San Francisco: Harper & Row, 1985), 180.

18. Neusch, *The Sources of Modern Atheism*, 211.

19. Meeks, *Origins of the Theology of Hope*, 18.

20. Moltmann, "An Autobiographical Note," 222, 204; Moltmann, *Theology of Hope*, 84.

21. Moltmann, *Theology of Hope*, 92; Moltmann, *God in Creation*, 202.

22. Moltmann, *Theology of Hope*, 35–6.

23. One distinction separates the two thinkers, however. Moltmann rejects any attempt to derive theological concepts from nature, human existence, or any dimension of the world as it already is. Rather than being already manifest in the existence or order of the world *as it is*, for Moltmann, God will be manifest only in the future Kingdom of Glory. Moltmann, *Theology of Hope*, 282. Yet Moltmann acknowledges that those who know God can derive evidence or anticipatory knowledge of God from the "traces of God" present in nature. Moltmann, *God in Creation*, 64.

24. Jürgen Moltmann, *The Experiment Hope*, trans. M. Douglas Meeks (Philadelphia: Fortress Press, 1975), 8.

25. Moltmann, *Theology of Hope*, 95–229.

26. Ibid., 102.

27. Ibid., 139–140, 203.

28. Ibid., 105, 85.

29. Ibid., 227.

30. Ibid., 84, 203.

31. Ibid., 32.

32. Moltmann, *The Experiment Hope*, 7, 8.

33. Jürgen Moltmann, "Theology as Eschatology," in *The Future of Hope: Theology as Eschatology*, ed. Frederick Herzog (New York: Herder & Herder, 1970), 10.

34. Bauckham, *Theology of Jürgen Moltmann*, 6.

35. Moltmann, *Crucified God*, 244.

36. Jürgen Moltmann, "The 'Crucified God': God and the Trinity Today" in *New Questions on God*, ed., Johannes Metz (New York: Herder & Herder, 1972), 35, 249.

37. That this is indeed Moltmann's view is argued by Christopher Morse, *The Logic of Promise in Moltmann's Theology* (Philadelphia: Fortress Press, 1979), 119.

38. Jürgen Moltmann, "The Trinitarian History of God," *Theology* 78 (December 1975): 644. See also, Moltmann, *Coming of God*, 330–32. In addition, unlike the process theologians Moltmann always keeps in view the transcendent, future nature of the Kingdom of Glory. Against the process view he asserts, "if there is no new creation of all things, there is nothing that can withstand the Nothingness that annihilates the world." Moltmann, *God in Creation*, 79. For a helpful discussion of Moltmann's doctrine of God vis-á-vis process theology, see John J. O'Donnell, *Trinity and Temporality, The Christian Doctrine of God in the Light of Process Theology and the Theology of Hope* (Oxford: Oxford, 1983), 159–200.

39. Moltmann, *Coming of God*, 325.

40. Ibid., 82.

41. Moltmann, *God in Creation*, 86, 98–103. See also Moltmann, *Coming of God*, 281–2, 297.

42. Moltmann, *God in Creation*, 91.

43. Jürgen Moltmann, *The Trinity and the Kingdom*, trans., Margaret Kohl (San Francisco: Harper & Row, 1981), 175.

44. Rahner's statement and a fuller explanation of it is to be found in Karl Rahner, *The Trinity* (New York: Seabury, 1974), 22.

45. Moltmann, *Crucified God*, 207.

46. Moltmann, *Trinity and the Kingdom*, 183, 160, 161.

47. Ibid.,161.

48. Moltmann, *God in Creation*, 279; Moltmann, *Trinity and the Kingdom*, 221.

49. Moltmann, *Trinity and the Kingdom*, 191–2.

50. Ibid.,17.

51. Moltmann, *Coming of God*, 295, 301, 307.

52. See the poetic note with which Moltmann concludes his volume on eschatology. *Coming of God*, 338–9.

53. See Bauckham, *Theology of Jürgen Moltmann*, 24–5.

54. Peter Fumiaki Momose, *Kreuzestheologie: Eine Auseinandersetzung mit Jürgen Moltmann* (Freiburg: Herder, 1978), 87. For this translation, we are indebted to Roger Olson.

CHAPTER 9

1. Wolfhart Pannenberg, "God's Presence in History," *Christian Century* 98 (March 11, 1981): 261.

2. For his own account of these experiences, see Pannenberg, "God's Presence in History," 260–3.

3. Wolfhart Pannenberg, "Die Theologie und die neuen Fragen nach Intersubjektivitaet, Gesellschaft, und religioeser Gemeinschaft," *Archivio di Filosofia* 54 (1986): 422–4.

4. Pannenberg, "God's Presence in History," 263.

5. Wolfhart Pannenberg, *Introduction to Systematic Theology* (Grand Rapids, Mich.: Eerdmans, 1991), 18–9.

6. Richard John Neuhaus, "Wolfhart Pannenberg: Portrait of a Theologian," in Wolfhart Pannenberg, *Theology and the Kingdom of God*, ed. Richard John Neuhaus (Philadelphia: Westminster, 1969), 16.

7. Wolfhart Pannenberg with Rolf Rendtorff, Trutz Rendtorff, and Ulrich Wilkens, *Revelation As History*, trans. David Granskow (New York: Macmillan, 1968), originally published in German in 1961.

8. Pannenberg's fight against grounding theology on a 'decision of faith' and on the attempt to create a separate sphere for theology alongside scientific endeavor is well-known, for the topic is broached in many of his essays. See "Insight and Faith" and "Faith and Reason," in Wolfhart Pannenberg, *Basic Questions in Theology*, trans. George H. Kelm (Philadelphia: Fortress Press, 1971), 2:43, 52–3; "Eschatology and the Experience of Meaning," in Wolfhart Pannenberg, *The Idea of God and Human Freedom*, trans. R. A. Wilson (Philadelphia: Westminster, 1973), 208. This concern arises in part from his interest in speaking to the contemporary atheistic alternative to belief, a topic discussed in several of Pannenberg's essays. See "Types of Atheism and Their Theological Significance" and "The Question of God" in *Basic Questions in Theology*, 2:184–233; "Anthropology and the Question of God" and "Speaking about God in the Face of Atheist Criticism" in *Idea of God*, 80–115.

9. See "The Crisis of the Scripture Principle," in Pannenberg, *Basic Questions in Theology*, 1:1–14.

10. Alfred H. Ackley, 'He Lives,' 1933.

11. See, for example, Wolfhart Pannenberg, *Anthropology in Theological Perspective*, trans. Matthew J. O'Connell (Philadelphia: Westminster, 1985), 71–3.

12. See, for example, Pannenberg, *Introduction to Systematic Theology*, 4–5.

13. Pannenberg, *Introduction to Systematic Theology*, 6. See also Pannenberg, "What Is Truth?" in *Basic Questions in Theology*, 2:1–27.

14. Pannenberg, *Basic Questions in Theology*, 2:1–27.

15. See "On Historical and Theological Hermeneutic" and "What Is a Dogmatic Statement," in Pannenberg, *Basic Questions in Theology*, 1:137–210.

16. See, for example, Carl E. Braaten, "Toward a Theology of Hope," in *The New Theology*, ed. Martin E. Marty and Dean G. Peerman, 10 vols. (New York: Macmillan, 1968), 5:90–2.

17. See, for example, Pannenberg, *Theology and the Kingdom of God*, 51–4.

18. Pannenberg, "Faith and Reason," in *Basic Questions in Theology*, 2:52–3.

19. Wolfhart Pannenberg, *Systematische Theologie* (Göttingen: Vandenhoeck and Ruprecht, 1988), 1:70–2. See also Pannenberg, *Basic Questions in Theology*, 2:1–27.

20. Pannenberg, *Introduction to Systematic Theology*, 8

21. See, for example, Pannenberg, *Theology and the Kingdom of God*, 55–6.

22. Pannenberg, *Introduction to Systematic Theology*, 12.

23. Ibid., 10.

24. See, for example, Pannenberg, "God's Presence in History," 263.

25. This is set forth in Pannenberg, *Systematische Theologie*, 1:283–483.

26. For a methodological preview of Pannenberg's doctrine of the Trinity, see Wolfhart Pannenberg, "The God of History," *Cumberland Seminarian* 19 (Winter/Spring 1981). Pannenberg's doctrine of the Trinity is discussed in Roger E. Olson, "Trinity and Eschatology: The Historical Being of God in Juergen Moltmann and Wolfhart Pannenberg," *Scottish Journal of Theology* 36 (1983):213–7; and Roger E. Olson, "Wolfhart Pannenberg's Doctrine of the Trinity," *Scottish Journal of Theology* 43 (1990): 175–206.

27. See Wolfhart Pannenberg, *Jesus—God and Man*, 2nd ed., trans. Lewis L. Wilkins and Duane A. Priebe (Philadelphia: Westminster, 1977), 181–3, 340.

28. Ibid., 324–49.

29. Pannenberg, *Introduction to Systematic Theology*, 61.

30. The concept of field is set forth in Wolfhart Pannenberg, "Theological Questions to Scientists," *Zygon* 16 (1981): 65–77; and "The Doctrine of Creation and Modern Science," *East Asia Journal of Theology* 4(1986):33–46.

31. Pannenberg, *Systematische Theologie*, 1:401–16.
32. Wolfhart Pannenberg, "The Spirit of Life," in *Faith and Reality*, trans. John Maxwell (Philadelphia: Westminster, 1977), 33.
33. See Wolfhart Pannenberg, "Spirit and Mind," in *Mind in Nature*, ed. Richard Q. Elvee, Nobel Conference 17 (New York: Harper, 1982), 137, 143; Pannenberg, *Anthropology in Theological Perspective*, 226–9, 235–6, 240, 384.
34. Pannenberg, *Introduction to Systematic Theology*, 43–7. The basis for his development of pneumatology is outlined in "The Spirit of Life," 32–7.
35. Pannenberg, *Anthropology in Theological Perspective*, 85–96.
36. Pannenberg, *Systematische Theologie*, 433–43; Pannenberg, *Introduction to Systematic Theology*, 48.
37. Pannenberg, *Introduction to Systematic Theology*, 49.
38. This conclusion is articulated in Neuhaus, "Wolfhart Pannenberg," 38.
39. Wolfhart Pannenberg, *The Church*, trans. Keith Crim (Philadelphia: Westminster, 1983), 165; Pannenberg, *Faith and Reality*, 138.
40. See the discussions in Wolfhart Pannenberg, *The Apostles' Creed in the Light of Today's Questions*, trans. Margaret Kohl (Philadelphia: Westminster, 1972), 152–5; Pannenberg, *Jesus — God and Man*, 372–3; Pannenberg, *Theology and the Kingdom of God*, 72–101.
41. William C. Placher, "Revealed to Reason: Theology as 'Normal Science,'" *Christian Century* 109/6 (February 19, 1992):195.

CHAPTER 10

1. Camilo Torres, quoted by Phillip Berryman, "Camilo Torres: Revolutionary-Theologian," *Commonweal* 96 (April 21, 1972): 164.
2. William M. Ramsay, *Four Modern Prophets* (Atlanta: John Knox, 1986), 52–3; *Twentieth-Century Dictionary of Christian Biography*, ed. J. D. Douglas (Grand Rapids, Mich.: Baker, 1995), 162.
3. For the full Instruction and commentary on it, see *Origins: NC documentary service* (published by the National Catholic News Service) 14/13 (September 13, 1984).
4. For the full text of the "Instruction on Christian Freedom and Liberation" see *Origins: NC documentary service* 15/44 (April 17, 1986). For an analysis of the Instruction from the viewpoint of liberation theology see Robert McAfee Brown, *Gustavo Gutiérrez: An Introduction to Liberation Theology* (Maryknoll, N.Y.: Orbis, 1990), 146–8.
5. Gustavo Gutiérrez, *The Power of the Poor in History*, trans. Robert R. Barr (Maryknoll, N.Y.: Orbis, 1983), 205.
6. Gutiérrez, *Power of the Poor*, 195.

7. For a representative work by Metz, see Johannes Baptist Metz, *Faith in History and Society, Toward a Practical Fundamental Theology*, trans. David Smith (New York: Seabury, 1980).

8. That Gutiérrez drew inspiration from this is evident in the introduction he wrote for the fifteenth anniversary edition of *A Theology of Liberation*. See Gustavo Gutiérrez, *A Theology of Liberation*, rev. ed., trans. and ed. Sister Caridad Inda and John Eagleson (Maryknoll, N.Y.: Orbis, 1988), xxvi.

9. See, for example, Paulo Freire, *Pedagogy of the Oppressed*, trans. Myra Bergman Ramos (New York: Continuum, 1982).

10. Dermot A. Lane, *Foundations for a Social Theology: Praxis, Process and Salvation* (New York and Ramsey: Paulist, 1984), 77.

11. Gutiérrez, *Power of the Poor*, 186.

12. Ibid., 193.

13. Brown, *Gutiérrez*, 39.

14. Gutiérrez, *Theology of Liberation*, 151.

15. Gutiérrez, *Power of the Poor*, 28.

16. Gutiérrez, *Theology of Liberation*, 54.

17. Ibid., 116.

18. Ibid., 18.

19. Ibid., xxix.

20. Ibid., xxxiv, 10.

21. Ibid., 156, xxvii.

22. Ibid., 83, 116.

23. Ibid., xxxviii, 36–7.

24. Gutiérrez, *Power of the Poor*, 64.

25. Gutiérrez, *Theology of Liberation*, 104, xlii.

26. Gutiérrez, *Power of the Poor*, 28.

27. Gutiérrez, *Theology of Liberation*, xliii.

28. See P. T. Bauer, "Western Guilt & Third World Poverty," *Commentary* (January 1976): 31–8.

29. Wolfhart Pannenberg, "Christianity, Marxism, and Liberation Theology," *Christian Scholar's Review* 18/3 (March 1989): 215–26.

30. Sam A. Portaro, Jr., "Is God Prejudiced in Favor of the Poor?" *Christian Century* (April 24, 1985): 404–5; J. Andrew Kirk, *Liberation Theology: An Evangelical View from the Third World* (Atlanta: John Knox, 1979), 193, 198.

31. Gutiérrez, *Power of the Poor*, 196.

32. Gutiérrez, *Theology of Liberation*, xlvi.

CHAPTER 11

1. Rosemary Radford Ruether, *Sexism and God-Talk: Toward a Feminist Theology* (Boston: Beacon, 1983), 193–4.

2. Rosemary Radford Ruether, *Women-Church: Theology and Practice of Feminist Liturgical Communities* (San Francisco: Harper & Row, 1986), 137.

3. Rosemary Radford Ruether, "What is Shaping My Theology: Social Sin," *Commonweal* 108 (January 30, 1981): 46; Rosemary Radford Ruether, "The Development of My Theology," *Religious Studies Review* 15/1 (January 1989): 2.

4. Ruether, "Development of My Theology," 1.

5. Ruether, "What Is Shaping My Theology," 47.

6. For her doctoral dissertation, see Rosemary Radford Ruether, *Gregory Nazianzus: Rhetor and Philosopher* (Cambridge: Cambridge University Press, 1969).

7. For a similar statement, see Mary Hembrow Snyder, "Rosemary Radford Ruether," in *A New Handbook of Christian Theologians,* ed. Donald W. Musser and Joseph L. Price (Nashville: Abingdon, 1996), 400.

8. Rosemary Radford Ruether, *Gaia and God: An Ecofeminist Theology of Earth Healing* (San Francisco: HarperSanFrancisco, 1992), 1–3.

9. See, for example, Rebecca S. Chopp, "Seeing and Naming the World Anew: The Works of Rosemary Radford Ruether," *Religious Studies Review* 15/1 (January 1989): 8.

10. Pamela Dickey Young, *Feminist Theology/Christian Theology: In Search of Method* (Minneapolis: Fortress Press, 1990), 15–7.

11. Ruether, *Sexism and God-Talk,* 18.

12. Ibid., 13.

13. Rosemary Radford Ruether, "The Future of Feminist Theology in the Academy," *Journal of the American Academy of Religion* 53 (December 1985): 706–9.

14. Rosemary Radford Ruether, "Feminist Theology in the Academy," *Christianity and Crisis* 45/3 (March 4, 1985): 59; Rosemary Radford Ruether, "Beginnings: An Autobiography," in *Journeys: The Impact of Personal Experience on Religious Thought,* ed. Gregory Baum (New York: Paulist Press, 1975): 44.

15. Ruether, "Development of My Theology," 2.

16. Ibid., 4.

17. Ruether, *Sexism and God-Talk,* 94–9.

18. Ruether, "Feminist Theology in the Academy," 59.

19. Ruether, *Sexism and God-Talk,* 61.

20. Ibid.,173.

21. Ibid., 178.

22. For a discussion of the sources for feminist theology, see Ruether, *Sexism and God-Talk*, 21–33.

23. More specifically, she is an ecumenical Roman Catholic Christian. See Rosemary Radford Ruether, "Asking the Existential Questions," in *Theologians in Transition*, ed. James M. Wall (New York: Crossroad, 1981), 163.

24. Ruether, "Development of My Theology," 3.

25. Ruether is convinced that male domination of women and domination of nature are interconnected. See Ruether, *Gaia and God*, 2, 258, 201; Ruether, *Sexism and God-talk*, 32.

26. Ruether, *Sexism and God-Talk*, 23.

27. William Oddie, *What Will Happen to God? Feminist and the Reconstruction of Christian Belief* (London: SPCK, 1984), 19.

28. Ruether, "Development of My Theology," 3.

29. Ruether, "Feminist Theology in the Academy," 61.

30. See, for example, Ruether, *Sexism and God-Talk*, 72–92, 112.

31. See Rosemary Radford Ruether, *Liberation Theology: Human Hope Confronts Christian History and American Power* (New York: Paulist, 1972), 16–20.

32. Ruether, *Sexism and God-talk*, 67–9.

33. Rosemary Radford Ruether, "Feminist Theology and Spirituality," *Christian Feminism: Vision of a New Humanity*, ed. Judith Weidman (San Francisco: Harper and Row, 1984), 9.

34. Ruether, *Sexism and God-Talk*, 86–7.

35. Ibid., 71.

36. Ruether, *Gaia and God*, 253–4.

37. Ruether, *Sexism and God-Talk*, 135, 116.

38. Ibid., 137–8.

39. Ruether, *Gaia and God*, 256, 141–2, 139; Ruether, "What Is Shaping My Theology," 47.

40. Ruether, *Sexism and God-Talk*, 8, 11.

41. Ibid., 9.

42. Elizabeth Achtemeier, "The Impossible Possibility: Evaluating the Feminist Approach to Bible and Theology," *Interpretation* 42 (January 1988): 57.

43. See, for example, Donald G. Bloesch, *The Battle for the Trinity. The Debate Over Inclusive God-Language* (Ann Arbor, Mich.: Servant, 1985), 84–5. This is likewise the essence of the several criticisms found in Kathryn Allen Rabuzzi, "The Socialist Feminist Vision of Rosemary Radford

Ruether: A Challenge to Liberal Feminism," *Religious Studies Review* 15/1 (January 1989): 7–8.

44. Young, *Feminist Theology/Christian Theology,* 74.

45. Ibid., 77.

CHAPTER 12

1. John Hick, *God Has Many Names* (Philadelphia: Westminster, 1980), ch. 1.

2. Hick, *God Has Many Names,* 14.

3. The actual, and narrower, traditional expression, enunciated by the Church Father Cyprian is: *Extra ecclesiam nulla salus,* "Outside the Church there is no salvation."

4. It is sometimes called "particularism" in an attempt to sidestep the harsh tone of "exclusivism."

5. This last title won the 1991 Graweneyer Award for the most significant new thinking in religion.

6. John Hick, *An Interpretation of Religion: Human Responses to the Transcendent* (New Haven, Conn.: Yale University Press, 1989), 235.

7. John Hick, "A Pluralist View," in *More than One Way? Four Views on Salvation in a Pluralistic World,* ed. Dennis L. Okholm and Timothy R. Phillips (Grand Rapids, Mich.: Zondervan, 1995), 45, 51.

8. Hick borrows the expression from previous thinkers. He cites, for example, the German philosopher Karl Jaspers, who spoke of the cultural *Achsenzeit.*

9. Hick, *An Interpretation of Religion,* 31.

10. Ibid., ch. 18.

11. John Hick, *Death and Eternal Life* (London: Macmillan, 1976), ch. 13.

12. Hick, *An Interpretation of Religion,* 240.

13. Ibid., 268.

14. Ibid., 292.

15. Ibid., 279.

16. Aquinas is quoted, for example, in a chapter subheading in *An Interpretation of Religion,* 153.

17. The appeal to Kant is found everywhere in Hick's pluralistic hypothesis, but see especially the section on "Kant's epistemological model," Ibid., 240–6.

18. See especially the section "Experiencing-as," Ibid., 140–2.

19. The "Nicene" Creed, familiar in today's church services, is actually the Constantinopolitan Creed of 381, a refined version of the Creed of Nicea, 325.

20. John Hick, "Jesus and the World Religions," in *The Myth of God Incarnate,* ed. John Hick (Philadelphia: Westminster Press, 1977), 178.

21. Hick, "Jesus and the World Religions," 172.

22. Ibid., 178–9.

23. John Hick, *A Christian Theology of Religions: The Rainbow of Faiths* (Louisville, Ky.: Westminster/John Knox Press, 1995). See also the give-and-take with which Hick participates in Okholm and Phillips, *More than One Way?* (Hick, "A Pluralist View.")

24. John Hick, *The Metaphor of God Incarnate: Christology in a Pluralistic Age* (Louisville, Ky.: Westminster/John Knox Press. 1993).

25. Henry Denzinger, *The Sources of Catholic Dogma,* 30th ed., trans. Roy J. Deferrari (St. Louis: Herder, 1957), sect. 714.

26. Walter M. Abbott, ed., *The Documents of Vatican II* (New York: America Press, 1966), 662–3.

27. Ibid., 663.

28. Ibid., 661–6.

29. Ibid., 346.

30. It goes without saying that an even more emphatic opening has occurred also in Roman Catholic relations to Eastern Orthodoxy and Protestantism.

31. This doctrine was formulated in response to the discovery by Columbus and others of vast numbers of people untouched by the Christian proclamation.

32. Paul F. Knitter, *No Other Name? A Critical Survey of Christian Attitudes toward the World Religions* (Maryknoll, N.Y.: Orbis, 1985), 123.

33. Karl Rahner, *Theological Investigations,* trans. Karl-H. Kruger (New York: Crossroads, 1983), 5:ch. 6.

34. Ibid., 133.

35. Hans Küng, *On Being a Christian,* trans. Edward Quinn (Garden City, N.Y.: Doubleday, 1976), 98.

36. Hans Küng, "The World Religions in God's Plan for Salvation," in *Christian Revelation and World Religions,* ed. Joseph Neuner (London: Burns & Oates, 1967), 31–7.

37. Küng, *On Being a Christian,* 123.

38. C. S. Lewis, *Mere Christianity* (New York: Macmillan, reprint 1967), 176.

Chapter 13

1. George A. Lindbeck, *The Nature of Doctrine: Religion and Theology in a Postliberal Age* (Philadelphia: Westminster, 1984), 7.

2. In the words of one student of liberalism, adherents of the movement "would have agreed on the necessity of giving renewed strength and cur-

rency to Protestant Christianity by adapting it to the spiritual wants of the modern man, even if much that the past had accepted without demur would have to be discarded." Bernard M. G. Reardon, *Liberal Protestantism* (Stanford: Stanford University Press, 1968), 10.

3. Lindbeck, *Nature of Doctrine*, 7.

4. For a short summary of Lindbeck's life, see Bruce D. Marshall, "George A. Lindbeck," in *A New Handbook of Christian Theologians*, ed. Donald W. Musser and Joseph L. Price (Nashville: Abingdon, 1996), 271–2.

5. Lindbeck, *Nature of Doctrine*, 16.

6. This crisis is presented in George W. Stroup, *The Promise of Narrative Theology* (Atlanta: John Knox, 1981), 21–38. See also Hauerwas's critique of the misuse of *sola Scriptura*. Stanley Hauerwas, *Unleashing the Scripture: Freeing the Bible from Captivity to America* (Nashville: Abingdon, 1993), 27.

7. See Paul Nelson, *Narrative and Morality: A Theological Inquiry* (University Park, Pa.: Pennsylvania State University Press, 1987), 100. Nelson cites Frank Kermode, *The Sense of an Ending: Studies in the Theory of Fiction* (New York: Oxford, 1967), 7.

8. For a succinct summary of Frei's contribution, see William C. Placher, "Hans Frei and the Meaning of Biblical Narrative," *Christian Century* 106/18 (May 24–31, 1989): 556–9.

9. Hans Frei, *The Eclipse of Biblical Narrative: A Study in Eighteenth and Nineteenth Century Hermeneutics* (New Haven: Yale University Press, 1974), 27, 51.

10. Michael Goldberg finds this to be Frei's basic thesis. *Theology and Narrative* (Nashville: Abingdon, 1982), 162.

11. Stanley Hauerwas, *Truthfulness and Tragedy* (Notre Dame, Ind.: University of Notre Dame Press, 1977), 30, 36.

12. For his understanding of this dimension, Stroup draws from the work of Hans-Georg Gadamer, especially his book, *Truth and Method* (New York: Seabury, 1975), as well as George Herbert Mead (Ibid.,109–10, notes 23, 24).

13. See, for example, Stroup, *Promise of Narrative Theology*, 249, 252.

14. Stanley Hauerwas, *The Peaceable Kingdom* (Notre Dame, Ind.: University of Notre Dame Press, 1983), 26.

15. Nelson, for example, describes Hauerwas as "the most significant and influential exponent of narrative among contemporary Christian ethicists." *Narrative and Morality*, 109.

16. That Hauerwas saw himself early on as loosely associated with Lindbeck as well as in some sense a postliberal is evident in the manner in which he appropriates Lindbeck's *The Nature of Doctrine*. See Stanley Hauerwas, *Against the Nations: War and Survival in a Liberal Society* (Minneapolis: Win-

ston, 1985), 1–9. See also Stanley Hauerwas, *Dispatches from the Front: Theological Engagements with the Secular* (Durham, N.C.: Duke University Press, 1994), 19; Stanley Hauerwas, *In Good Company: The Church as Polis* (Notre Dame, Ind.: University of Notre Dame Press, 1995), 16. For an autobiographical statement of his own intellectual development, see Stanley Hauerwas, "The Testament of Friends," *Christian Century* 107/7 (Feb. 28, 1990): 212–6.

17. Hauerwas, *Truthfulness and Tragedy*, 75–7; Stanley Hauerwas, *The Community of Character* (Notre Dame, Ind.: Notre Dame University Press, 1981), 144.

18. This is evident, for example in his contribution to the *Festschrift* for Hans Frei. See Stanley Hauerwas, "The Church as God's New Language," in *Scriptural Authority and Narrative Interpretation*, ed. Garrett Green (Philadelphia: Fortress Press, 1987), 179–98.

19. For a description of an ethic of doing versus an ethic of being, see William Frankena, *Ethics* (Englewood Cliffs, N.J.: Prentice-Hall, 1973), 61–9.

20. Hauerwas, *Peaceable Kingdom*, 16. See also Hauerwas, *Vision and Virtue*, 2–3, 29, 36, 59, 67, 73–4; Hauerwas, *Truthfulness and Tragedy*, 29. The centrality of these concepts in Hauerwas's thought has also been noted by Goldberg, *Theology and Narrative*, 174.

21. Hauerwas, *Community of Character*, 1–4, 95–6.

22. Hauerwas, *Peaceable Kingdom*, 16, 24–30, 54; Hauerwas, *Community of Character*, 63, 66.

23. Goldberg, *Theology and Narrative*, 192.

24. Nelson, *Narrative and Morality*, 142.

25. See, for example, his article in the *Festschrift* for his Yale colleague Hans Frei. George A. Lindbeck, "The Story-Shaped Church: Critical Exegesis and Theological Interpretation," in *Scriptural Authority and Narrative Interpretation*, ed. Garrett Green (Philadelphia: Fortress Press, 1987), 161–78.

26. Lindbeck, *Nature of Doctrine*, 34, 118.

27. George Lindbeck, "Scripture, Consensus, and Community," in *Biblical Interpretation in Crisis: The Ratzinger Conference on Bible and Church*, ed. Richard John Neuhaus (Grand Rapids, Mich.: Eerdmans, 1989), 74–101.

28. Lindbeck, *Nature of Doctrine*, 80.

29. Ibid., 36–7.

30. Ibid., 32. On the next page he declares, "a religion can be viewed as a kind of cultural and/or linguistic framework or medium that shapes the entirety of life and thought."

31. Ibid., 39.

32. Ibid., 40.

33. For a short summary of Wittgenstein's view, see Stanley J. Grenz, *A Primer on Postmodernism* (Grand Rapids, Mich.: Eerdmans, 1996), 112–4.

34. Lindbeck, *Nature of Doctrine,* 18, 74.

35. Ibid., 80, 64.

36. Ibid., 69.

37. Ibid., 118, 113.

38. Ibid., 69.

39. the helpful critique in Terrence W. Tilley, *Postmodern Theologies: The Challenge of Religious Diversity* (Maryknoll, N.Y.: Orbis, 1995), 91–113. Tilley, writing with Stuart Kendall, claims that Lindbeck is "premodern."

40. This was a central point of contention in the encounter between Carl F. H. Henry and Hans Frei at Yale. See Carl F. H. Henry, "Narrative Theology: An Evangelical Appraisal," *Trinity Journal* 9 (Spring 1987): 19. For a similar critique, see Alister E. McGrath, "An Evangelical Evaluation of Postliberalism," in *The Nature of Confession: Evangelicals and Postliberals in Conversation,* ed. Timothy R. Phillips and Dennis L. Okholm (Downers Grove, Ill.: InterVarsity, 1996), 35–9. Clark Pinnock notes this objection but then erroneously concludes that Lindbeck is not denying that doctrines make first-order truth claims. *Tracking the Maze: Finding Our Way through Modern Theology from an Evangelical Perspective* (San Francisco: Harper & Row, 1990), 59. For a sympathetic treatment of this issue, see Bruce D. Marshall, "Absorbing the World: Christianity and the Universe of Truths," in *Theology and Dialogue: Essays in Conversation with George Lindbeck,* ed. Bruce D. Marshall (Notre Dame, Ind.: University of Notre Dame Press, 1990), 69–102.

41. Hauerwas has found it repeatedly necessary to respond to this charge. See his shorter rebuttals in, for example, Stanley Hauerwas, *Christian Existence Today: Essays on Church, World, and Living In Between* (Durham, N.C.: Labyrinth, 1988), 7–8; Stanley Hauerwas, *After Christendom?* (Nashville: Abingdon, 1991), 15–9. See also Hauerwas's more autobiographical response in *Dispatches from the Front,* 18–25. For what is perhaps his lengthiest reply, see Stanley Hauerwas and William Willimon, *Where Alien Residents Live: Exercises for Christian Practice* (Nashville: Abingdon, 1996), 29–45.

42. See, for example, David H. Kelsey, "Church Discourse and Public Realm," in *Theology and Dialogue,* 7–34.

43. Pinnock, *Tracking the Maze,* 59.

INDEX

CPSIA information can be obtained at www.ICGtesting.com
Printed in the USA
LVOW121701221211

260744LV00001B/69/A